Third World Cities
in Global Perspective

Third World Cities
in Global Perspective

The Political Economy
of Uneven Urbanization

David A. Smith

WestviewPress

A Division of HarperCollins*Publishers*

Copyright © 1996 by Westview Press, Inc., A Division of HarperCollins Publishers, Inc.

Published in 1996 in the United States of America by Westview Press, Inc., 5500 Central Avenue, Boulder, Colorado 80301-2877, and in the United Kingdom by Westview Press, 12 Hid's Copse Road, Cumnor Hill, Oxford OX2 9JJ

Library of Congress Cataloging-in-Publication Data
Smith, David A. (David Alden), 1956–
    Third world cities in global perspective : the political economy
    of uneven urbanization / David A. Smith.
        p. cm.
    Includes bibliographical references and index.
    ISBN 0-8133-8720-5 (hc)—0-8133-2998-1 (pbk)
    1. Cities and towns—Developing countries.   2. Urbanization—
Developing countries.   I. Title.
HT149.5.S65   1996
307.76'09172'4—dc20   95-43521
                                                                                                        CIP

The paper used in this publication meets the requirements of the American National Standard for Permanence of Paper for Printed Library Materials Z39.48-1984.

10   9   8   7   6   5   4   3   2   1

For my parents, Alden and Betty Smith

Contents

vii

Tables and Figures

Preface

This book is the final product of a long process that began over a decade ago when I was a graduate student at the University of North Carolina at Chapel Hill. The initial idea of placing Third World urbanization and development in the context of world-system analysis was the driving motivation behind my dissertation research. In subsequent years the project has gone through various permutations, expansions, and revisions. These reflect responses to readers' comments and criticism, changes in my own perspective as my scholarship matured, and shifting theoretical debates in comparative urban research. Early drafts were innovative but preliminary efforts to synthesize a fresh framework for examining cities and underdevelopment from the emerging world-system perspective and the nascent "new urban sociology." Now, in the mid-1990s, the paradigm shift is complete. So this book is a somewhat more staid, less controversial, but hopefully more fully explicated, statement of an increasingly accepted view of cities and social change.

Over the years, many people have helped me on this project. First, I must thank those who contributed back in the Carolinas. Alejandro Portes' graduate seminar on "Cities and Social Change" at Duke University provided an intriguing introduction to this topic. My doctoral committee at UNC, chaired by Amos Hawley, and including Gary Gereffi, Gerhard Lenski, Peter Marsden, and Barbara Stenross, was a stellar constellation of scholars. I was very lucky: They provided not only steady guidance, commentary and critique, but also a great deal of latitude to develop the project as I saw fit. Other graduate students in Chapel Hill—among them Karen Campbell, Valerie Haines, Mike Kennedy, Dave Maume, Roger Nemeth, and Shelley Pendleton—added to the stimulating and supportive environment. Josie Rush and Darla Ladkau at the University of South Carolina took on a major word-processing job (back when I was just learning Wordstar) to get out an early draft.

The major work done over the long haul to actually produce this book was carried out here at the University of California at Irvine. I particularly would like to thank colleagues who read portions of the manuscript: Francesca Cancian, Judy Treas, Sam Gilmore, and Judy Stepan-Norris. Jószef Böröcz, Nancy Naples, Dorie Solinger, and Steve Topik deserve some credit, too—they are faculty who have made Irvine an intellectually exciting place for me. While not directly involved with this project, my own doctoral students in our Social Relations Ph.D. program provided a steady stream of new insights that enriched my perspective; I would especially like to thank Ku-Sup Chin, Angela Crowly, Dennis Downey, Linda Miller Matthei, and Yoonies Park. Finally, thanks to the staff of the School of

Social Sciences who helped in big and small ways to get this research and writing completed. Two deserve special recognition. Cheryl Larsson is an invaluable resource who typeset the final camera-ready text. Linda Cleland, the administrative assistant for the Department of Sociology, was always there to provide various types of support—emotional as well as instrumental—as this project made its way toward publication.

Of course, scholarly work also relies on academic communities that are not localized. I was fortunate to have good access to intellectual luminaries such as Immanuel Wallerstein, Andre Gunder Frank, Saskia Sassen, and Terry McGee via correspondence and conversation, as well as their written work—I hope their influence is clear in the book. Several colleagues at other universities contributed even more directly. Christopher Chase-Dunn, Joe Feagin, Bruce London, and Michael Timberlake provided early support for this project—all have consistently shared their own work and constructively critiqued mine. More specifically, Chris and Joe provided constructively critical reviews of earlier drafts of this manuscript; Bruce was gracious enough to send me updated data used to do the analysis reported in Chapter 2. I got to know York Bradshaw and Su-Hoon Lee while we each did graduate work on related topics at different universities; York and I continue to correspond and share data and papers about comparative urban dynamics (as well as commiserate about tenure and career paths); Su-Hoon has even more directly aided this project by graciously hosting me (at the Institute for Far Eastern Studies of Kyungnam University in Seoul) on three seperate research trips to Korea.

When I decided to seek a publisher for this project I was a total novice in the world of book publishing. Like most writers I had my share of summary rejections and at least one devastatingly unfair reader review. But it has been a great pleasure to work with Dean Birkenkamp, senior editor, Jill Rothenburg, associate editor, and Melanie Stafford, assistant editor, at Westview Press. Although they never wavered in their faith in me and the project, they also firmly insisted on changes that resulted in major improvements in this published book. I would also like to thank Joan Sherman who did a magnificent job copy editing the final draft.

Having good friends to lean on is important for any author. Gail Boyarsky and Walter Fowler, Harry Hunt, Dave Parsel, Lianne Oakes, Lou Thompson, and Rick Wagner all provided crucial support at critical times over the years. My biggest debt of gratitude goes to my family. My parents, to whom I have dedicated this book, have provided tangible and intangible support for all of my endeavors, and were a steady source of encouragement throughout the years I worked on this volume. Beatrice, my daughter, has been a constant source of love, hope, and inspiration over the last three years, and a increasingly talkative companion (though, as yet, our discussions have not centered on scholarly pursuits). Needless to say, I reserve my fondest thanks for my wife, Tonya Schuster. In addition to being my partner and the central source of sanity and stability in my life, she and I share a passion for sociological ideas. Though as a sociologist her interests are about as different from mine as they possibly could be, Tonya has patiently served as a sounding board for my ideas and acts as one of my most formidable critics—all while she actively pursues the difficulties of her own career and research agenda. Without her love, support, and understanding this book would have been impossible.

David A. Smith

Third World Cities
in Global Perspective

Introduction

The recent *Los Angeles Times* headline was stark: "The Rush to the Cities Is Straining the Social Fabric of Nations."[1] The article reports:

> In 1800, only 3% of the world's population lived in cities. In 1900 it was 10%. By the beginning of the 21st Century—for the first time in history—at least half of the people of the world will be urbanized.
>
> The impact of that transformation, which is occurring at its most uncontrolled in Third World countries least able to handle it, is staggering—on the people pouring into the cities, on the cities themselves and on the nations of a world grown so interconnected that few will escape the shock waves from one of the greatest migrations of human history.

The *Times* reporter proceeds to argue that this "run-away urbanization" is creating a "social disaster" of "marginalized people" and "impoverished megacities," which have completely outstripped the ability of public or private institutions to control their growth or cope with the problems of their burgeoning populations. In good journalistic fashion, the reporter tells the stories of the sights and sounds of African squatter settlements in Johannesburg and Maputo and details the varying business of the vendors of Lima's "informal sector" where "merchants offer fruit, underwear, toys, watches, each business neatly laid out on the sidewalk. Near one vendor, a child taps out tunes on empty Coke bottles." The human dimension of seemingly sterile statistics and bar graphs on urban population growth are vividly (and poignantly) animated by reference to faces and images of the struggle for everyday existence. In these giant conurbations, there are literally millions of stories of uprooted people battling poverty. Yet one of the truly interesting, if paradoxical, elements of these giant urban areas is that, despite all this human suffering and despair, they are concurrently places of tremendous wealth and opulent consumption. These cities of the poor are also sites for gleaming skyscrapers, suburban "gated communities," and five-star hotels that house societal and multinational elites as they work and play. Often, the shantytowns or slums are physically in the shadow of these monuments to opulence. "Underdevelopment" and "overdevelop-ment" literally exist side by side.

Jakarta, Indonesia's capital and largest city, is a striking example.[2] Now home to over 10 million people, it is a crowded city of jarring contrasts. From a vantage point atop one of the city's shimmering high-rises, other modern skyscrapers displaying the corporate logos of multinational businesses and bustling six-lane highways filled with cars and trucks stretch out for miles through the smoggy haze. At street level along the major avenues, the sights, sounds, and smells of heavy vehicle traffic remind a visitor of Southern California freeways (and are about as inviting for pedestrians). Although there are very few trees or green areas in this city of concrete and glass, there is a veneer of great commercial activity, prosperity, and growth. The sprawling downtown area of tall buildings is home to scores of luxury hotels and restaurants (bearing familiar names like "Hilton" and "Hard Rock Cafe"), sleek office buildings, and upscale shopping arcades. Elegantly dressed men and women cut deals, manage commerce, coordinate production systems, recreate, shop, and dine in the ornate, air-conditioned buildings of this area.

But in the less visible parts of the city—in slums off the main avenues and sprawling squatter settlements and shantytowns on the outskirts of the metropolitan area—the masses of Jakartans live starkly different lives. The fortunate few work in manufacturing industries producing commodities like clothing or athletic shoes for global markets where pay is about the rupee equivalent of US $2 a day; others are employed as "entrepreneurs" in less formal enterprises like vending and driving bajai taxis (small, noisy, three-wheel cabs). Images of a polarized city are unmistakable. A foreign businessman who operates a large export garment factory complains that his rising wage costs have now reached about $100 per month per worker—over a sumptuous buffet meal and drinks for two in an elegant restaurant that costs about that amount. The tour guide on a bus excursion for European and North American tourists to the old port of Batavia points out a particularly wretched-looking slum along the way: Shacks teeter on stilts along the bank of a local river that smells more like a fetid open sewer as the group passes by in the comfort of their air-conditioned coach.

The sights and smells, sounds and faces of Jakarta, Lagos, Calcutta, Manila, Lima, and all the other rapidly growing cities of the poor countries are the reality that I ultimately attempt to explain in this book. My strategy is to attempt to tease out the deeper macrostructural political and economic dynamics of this pattern of urbanization and its relationship to "national development." A major argument advanced in the volume is that a complete understanding of the social dynamics and structure of Third World cities must begin with an attempt to situate these places in the global political economic system and from there to explore the "articulation" between that seemingly very abstract level and national and municipal dynamics, ultimately linking up with what happens "on the ground" in the local neighborhoods where people live. The alternative strategy of starting with a deep description of urban lives and times can only lead us so far, unless we comprehend the way that these cities are inserted into the contemporary world-system. Journalistic or ethnographic accounts that fail to explicitly incorporate a global political economy perspective will be incomplete. The type of macrosociological analysis offered in the following pages sometimes seems too abstract and remote from the flesh-and-blood realities of ordinary people. But it is these people—the impoverished urban masses of the Third World, carrying the weights of the world but also poised like poet Edward Markham's "man with a hoe" to throw off the shackles of their misery—who are the ultimate subjects of this book.

As the newspaper article suggests, the growth of cities across the globe during the twentieth century represents the most massive geographic shift of human population since the beginning of recorded history. Between 1920 and 1980, the global population of urban areas skyrocketed from 36 million to over 180 million—a fivefold increase (Armstrong and McGee, 1985: table 1.1). Significantly, the locus of urbanization has moved from the economically advanced nations of the West to the relatively underdeveloped countries of the world (Davis, 1972). These societies are now undergoing an "urban revolution" that is drastically altering the fabric of their predominantly rural agrarian societies (Mountjoy, 1978). Particularly since 1950, city growth in the Third World has been staggering, with the proportion of the total population in urban areas doubling and the per annum population increases of many metropolises exceeding 5 percent (Gilbert and Gugler, 1982: 5). In terms of both the average rate of urban growth and the absolute number of added residents, contemporary Third World urbanization easily outstrips the growth of nineteenth-century cities in Europe and North America (Bairoch, 1975: chapter 8; Light, 1983: 128; Timberlake, 1987: 41). These unprecedented rates of increase are expected to continue or even accelerate through the year 2000 (Drakakis-Smith, 1980: 3; Todaro, 1981).

While city growth is intrinsically interesting and important, it is also a strategic entry point to wider theoretical disputes about social change in general. Urbanization is an integral part of broader currents of social transformation. Although their specific formulations vary widely, writers from a number of disciplines, some holding radically different political and ideological views, have agreed on the importance of linking urbanization with more general processes of macrostructural change. Because of the reciprocal causal relationship between city growth and national, social, and economic development, theoretical approaches to urbanization are usually variations on more general perspectives aimed at explaining social change.

Urbanization Theory

Developmentalism and Its Inadequacies

The study of cities and development is one of the many aspects of social change that has been influenced by the paradigm shift in comparative sociology that Peter Evans and John Stephens (1988) call the rise of the "new international political economy" perspective. During the 1970s, the dominant developmentalist approach came under blistering attack, primarily from proponents of world-system and dependency theories (see Portes, 1976, for a seminal statement). This volume contributes to further refinement and evaluation of the emerging political economy perspective on urbanization, with its focus on global inequality and dependency as the context for city growth in the Third World.

But it is important to understand that although the basic premises of the political economy of the world-system approach are now widely accepted, comparative urban sociology remains heavily influenced by the earlier developmentalist assumptions of modernization theory and human ecology. There are two basic reasons for this situation. First, it reflects an old and deeply ingrained heritage in urban studies. The basic assumptions of stages and phases of urbanization were implicit in the classical sociological theories of the nineteenth century (such as those of Marx, Weber, and Durkheim) and explicitly formulated in Adna Weber's (1899) influential book *The Growth of Cities in the Nineteenth Century*. The structural-functional and developmentalist assumptions were further codified in the basic writings of the founders of the "Chicago School" of human ecology in the early decades of the twentieth century (Park, 1916; Park and Burgess, 1925; McKenzie, 1933). Second, urban sociology, geography, and planning have tended to become very specialized, empirically oriented fields, increasingly dominated by researchers who are primarily concerned with data collection, model testing, and more and more sophisticated techniques of demographic analysis. Studies of urbanization in less developed countries are often designed to demonstrate the extent to which Third World patterns replicate city growth in the "advanced" nations, often using conceptual and/or statistical models of patterns such as "polarization/polarization reversal" (for examples, see Fuchs, Jones, and Pernia, eds., 1987; Richardson and Hwang, eds., 1987). Given its narrow focus, this research is relatively insulated from current theoretical debates and developments in comparative social science. The result is images of urbanization in regional science and urban geography/sociology that unselfconsciously rely on modernization theory assumptions.

Working within the broad rubric known as modernization theory, many social scientists in the 1950s and 1960s assumed that the urbanization process in less developed areas would evolve through a progression of stages approximating the phases of city growth in Western urban history (for an example, see Reissman, 1964). This approach emphasized the similarities between the dynamics of urban growth in the contemporary Third World and the historical process in the advanced nations during the nineteenth century. Following the European and North American model implied that urbanization was tied to industrialization and economic growth (see Roberts, 1978a: 10–11). Although scholars in this school acknowledged the possibility that cities could exert a short-run "parasitic" effect in special circumstances—slowing national economic development—the general thrust of this literature emphasized the long-term "generative" influence of cities as catalysts to development (see Hoselitz, 1954). Cities were foci of modernization and dynamism because they served as conduits for information to developing societies and as loci for innovation, opportunity, and political transformation (Friedmann, 1978: 87; Murphey, 1988).

In the 1970s, research undertaken from the modernization theory perspective was the object of much criticism.[3] The basic problem was simple: The empirical reality in the Third World did not square with the theory. Specifically in reference to urbanization, there was a growing consensus among social scientists that the process of city growth, in both structural form and social consequences, differed from urbanization in the developed world (Berry, 1973: 73; Berry and Kasarda, 1977: 375; Roberts, 1978a: 11; for more recent reiterations of this theme, see Sachs, 1988; Teune, 1988). By the early 1980s, even normally orthodox development planners employed by international agencies like the World Bank were expressing skepticism about the putative generative effect of city growth in underdeveloped areas. Recent academic research has returned to a focus on the negative implications of overurbanization (Gugler, 1982, 1988; Timberlake and Kentor, 1983; Bradshaw, 1987; Smith, 1987a; London and Smith, 1988).

One possible mechanism linking rapid urbanization to economic and social stagnation is the distinctive form that city growth takes in these societies. Empirical studies indicate that urbanization in the contemporary Third World is characterized by uneven growth and inequality (Castells, 1977: chapter 3; Roberts, 1978a, 1987b; Gugler, 1982; Armstrong and McGee, 1985). These inequalities are manifest at three basic levels:

1. The imbalances between life chances in the urban and rural sectors,
2. Among cities, the concentration of limited resources in the capitals and/or primate cities, and
3. Within cities, the economic disparity between the masses and a small wealthy elite (Gugler and Flanagan, 1977: 273, cited in London, 1980: 5).

In addition to their intrinsic evils, these imbalances also may retard national economic efficiency and prospects for growth (Gugler, 1982; see also Bairoch, 1988).

Various authors focus on different levels of this structural inequality. Michael Lipton (1977, 1984) identifies "urban bias" as the major cause of persistent poverty in the Third World. He argues that Third World societies are ruled by urban elites who misallocate scant resources by disproportionately investing them as subsidies to urban living. This sort of inequality, while doubtlessly important, is not unique to the contemporary underdeveloped world. The exploitation of the countryside by the city in the process of societal development was recognized by classical social theorists such as Marx (1959: 352) and Weber (1958), as well as developmentalists such as Keyfitz (1965). Not only did this process occur in the West, it also may have been a prerequisite for capital accumulation (see particularly Nathan Keyfitz, 1965; Hawley, 1971: 283). Therefore, the existence of urban bias presents little problem for those subscribing to the modernization theory view that urbanization follows a universal sequence of steps initially undertaken in the advanced nations.

A tendency that less clearly replicates the Western historical experience is the phenomenon of urban primacy. In many Third World countries, population tends to be concentrated in one very large city. Urban primacy and the uneven patterns of growth associated with it are important concerns in comparative studies of urbanization in the underdeveloped countries. The causes and consequences of the growth of giant, sprawling cities in the Third World is the source of some debate. Consistent with the need for urban capital accumulation, some scholars claimed that the growth of very large cities and the asymmetrical flow of resources to them from their hinterlands is necessary to stimulate national economic development (J. Friedmann, 1978; Mera, 1978). Earlier work pointed to the long-run parasitic role of these inordinately large cities, claiming that they have a retarding (or even debilitating) effect on efforts directed toward development and economic growth (for a summary, see Mehta, 1969). Others suggested a more nuanced, complex relationship between primacy and economic takeoff (Linsky, 1969; El-Shakhs, 1974). While the effect of private cities may be debatable, there is a consensus among researchers that only in a few underdeveloped countries is the growth of small or medium-sized cities keeping pace with the increasing size of the largest cities (Hawley, 1971: 277–278; Roberts, 1978a: 107; Bairoch, 1988: 436–440).

The final level of uneven and imbalanced growth is the inequality of the internal structure of large, rapidly growing Third World cities. These urban areas are simultaneously places of sumptuous wealth and incredible poverty, exclusive privilege and utter degradation (Fanon, 1965: 39). Reports in both the social scientific literature and the popular press are replete with descriptions of sprawling cities teeming with unemployed men and women and dominated by mushrooming shantytowns and slums (see, for instance, Abrams, 1978; Hollensteiner and Lopez, 1976; Mountjoy, 1978). Yet amid the squalor, the wealthy and powerful live in segregated areas of considerable opulence (Portes and Walton, 1976: chapter 1; Gugler and Flanagan, 1978: 45). The employment structure seems to replicate the inequality of settlement patterns in these cities. The urban economy reflects a "dualistic" nature: There is a basic split in labor pools, working conditions, and earning capacities, between a small group of skilled workers and managers and the masses of citizens involved in the "informal sector" or "petty commodity production" (for discussions, see Roberts, 1978a: chapter 5; Portes, 1983, 1985a; Bairoch, 1988: chapters 29 and 30).

Toward a New Theoretical Approach

By the 1970s, the growing inequality and the continued economic stagnation in much of the Third World, especially manifest in cities, led many comparative urbanists to reevaluate the conventional developmentalist assumptions of modernization theory (Walton, 1977). It was becoming obvious that Third World patterns and processes were not conforming to the models of urbanization borrowed from the Western experience, with its emphasis on "generative" cities and intersocietal convergence (Roberts, 1978a: chapter 1). Further evidence mounted that highlighted different trajectories of urban growth *within* the Third World. The search for a more adequate theoretical basis for comparative study of urbanization was under way in earnest.

In the late twentieth century, the dependency/world-system perspective has developed and proven to be a particularly powerful tool for analyzing problems involving macrostructural change. In the late 1970s, a number of pioneering efforts were made to apply the general logic of this international political economy approach to comparative research on cities and urban systems (Castells, 1977; Walton, 1977; Slater, 1978; Roberts, 1978a). Recently, more refined, programmatic statements outlining the world-system perspective on urbanization have appeared that both synthesize the most useful parts of the early formulations and draw on a growing body of empirical research to correct and extend them (Walton, 1982; Chase-Dunn, 1984; Timberlake, 1987).

In this book, I adopt and refine this international political economy approach to cities. I critique the conventional ecological view of the city not by rejecting traditional analyses out of hand but by reformulating the crucial questions. The conventional ecological perspective assumes an equilibrium model in which very rapid city growth and the various types of urban imbalances are transitional phases on the path to modernity. The comparative political economy approach, by contrast, conceptualizes uneven development and inequality as inevitable results of the expansion of the capitalist world-system. Similarly, whereas demographic "push and pull" and the technology of transportation and communication are paramount factors for ecological theory, my approach focuses on the social, economic, and political factors that lie behind population dynamics or the provision of infrastructure. After all, individual and family migration and fertility decisions are the results of complicated processes that are strongly influenced by macrostructural contexts of political policies and economic realities. In much the same way, the crucial point about infrastructure is that communication and transportation networks are differentially allocated across space—elites in one area often are able to marshal resources for roads, telephones, and electricity while those in another area are not. The comparative political economy approach prompts researchers to seek the relations of dominance and subordination between and among actors in different local regions to explain these differences. The approach also acknowledges the importance that global links of dominance and dependency play.

In Chapter 1, I will selectively review the theoretical and empirical literature that focuses on the political economy approach to urbanization in the world-system and present a synthetic model of the process. Here, I want to briefly indicate the distinctive thrusts of this theoretical perspective.[4] First, the current mode of production operates at the global level, incorporating most areas of the world (including seemingly remote regions of underdeveloped countries) into a world-system of hierarchial social, economic, and political relationships. City growth must be analyzed in this context. In the capitalist world-economy, the fundamental units of rational profit-and-loss calculation are usually extralocal (depending on the historical period: colonial empires, mercantile companies, multinational corporations). Therefore, the development needs of specific countries, cities, and communities are not likely to be very relevant to key decisionmakers at the globally important levels. Second (in sharp contradistinction to the functionalist models of human ecology), space—particularly the geography of cities—is socially structured by class relations of dominance and subordination in articulation with the logic of the mode of production. Third, despite the indisputable importance of global economic relationships, urbanization is also critically linked to political processes. The state (whether national or local) generally plays a critical role in fostering development and capital accumulation. As such, it is a critical locus of formulation and implementation of both explicit and (probably more critically) implicit urban policy. Finally, structural similarity between nations or regions in the global hierarchy may lead to parallel patterns of urban growth. But this will not always be the case. Macrostructural change is a complicated process that is influenced by multiple factors. Some of these may be historically specific; in other cases, the notion of conjunctural causation (see Ragin, 1987) may be particularly relevant. The real challenge is to identify the ways in which social relations and outcomes on the local level are linked to macrostructural processes, including those of the global political economy. This necessitates a multiple-method approach that includes global comparative analysis as well as detailed historical case studies.

After developing this theoretical approach more fully in Chapter 1, I will begin an empirical analysis that takes on the methodological challenge. In Chapter 2, the results of the cross-national quantitative analysis are reported and discussed. Chapter 3 provides a brief overview of the logic of research employing comparative case studies. The next four chapters deal with urbanization in West Africa and East Asia, respectively, using a case-oriented approach. In the concluding chapter, I will summarize and reappraise the global perspective on urbanization in light of the preceding analysis; I will also discuss the policy relevance of my results and suggest research priorities.

1

Developing an International Political Economy Approach

Dominance and Dependency: A Theoretical Reprise

Notions about the emergence of hierarchy and dominance within urban systems are very old in U.S. social science. Early writings by Norman S.B. Gras (1922) and Roderick McKenzie (1933) on "metropolitan dominance" pointed to the linkage between the ascension of a city to a position of economic and political importance and the concomitant subordination of surrounding secondary towns and rural areas to this center. In fact, some of McKenzie's observations were particularly prescient in terms of the new global political economy perspectives (see D. Smith, 1995, for a complete discussion). In papers addressing "industrial expansion" and the emergence of "dominance in world-organization," he highlighted the "predatory and exploitative" history of European expansion, discussed economic "penetration" of less developed countries, and suggested a core/periphery structure and a cyclic pattern of uneven development in which cities and urbanization play key roles (McKenzie, 1927, 1933). More recently, in a major work on twentieth-century urban patterns in the United States, Otis Dudley Duncan and his collaborators (1960: 133) emphasized the importance of studying "the structural geographic patterns of flows" between U. S. cities in shaping the emerging national "urban hierarchy." The emergence of dominance relations within large-scale social systems is a basic principle of the human ecology approach (Hawley, 1968a: 333).

Dependency theory initially emerged in the form of a vitriolic attack on the culturalist and developmentalist assumptions of modernization theory by a group of Latin American social scientists.[1] Like human ecologists, some early proponents of this approach were also interested in the development of an exchange system with asymmetrical relationships between the parts. In this case, however, the boundaries of the system have been set by the imperialism and neo-imperialism of the advanced nations. In the language of urban systems, Andre Gunder Frank

(1969: 6–9) described the result as "a chain of constellations of metropolis and satellites" that relate

> all parts of the whole system from its metropolitan center in Europe or the United States to the farthest outpost in the Latin American countryside . . .. When we examine this metropolis-satellite structure, we find that each of the satellites . . . serves as an instrument to suck capital or economic surpluses to the world metropolis of which all are satellites . . . within this world embracing structure, the metropolis tends to develop, and the satellites to underdevelop.[2]

Dependency theorists argued that as a result of the penetration of foreign political and economic influence, many formerly undeveloped areas became incorporated as "peripheral" or "dependent" underdeveloping appendages to the colonial core states. This type of perspective sensitized the researcher to the importance of international exchanges such as trade and foreign aid and investment. It suggested that "unequal exchange" between colonial cities and core metropoli benefits the latter and leads to the stunted or distorted growth of the former.

In its earliest formulations, dependency theory was intended to be a rather narrow framework for dealing with the problems of contemporary underdevelopment in peripheral areas, particularly in Latin America. One problem, especially in the least sophisticated versions of this approach, was the rather limited attention given to the two-way relationship between the imperial (or neo-imperial) core nation and the colonized (or neocolonized) peripheral country. Additionally, the terminology of dependency theory seemed to imply an either-or situation— dependent or autonomous, metropolis or satellite, core or periphery. These deficiencies are at least partially corrected when a more comprehensive conception of the world economic system, like that proposed by Immanuel Wallerstein, is accepted (Evans, 1979a: 16). While this "world-system" perspective still focuses on external conditions affecting the development of peripheral areas, the emphasis is on "the consequences of occupying a given structural position within the world system as a whole" (Evans, 1979a: 15). This reconceptualization further allows for (1) an intermediary stratum of semiperipheral countries as "a necessary structural element in the world economy" (Wallerstein, 1974a: 349) and (2) the possibility of mobility in the international system through dependent development (see Cardoso, 1973; Evans, 1979b).

Even with the advantages that the world-system reformulation enjoys, this approach has some important weaknesses. One major problem for the entire dependency/world system school involves a tendency to place a disproportionate emphasis on the exchange aspect of the world-economy and to give inadequate attention to the internal dynamics of areas that are labeled "dependent" (Portes, 1979: 5–6). This issue of "internal" versus "external" determination has become a central concern for scholars adopting the dependency/world-system approach

(Frank, 1979). A major thrust of this perspective is that the exclusive intrasocietal perspective of modernization theory (or, for that matter, orthodox Marxism) is incorrect. But too much emphasis on the exchange relations between nations has led to charges of "economic reductionism" (Skocpol, 1977) and "neo-Smithian Marxism" (Brenner, 1977).

One remedy for the problem is to also analyze the relationship between exchange and the local modes of production and class structures (Evans, 1979a: 19; Cardoso and Faletto, 1979: XVI). Linking class structure and local policymaking with variables that the human ecological approach emphasizes, particularly changes in transportation and communications systems and technology (see Hawley 1950, 1971), offers a particularly promising strategy. The tie to human ecological theory is particularly germane for comparative urban research since cities and urban systems are major foci of this school. In light of these suggestions, a useful way to conceptualize a more adequate, synthetic theory of macrosocial change views the external world-system interrelationships as setting the broad parameters for processes such as urbanization and development, while the internal political, economic, and ecological variables help to explain more specific outcomes.

Another way to move away from economic reductionism is to recognize that the world-system is also an "interstate system" (Chase-Dunn, 1981b). Two of the most damaging critiques of the world-system perspective during the late 1970s focused on the economistic nature of exchange-based "neo-Smithian Marxism" with its lack of attention to political and class forces (Brenner, 1977; Skocpol, 1977). These attacks, directed at the early writings of A. G. Frank and Wallerstein's (1974a) explanation of the European transition to capitalism, had considerable merit. Further theoretical elaboration and mounting empirical research now clearly demonstrate the inadequacies of economic reductionist arguments that consign politics to a derivative or epiphenomenal status. This led to a major effort to "bring the state back in" to a theoretical synthesis labeled the "new comparative political economy" (Evans, Rueschmeyer, and Skocpol, 1985; Evans and Stephens, 1988). In the case studies in this volume, the role of the state and contending classes in the struggle for dependent development are assumed to be central to the political economy of urbanization in the contemporary Third World.

A major emphasis of the dependency/world-system literature is on the importance of the historical context of social change. Because world capitalism has been an expanding system since its emergence in Europe in the sixteenth century, a full understanding of its operations must take the changing needs of the system and the shifting mechanisms of capital accumulation into account. Therefore, dependency/world-system theorists have found it useful to delineate stages or phases of capitalist development (Wallerstein and Hopkins, 1977: 125; Valenzuela and Valenzuela, 1978: 546; Frank, 1979: 9).[3] Because of the importance given to the changing nature of capitalism and the need to blend an analysis of changes in the world-economy with an analysis of local dynamics, researchers must adopt a "historical-structural" approach (Cardoso and Faletto, 1979). The critical aspect of this methodology is that it attempts to examine the history of specific societies in such a way that the linkages between the external and internal factors shaping change are both illuminated.

Cities in the World-System: Previous Research

Research directed specifically at urbanization from the dependency/world-system perspective started to appear in the late 1970s. This work began with the premise that the contemporary patterns and processes of urbanization can only be fully understood as part of the expansion of the capitalist world economy. The patterns of urban growth are shaped by the historical contexts of a region's initial incorporation into and changing role within this world-system (Walton, 1977: 12–13; Slater, 1978: 27). "The process of urbanization becomes, therefore, the expression of this social dynamic at the level of space, that is to say, of the penetration by the capitalist mode of production, historically formed in the western countries, of the remainder of the social formations at different technological, economic and social levels (Castells, 1977: 44).

The earliest articles developing this "international political economy of cities" approach were primarily intended as attempts at theoretical reconceptualization. They pointed to a number of potentially fruitful avenues of research, but the actual analyses performed were more suggestive than conclusive.

Recent research has attempted to apply the perspective more rigorously to empirical situations. In an introduction to a major compilation of studies, Michael Timberlake (1985: 10) succinctly summarized the shared premise of this research:

> Urbanization must be studied holistically—part of the logic of a larger process of socioeconomic development that encompasses it, and that entails systematic unevenness across regions of the world. The dependence relation is an important theoretical concept used to pry into ways in which the processes embodied in the world-system produce various manifestations of this unevenness, including divergent patterns of urbanization.

Within the developing literature devoted to this approach, two distinct modes of analysis are apparent—arising from a methodological division among dependency/world-system analysts in general (for a more detailed analysis, see D. Smith, 1991).

Quantitative Cross-National Analysis

One strain of research on cities in the world-system particularly popular with U.S. trained sociologists stresses a comparative statistical analysis of urbanization and development. Scholars in this school are attempting to formulate hypothesis-testing procedures for the effects of dependency on patterns of urbanization. Specifically, dependency is expected to affect overall levels of urbanization, urban primacy, or "overurbanization," through intermediary variables such as tertiary sector employment, state power, and so forth. In attempting to perform quantitative cross-national "tests" of dependency/world-system formulations, researchers are expanding on a groundswell of similar studies in the late 1970s.[4] These studies tried to assay the effect of international dependence, operationalized using measures of trade concentration or direct foreign investment and/or aid, on various indicators of national development.

The first real attempt to relate dependency to patterns of urbanization using such a rigorous cross-national approach was offered by Timberlake (1979). He hypothesized that overall urbanization, urban primacy, and tertiary sector employment are critical intermediate variables that help explain the effects of dependence on economic development, income inequality, and political violence. Using multiple regression and causal analysis, Timberlake found only modest support for most of his models. The mixed results of this study may be attributable to several factors. First, the author himself admitted "that dependency is a concept in need of greater specification" (Timberlake, 1979: 141). He argued that one must differentiate between various types of dependency—and the mechanisms through which these forms are likely to affect processes like urbanization. Second, the study faced a familiar problem in cross-national research: a tremendous amount of missing data. Only a handful of nations had complete information on the variables of interest. As a result, Timberlake's regression equations covered between 14 and 27 cases—which leads to great difficulty in interpreting results. Finally, the study used a fairly easy to calculate but widely criticized measure of urban primacy employing data on only the four largest cities, called the Davis Index (see Davis, 1970). This indicator has been criticized as a very crude operationalization of the concept of an even/skewed city-size distribution (C. Smith, 1982b; Walters, 1985). Yet despite its flaws and lack of conclusive results, Timberlake's work was a pioneering attempt to systematically apply the dependency/world-system approach to global urbanization.

Following Timberlake's lead, Christopher Chase-Dunn and his associates systematically developed the quantitative approach to urbanization in the world-system (see Chase-Dunn, 1979, 1982). They sought to redress problems involving lack of data and inadequacy of measures by expending considerable time and energy collecting and compiling time-series measures of these variables.

to affect urban development. But in examining Latin America and Africa, he also noted a general pattern of imbalance and uneven growth and claimed that "urbanization, because of the accumulative processes which engender it, is attended by greater socio-spatial polarization" (Walton, 1977: 12). Walton (1977: 14–15) argued that later incorporation into the world economy and more active state planning may lead to more even and equitable urban growth in the latter.

Coming from a more orthodox Marxist perspective, David Slater attempted to formulate a general approach to urbanization in "peripheral capitalist societies." Despite many similarities to Walton (for instance, an emphasis on the importance of timing of incorporation into the world economy), Slater differentiated himself from world-system approaches by insisting that scholars must be more sensitive to the internal class dynamics affecting urban processes. Additionally, in his historical case study of Peru, Slater urged more careful consideration of the relationship between urbanization and other demographic phenomena, particularly general population growth. But he took pains to rebut the "spatio-demographic determinism" of traditional human ecological descriptions of urban evolution. He stressed that state policies, not disembodied "technology," shaped the Peruvian transportation system, which, in turn, structured the growing urban system.

Obviously, most historical analyses of comparative urban development have focused on particular countries or regions. Not surprisingly, many of the early case studies (including Slater's cited earlier) concentrated on Latin America (Portes and Walton, 1976; Roberts, 1978a and 1978b; C. Smith, 1978, 1982a). This work defies perfunctory summary since an animating theme was the importance of a nuanced study of particular historical conjuctures. Most writers discussed specific class alliances between urban-based elites in peripheral societies and core economic and political actors, as well as the way in which these overlapping interests shape policies affecting city and regional growth in particular societies. Nevertheless, the work of two researchers—Carole Smith and Brian Roberts—offer particularly important theoretical insights.

An anthropologist who studies Guatemala, Smith addressed the evolution of extreme urban primacy in that Central American country. Unsatisfied with the claim that skewed urban systems are generic characteristics of formally colonized, export-dependent, peripheral countries, she developed a "class relations theory of urban primacy" (most clearly developed in C. Smith, 1985). To fully understand Guatemalan primacy, she asserted, one has to analyze how the particular mercantile elite, in *both* the capital and the provincial centers, developed historically. Primacy is explained by the movement of rural migrants toward places of economic opportunity. Guatemala City, with an open labor market characterized by many informal sector enterprises, does attract migrants. Equally important, however, are the relatively closed labor markets in the secondary centers controlled by an older commercial elite. This provincial mercantile elite has managed to maintain a monopoly over business and commerce in these smaller cities—thus leaving no openings for new workers from the countryside. Contradictory class relations, in this case between the externally oriented national bourgeoisie and an older, entrenched provincial merchant class, have led to "a relatively poorly integrated urban system (and immature city-size distribution) with a single major (primate) center" (C. Smith, 1985: 143). Smith (1982a) provided a theoretical typology. She distinguished between "premodern," "transitional," and "modern" forms of urban primacy. Her point was that "the underlying cause of the selective urban growth that produces primacy, urban migration, is of a fundamentally different nature in precapitalist and capitalist economies" (C. Smith, 1985: 79). Transitional urban primacy is found in the contemporary Third World. It results in huge cities that are "overlarge in population and oversmall in urban functions" (C. Smith, 1982a: 85). There is no simple relationship between lognormal city-size distributions and development, as scholars like Brian Berry have suggested (see Berry, 1971). Instead, the crucial variable is the manner and degree to which the penetration of capitalism gives rise to free wage labor.

> I wish to emphasize the importance of free labor. As long as producers are tied to particular enterprises and to particular elites, and as long as producers are overworked by their overseers when labor is scarce or underworked by them when labor is abundant (but the labor is kept on to maintain the prestige and political power of the elites who control them), one will *not* find the cities in an urban system growing in relationship to the sizes of cities around them, the urban growth pattern that produces lognormalcy. Thus, I assert, one does not find "modern" urban systems until one finds the conditions which give rise to modern capitalism— abundant, free, wage labor (C. Smith, 1982a: 82).

This linkage between dependency, class alignments, and the emergence of free wage labor (i.e., "the proletarianization of the labor force") may explain a variety of the macrostructural transformations in underdeveloped societies—including, but not limited to, the unbalanced pattern of urban development considered here.[6]

Perhaps the most important and comprehensive historical-structural treatment of dependent urbanization in Latin America was provided by Roberts (1978a, 1978b). In *Cities of Peasants: The Political Economy of Urbanization in the Third World*, he explicitly identified his goal of showing how European economic expansion

> from the sixteenth century onwards has shaped the patterns of growth in underdeveloped areas of the world. . . . I will suggest that the most convincing framework for our analysis is that of the economic interdependency of nations and regions within nations. . . . The potential of any one area, such as its urban or industrial growth, is formed by that area's position within a wider world economic system (Roberts, 1978a: 1–2).

Roberts insisted on viewing urbanization as being closely tied to other social transformations affected by world-system position and dynamics. But his major focus was the "internal structure of class relationships which work to the economic advantage of the metropolis and to the progressive underdevelopment of the periphery" (Roberts, 1978a: 14). Much of the substance of the book emphasized the manner in which patterns of urbanization, migration, and urban economic and class structure are affected by changing contexts of industrialization, elite power, and state centralization in Latin American countries. Beginning with a chapter on the colonial period and the historical process of integration into the European economy, this analysis was extremely sensitive to the importance of both the initial penetration by and the subsequent development of world and local capitalism. Discussing topics like agrarian structure, urban "dual economies," and poverty and "marginality," Roberts took great pains to sketch the links upward to the area's and nation's role in the world economy. Dependent development is a dynamic process that unfolds in particular ways in the various Latin American countries. Because of the different roles that nations play in the international system and their distinct historical heritages, all underdeveloped societies are not characterized by identical class and state structures. In turn, these particular configurations of dependent societies' political economies will lead to differential urban outcomes.

For instance, it is a truism that the growth of manufacturing has promoted urbanization in nearly all nations where it has occurred (Mills and Song, 1979: 10). Roberts (1978a), however, pointed out that there are both different types of industrialization *and* urbanization in Third World countries. Certain forms of manufacturing—particularly import substitution industrialization (ISI)—are likely to spawn primate urban systems characterized by high levels of income concentration (Roberts, 1978a: 81). Countries that do not follow the ISI path are less likely to exhibit similar patterns of uneven growth.

Not surprisingly, in-depth case study research on the historical development of dependent urbanization in Africa and Asia is much spottier than that for Latin America. Ademola Salau (1978) presented a theoretical survey of cities in tropical Africa, concluding that a city's effect on national economic development is contingent on the role the urban place plays in the world economy. He argued that most large African cities are direct products of capitalist expansion and perform an intermediary role in a hierarchy of exploitation that has its apex in metropolitan cities and its roots in the African hinterland. Paul Lubeck's (1977) case study of northern Nigeria and Josef Gugler and William Flanagan's (1977) survey article were other early attempts to flesh out a political economy approach to urbanization in Africa. The literature developing from this perspective on Asia was arguably even thinner, despite the prescience of T. G. McGee's classic, *The Southeast Asian City* (1969). Even in the 1960s, McGee was already developing many of the basic elements (the key role of colonialism, the pervasiveness of Third World inequality, the paradoxical nature of "the bazaar economy") of the world-system approach (see also McGee, 1971, 1973).

Nevertheless, one little-noticed but significant in-depth historical analysis of a particular case of uneven urban growth in the Third World did focus on Asia. London's (1980) major concern was to explain a case of extreme urban primacy—Bangkok, Thailand. In this book and in an earlier article, this researcher explicitly tried to develop "a more 'politically' comparative urban sociology" (London, 1979: 485). His work offered an extensive historical treatment of the politics of urban concentration. Noting the overwhelming power of the Bangkok elite since the mid-nineteenth century, London detailed how policy decisions bearing on governmental reorganization, fiscal and economic strategy, education, and transportation all tended to reinforce the metropolis's functional and demographic dominance. A major weakness of his analysis is its failure to adequately locate the "internal colonialism" carried out by the Bangkok elite in the context of this group's and the nation's role in the world economy. For the analysis to be complete, it would be necessary to better locate Thailand in the international system and explain the transnational alliances of the Thai elite. Needless to say, the creation and survival of the Bangkok elites was tied to the relations they maintained with other power centers in the world economy and politics. Despite this analytical weakness (and an occasionally slip into a culturalist mode of explanation), London's case study helps explain the kinds of historical dynamics that affect the rise of urban primacy in the underdeveloped world. Its most important contribution is an insistence that cities are shaped not by vague social forces but by the concrete policymaking of political and economic elites.

World-System Hierarchy and Vertical
Linkages: Beyond Core and Periphery

Having reviewed some of the literature of both the quantitative cross-national approach and the qualitative historical-structural strategy, it is now time to attempt a synthesis. Both approaches are legitimate ways to study the political economy of urbanization in the modern world-system. In fact, although they vary in their basic foci and perhaps even in some epistemological assumptions, I would argue that these two modes of analysis can be used in a complementary fashion (see also D. Smith, 1991). The search for generalizable causal relationships between a nation's position in the world-system and their urban patterns and processes is best carried out using some sort of hypothesis-testing strategy. Trying to discover probabilistic "laws" of world-system development through the use of the comparative method is a legitimate goal of macrosociological research (Chase-Dunn, 1981a; see also Lenski, 1976). But historical case studies are also vital. They allow social scientists to understand the *mechanisms* that operate within and between societies to bring about large-scale changes. This latter research methodology can provide a concrete analysis of the ways in which class relationships, ecological factors, and other important local characteristics are articulated with the international system and how they interact to produce specific outcomes in processes such as urbanization. It seems appropriate to formulate a research design that incorporates aspects of both of these approaches.[7]

Roberts's (1978a) insistence on multiple patterns of urbanization and development in Latin America presented a problem for oversimplified versions of dependency theory. Many North American social scientists of the quantitative ilk have reduced the concept of dependence to a continuous measure of the degree of foreign penetration into Third World economies or scores of various types of trade concentration. Most of the studies based on multiple regression that were discussed earlier have operationalized dependence in this way. In an analogous fashion, researchers working from a more qualitative historical bent often emphasized the dichotomy between core and periphery or dependent and autonomous. Slater (1978: 29), for instance, while acknowledging the need to distinguish between various types of underdeveloped countries, set out to understand urbanization in the context of "the unity of dependent, or what I prefer to call peripheral, capitalism."

Obviously, these types of approaches do not adequately specify the important differences between dependent countries that Roberts claimed are critical for truly comprehending the processes of urbanization and development. The problem is that "dependency needs to be analyzed in terms of discrete, structurally-similar 'situations' . . . rather than as a continuum" (Gereffi, 1979: 4). Dependence should be viewed as a referring to "general referential contexts" (Duvall, 1978: 39)—not simply as either the general condition of all Third World societies or a variable property of those nations. Those who claim to measure "degrees of dependency" or assume that all forms of dependence are similar miss part of the theoretical kernel of dependency theory (Cardoso and Faletto, 1979: XII).

When the concept of dependence is used as a "general referential context," it closely resembles Wallerstein's notion of countries holding structural positions in the world economy. Most previous research on dependent or peripheral urbanization has failed to systematically utilize the notion of a capitalist world-system organized into a hierarchy of discrete positions of core, periphery, and semiperiphery. Wallerstein (1974a and 1974b, 1980, 1989) and others (for instance, Evans, 1979b; Chase-Dunn, 1980; Gereffi and Evans, 1981) have argued that the tripartite division between core, periphery, and semiperiphery makes theoretical sense and is useful in empirical analyses. The crucial insight here is not the number of layers but the idea of countries occupying structurally isomorphic levels in a coherent world-system. Nations holding similar positions and ostensibly playing similar roles in the world division of labor should exhibit parallel patterns of macrostructural change. The observation by Roberts (1978a) that urbanization patterns and processes varied in Latin America according to type of industrial growth may be suggestive in this regard. If nations can be meaningfully differentiated by world-system position and if these strata play certain identifiable roles in the world economic system, then one would expect *both* industrialization and urbanization to systematically vary by structural position.

The use of a model of the world-system that incorporates this idea of a three-tiered hierarchy of structural positions would be a significant change from either the discrete or continuous bipolar conception of dependency. This type of model squares with the general human ecological notion of the ubiquity and structural necessity of hierarchies within highly differentiated systems (see Hawley, 1968a: 333). It also suggests that the roles countries play in the international system—and, by extension, aspects of their related internal structures and dynamics—are defined by the countries' positions in this global division of labor (Evans, 1979a). This suggests that urbanization and other macrosociological configurations and processes are likely to be different in the periphery than in the semiperiphery. A serious examination of a layered model of the world-system may help comparative urban researchers to sort out and explain the apparent diversity of patterns in the contemporary underdeveloped world.

A basic premise of the research presented in this volume is that the role a nation plays in the world-economy will affect the pattern of urban development. Nations in the periphery and semiperiphery will be expected to exhibit differing urbanization patterns, with the most uneven patterns likely to occur in the periphery. But I will not argue that world-system position *determines* urban patterns. Instead, position in the international economic system is seen as limiting and constraining patterns of development, including urbanization. That is, world economic position and the roles societies play in the world-system will narrow the arc of possible development trajectories rather than mechanistically determine patterns of change. Therefore, it is expected that a quantitative analysis of the relationship between world-system position and various measures of development and urban configuration will reveal systematic relationships between the former and the latter.

But arriving at such generalizable patterns is only the beginning of the research agenda designed to explore the political economy of dependent urbanization. To look exclusively at world-system, structural properties is to assume that a sort of external determination of development processes proceeds within societies. This approach, by itself, is one-sided and inadequate. Fernando Cardoso and Enzo Faletto (1979: XV–XVI) eloquently explain:

> We do not see dependency and imperialism as external and internal sides of a single coin, with the internal aspects reduced to the condition of "epiphenomenal"
> . . ..
> We conceive the relationship between external and internal forces as forming a complex whole whose structural links are not based on mere external forms of exploitation and coercion, but are rooted in the coincidence of interests between

local dominant classes and international ones, and, on the other side, are challenged by local dominated groups and classes.

A comprehensive treatment of the process of urbanization in the world-economy necessitates a historical-structural approach to complement the cross-national quantitative research. It must stress the importance of the world-system context of local areas and class structures, the dynamics of internal politics, the material interests of elite groups, and the concentration of state power and autonomy that have a considerable impact on urban structures. Therefore, the greater portion of this volume is devoted to developing historical case studies of particular world regions and nations within them. While cross-national research gives us broad generalizations about the relationship between world-system position and urban patterns, this historical-structural analysis should provide information about the more proximate causes of specific patterns of urban growth. This portion of the book focuses on the mechanisms determining urban configurations. Here, in other words, an attempt is made to show how particular historical processes in "local" areas worked to produce the world pattern of urbanization that emerges from the cross-national analysis of the contemporary period. In a suggestive early article, Walton (1979a: 164) noted:

> What is called for, and beginning to emerge in recent urban research, is a new unit of analysis based on distinctive *vertically integrated processes* passing through a network from the international level to the urban hinterland. Another definitive feature of the new urban research is a closer integration of historical and contemporary analyses, particularly greater emphasis on the manner in which the colonial heritage and process of incorporation into the world economy variously condition the social, economic, and spatial organization of cities.

This research agenda will be carried out by focusing first on the nature and time of the original contact that a colonial area or nation had with the European world economy' the area's initial role in the world-system may have led to the growth of certain types of cities. The manner in which urban patterns in such areas have been either altered or maintained as the areas' roles in the world-system changed is also explored. A basic linkage, in this regard, is the relationship between structural positions in the world-economy and the functional role that a region's or nation's urban system plays. As certain parts of the former periphery become semiperipheral, does this systematically affect the regional or national urbanization patterns?

The emphasis in these case studies will be on the political economy of urbanization. Urbanization is a process of decisionmaking. Taking a cue from human ecological research, I will pay particular attention to the development of transportation and communication systems. But it is critical that processes such as the creation of transport networks are not viewed in a vacuum since these changes themselves are the result of political processes. The dependency/world-system perspective suggests that local and national political elites and dominant economic groups in the underdeveloped or dependent areas of the world have close class linkages to the international elites (for instance, see Cardoso and Faletto, 1979; Evans, 1979b). A major hypothesis of this research is that the mechanism by which structural position in the world-system affects urbanization involves the articulation of these local and international class structures.

A critical issue to explore is whether power is concentrated in the hands of urban elites and what class interests these elites represent locally *and* internationally. The coincidence of the material interests of local urban elites and the dominant classes globally will have an effect either on policy decisions bearing on infrastructural development or on the distribution of power and resources within the dominant city or throughout the urban hierarchy. In turn, these decisions will have a great impact on urban growth, urban primacy, and intra-urban inequality.

Summary and a General Model

In this chapter, I have presented an overview of approaches to the political economy of dependent urbanization. I have highlighted the points of convergence and divergence with more traditional human ecological analyses of urban systems/developmentalist perspectives on macrostructural change. My approach is different from these, but it does not categorically reject the potential insights found in this literature. Previous research in the world-system analysis of cities has followed two distinct methodological paths, which were reviewed earlier.

Before turning to the empirical evidence, I will outline a general theoretical model for urbanization in the world-economy based on the preceding discussion. This model is schematically depicted in Figure 1.1. I will return to this figure in Chapter 8. Briefly, the argument contends, in agreement with traditional human ecological approaches, that technological and economic infrastructures are very important causal agents generating patterns of urban structure. Networks of transportation and communication are critical proximate influences shaping the growth of an urban system or an individual city. But roads, railroads, port facilities, and telegraph and telephone lines are constructed to fit the needs and interests of the powerful in various societies. Therefore, class structures and the state are also critical determinants of urban configurations. Class alignments and states, however, can only be understood in the context of a nation's role in the global system. And the types of niches available in the international division of labor are dependent on the world historical characteristics of particular periods of world-system expansion and contraction. Tracing the linkages backward, I contend that urban patterns arise in response to infrastructural changes that are implemented to fulfill the needs of elite groups whose formation and interests are fully explicable only by

Figure 1.1   Urbanization in the World-System: Model of How Macrostructures Set the Parameters for Urban Development

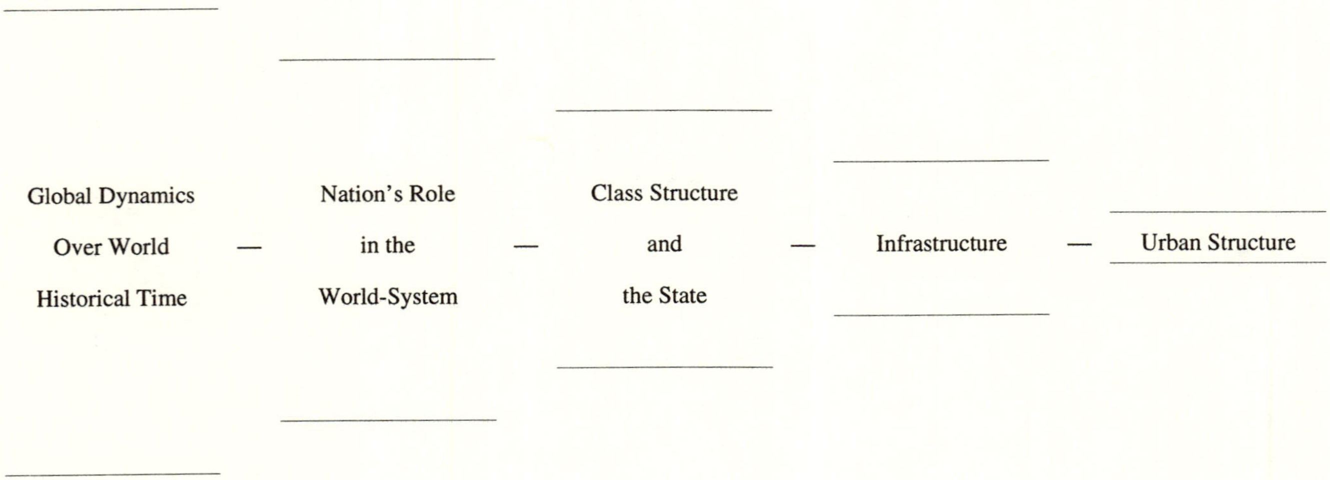

| Global Dynamics
Over World
Historical Time | — | Nation's Role
in the
World-System | — | Class Structure
and
the State | — | Infrastructure | — | Urban Structure |

understanding ing the historical relationships between them and their society and the evolving capitalist world-system.

The next chapter begins the real task of this book: analyzing empirical data about cities and urban systems. The quantitative work reported there offers an overview of the global picture of urban patterns and trends. It sets the broad context for the in-depth historical case studies that make up the balance of the volume.

2

Global Patterns: A Cross-National Analysis of Urbanization

The key theoretical premise of the political economy of the world-system analysis is that the roles countries play in the international division of labor have critical effects on national development trajectories. Various types of macrostructural dynamics within a society are posited to be related to a country's membership in the core, periphery, or semiperiphery.

Chapter 1 suggests that this general hypothesis should hold in relation to urban patterns. The rise of cities and systems of cities is an integral part of wider processes of societal growth and development. Placing urbanization in an international political economy context implies that there will be essential differences between urban dynamics in the distinct world-system zones.

Most cross-national studies of the effects of the international division of labor on Third World societies use continuous variables such as "trade dependence" or "foreign direct investment" as proxies for "role in the world-system" (see Bornschier and Chase-Dunn, 1985, for an exhaustive review). While the idea of a role is relational by definition, operationalizing dependence as an attribute of a particular country has a number of practical advantages. The data on gross characteristics such as trade, aid, and investment are usually more readily available. Also, the continuous nature of the measures are easily accommodated to the type of linear models with which many quantitative social scientists are most familiar.

Despite the pragmatic advantages of attributional measures of penetration or dependence in cross-national research, this approach has its shortcomings as a faithful operationalization of world-system concepts. Most theoretical elaborations emphasize the need to study the *relationships* between various societies and regions, and they highlight the degree to which local and national dynamics must be understood as embedded and intermeshed within a complex global system. Social changes in various societies are seen as "the consequence of occupying a given structural position within the world-system as a whole" (Evans, 1979b: 15). Wallerstein (1974a, 1979) argues that there are three strata that play distinct economic and political roles in the international system: the core, periphery, and semiperiphery. These world zones are a historical product of the expansion of the world capitalist system and various forms of imperialism. The core countries are the advanced industrial states literally at the center of various political, economic, and cultural networks. The countries of the periphery are at the other extreme: often tied to the entire system through strong dependence ties with a single core nation. The countries of the semiperiphery differ politically and economically from either the core or the periphery nations. They form a middle category in terms of commodity mixes of production and trade, and they function as a political buffer between the two extremes of the world-system. This "structural" view of a relational international system suggests that a network analytic approach to measuring "roles" in the system more accurately captures the essence of the Wallersteinian view. Such a measure is used here.

Since the world-system paradigm stresses the distinct developmental dynamics of the three zones, my main hypothesis is that there will be significant and persistent differences between urbanization in the core, periphery, and semiperiphery. This expectation, of course, runs directly counter to that of the more traditional developmentalist or modernization theory approach to cities in less developed areas. This approach suggests that all societies evolve through a sequence of stages approximating the phases of city growth in Western urban history (see, for example, Reissman, 1964). Modernization theorists saw the Third World city as a locus for innovation, opportunity, and political transformation (Friedmann, 1978), with a net generative influence on the host societies (Hoselitz, 1954). Using the advanced nations as their model, these scholars assumed that urbanization is an ineluctable part of industrialization and economic growth (see Roberts, 1978a: chapter 1). Since urbanization, in this view, is a unified and universal phenomenon, developmental theory suggests an eventual *convergence* in urbanization patterns across the globe.

In this chapter, I will report the findings of a simple test of this convergence hypothesis using cross-national statistical data on urban patterns.[1] I will begin with simple descriptive statistics (averages across various zones and regions) and move to a very straightforward regression analysis designed to untangle causality. This approach reveals the association between the world-system status of countries and their generic patterns of city growth. A global analysis gives an overview of the gross patterns of urbanization in the world-system, which serves as a context for the more in-depth historical-structural analysis of specific cases later in this volume.

Measuring Urbanization and World-System Status

While urbanization is a very concrete demographic and physical reality, some basic problems arise in making cross-national comparisons of data on cities. The first is primarily one of classification: What is the minimum population a settlement must reach before becoming officially designated as "urban"? (For a wide range of size definitions, see United Nations, 1980: annex 1.) Since most statistics on the size and structure of urban places are collected by various national governments (with wide-ranging cultural and operational definitions of what constitutes a "city"), some of these data must be interpreted very cautiously. The second problem is in some ways more serious: This is the issue of urban boundaries. Cities are politically defined areas as well as sociologically meaningful units of analysis. But rarely do the political boundaries and the extent of the city as a social system exactly coincide. Cities undergoing rapid growth, like those of Third World countries, are particularly likely to spread geographically beyond juridical limits. Many countries have adjusted for urbanization outside the legal boundaries of their cities by providing data and/or estimates for metropolitan areas as well as for central cities. In this volume, these sources are utilized wherever possible. But countries also vary in terms of their definitions of a "metropolitan area" or an "urban agglomeration." These caveats should be kept in mind when interpreting the results of the analysis in this chapter.[2]

Data relevant to this study are available from international data sources published by the United Nations and the World Bank. Data on many aspects of urbanization (i.e., data on intracity inequality or regional income distribution, housing provision, or the extent of urban poverty) are not available, exist only for very few countries, or are impossible to find in even the most roughly comparable form. But a number of important characteristics of cities and city systems can be tapped using these sources. The challenge is to translate the available data into operationalizeable variables measuring the concepts of most interest to urban researchers. In this chapter, I examine the overall level of urbanization, lead-city primacy, and urban bias.[3]

Level of Urbanization

The most obvious measure of national urbanization is simply the percentage of the population living in areas classified as cities. This is a familiar index used by a wide array of scholars. These data are taken from the most recent *World Urbanization Prospects: The 1992 Revision* (United Nations, 1993). Unfortunately, they reflect differing national definitions of the term *urban*, including data for cities of various size thresholds.[4] The 1990 percentage, one of the most recent indicators available, is chosen to maximize the time lag in the data, to allow the best possible test of possible convergence (see London, 1987). Obviously, these data need to be interpreted with special caution since they are not completely comparable. Despite potential reliability problems, these data provide the most adequate recent information on population distribution between rural and urban populations for a large number of countries. In Table 2.1 URB60, URB83, and URB90 represent the

TABLE 2.1   Mean Urban Characteristics by World-System Region, 1960–1990

	PRIMACY			*URBAN BIAS*			*% URBAN*	
PRIM60	*PRIM80*	*PRIM90*	*GSECT60*	*GSECT70*	*DISP65*	*URB60*	*URB83*	*URB90*
CORE*								
3.25	3.03	2.56	14.0	10.8	2.29	67.3	72.3	76.4
(17)	(17)	(13)	(17)	(17)	(15)	(15)	(17)	(17)
SEMIPER								
4.50	4.20	4.20	24.6	21.9	3.64	40.1	57.1	58.3
(25)	(27)	(22)	(22)	(23)	(18)	(28)	(27)	(28)
PER								
4.27	4.58	4.53	32.9	34.5	6.71	27.6	39.9	44.3
(27)	(41)	(22)	(48)	(57)	(47)	(67)	(62)	(67)
MEAN								
4.10	4.15	3.95	27.1	27.4	5.19	36.2	49.5	52.7
(71)	(85)	(56)	(87)	(97)	(80)			
AFRICA								
5.81	4.41	3.67	36.8	41.0	9.29	15.3	25.5	30.3
(7)	(18)	(7)	(34)	(27)	(30)	(48)	(33)	(48)
ASIA								
2.40	2.25	4.65	23.5	22.5	3.87	19.9	38.2	32.9
(12)	(13)	(10)	(11)	(14)	(15)	(21)	(19)	(21)
LAT-AM								
6.70	7.32	5.58	26.6	25.1	3.65	44.2	56.9	54.6
(12)	(15)	(10)	(21)	(21)	(17)	(30)	(20)	(32)
EUROPE								
4.05	3.61	3.42	17.7	13.4	2.47	54.1	64.0	70.8
(22)	(23)	(18)	(20)	(20)	(14)	(24)	(25)	(27)
NOR-AM								
1.70	1.40	1.30	6.5	3.7	1.95	69.5	74.5	76.0
(2)	(2)	(2)	(2)	(2)	(2)	(2)	(2)	(2)
OCEAN								
4.00	3.93	3.93	17.2	18.3	4.73	30.7	55.5	40.8
(3)	(3)	(4)	(2)	(4)	(3)	(9)	(4)	(6)
USSR								
1.80	1.80	—	—	—	—	49.0	65.0	64.0
(1)	(1)	(1)	(1)	(1)				
DESERT**								
3.02	2.06	2.78	33.1	33.9	6.95	41.9	57.0	66.1
(12)	(14)	(9)	(11)	(16)	(12)	(19)	(18)	(19)
MEAN								
4.02	4.11	3.88	28.0	28.5	5.75	32.7	47.3	48.1
(71)	(89)	(60)	(101)	(114)	(93)	(154)	(122)	(159)

Number of cases for each cell in parenthesis., Urban variables and data sources are described in text.

*Core, periphery and semiperiphery are based on Bolle's (1983) classification.

**This world region includes the Middle East and North African countries that border the Mediterranean Sea.

level of urbanization in 1960, 1983, and 1990, respectively. Since the distribution of these variables is skewed, however, they are logarithmically transformed for the regression analysis presented in Table 2.2 (LURB60, LURB83, LURB90).

Urban Primacy

As the discussion in Chapter 1 makes clear, the shape of national city-size distribution has been an enduring and recurring issue in comparative urban research (Jefferson, 1938; Friedmann and Lackington, 1967; Linsky, 1969; Berry, 1971; McGreevey, 1971; Mera, 1978; C. Smith, 1985). Some scholars believe urban primacy—the demographic and/or functional dominance of the most populous city—is likely to have dire effects on national development (Friedmann and Lackington, 1967; Linsky, 1969); others see no ill effects (Mera, 1978), and still others reach inconclusive results (Timberlake, 1979).

Here, primacy is conceptualized as a structural characteristic of a city system and an indicator of a sort of uneven urbanization, without an evaluation of its positive or negative effects. The measure I use is a simple one: the population of the largest city divided by the population of the second largest city.[5] Once again, the source for the 1960 and 1980 data is the United Nations (1980). Because of a change in the way the United Nations compiles its data, urban primacy measures for 1990 were calculated using two separate sources (United Nations, 1992, 1993). Data for its *World Urbanization Prospects* series no longer include populations of secondary cities with fewer than 1 million inhabitants in 1990; therefore, it was necessary to augment this standardized source with information from national censuses from approximately 1990 (ranging from 1987 to 1992). Unfortunately, even this strategy resulted in much missing data—only sixty countries have scores for urban primacy at this most recent time point. Like the overall level of urbanization measure, this variable is also logged to correct for skewness in Table 2.2. In Table 2.1, it is labeled PRIM60, PRIM80, and PRIM90; in Table 2.2, the monikers LPRIM60, LPRIM80 and LPRIM90 are used.

Urban Bias

One of the seminal monographs on Third World urbanization of the 1970s was Michael Lipton's *Why Poor People Stay Poor: Urban Bias in World Development*. His thesis is that political forces and elites that funnel resources toward cities, to the neglect and impoverishment of rural areas, are integral components of underdevelopment in many less developed countries. The urban concentration of financial and human resources not only leads to rural-urban inequality but also retards positive efforts to attain national development. Clearly, this concept of urban bias is related to the emphasis on the *political* underpinning of city growth discussed earlier.

TABLE 2.2   Regression of Urban Characteristics on Level of Economic Development and World-System Status

	LURB83	*LURB90*	*GSECT70*	*LPRIM80*	*LPRIM90*
Lagged D.V.	.46**	.64**	-.75**	.78**	.82**
LGNP65	.55**	.39**	-.22**	.20*	-.003
SEMIPER	.21**	.19**	-.07	.21*	.O7
PER	.26**	.23**	.02	.20*	.27*
R^2	.68	.79	.85	.62	.71
Adj. R^2	.67	.78	.84	.59	.68
N	86	89	80	60	43

Variables defined in the text

*indicates parameter at least 1.5 times its standard error (p <.10)

**indicates parameter at least twice its standard error (p <.05)

Measuring this variable requires constructing an index that will operationalize sectoral inequality between urban and rural areas within countries. Ideally, the urban bias variable would *directly* gauge the relative distribution of resources and investment to the cities versus the resources and investment flowing into the countryside. Unfortunately, good data on the spatial allocation of material inequality are unavailable for most countries. Instead, two proxy measures must be used. The first is the measure of rural-urban disparity constructed by Bradshaw (1987). This variable, explicitly based on Lipton's argument, divides the ratio of output for each nonagricultural worker to the output for each worker in agriculture (Bradshaw, 1987: 230–231), and is measured for 1965 (DISP65 in Table 2.1). The second index is a gini coefficient of sectoral inequality that uses data on product per worker in agriculture, service, and manufacturing to measure "the imbalance between the rural subsistence farming sector and the urban commercial and manufacturing sectors of a dual economy characteristic of a developing country" (Taylor and Jodice, 1983: 139). Because of data limitations, it is only possible to construct these variables for 1960 (GSECT60) and 1970 (GSECT70).

World-System Status

To preserve its relational nature, world-system status is derived from the network analysis of the international system originally done by David Snyder and Edward Kick (1979) and revised by Kenneth Bollen (1983). This attempt to "empirically ground" Wallerstein's model involved examining four types of international transaction flows: trade, treaty membership, military intervention, and diplomatic exchange (Snyder and Kick, 1979). A mathematical algorithm clustered countries into nine "structurally equivalent" blocks, and further analysis demonstrated that these clusterings were reducible to the familiar tripartite division of core, periphery, and semiperiphery. Bollen (1983) later reclassified six nations that he felt were misspecified by the Snyder and Kick analysis.

This classification scheme has been widely criticized on both theoretical and methodological grounds (see, for example, Nemeth and Smith, 1985a), and I have developed an alternative network measure of world-system roles (Smith and White, 1992). But there are some compelling reasons to use it nevertheless. First, it has become the standard quantitative categorization of world-system status and is widely used in cross-national research. Utilizing this measure allows scholars to compare their results with other studies, and it makes a cumulative comparative social science possible. Second, the alternative schema that I am developing, focusing exclusively on international commodity trade, shows considerable promise but at this point still has some problems of its own. Probably the most important limitation for work of the type presented here is the limited number of cases included. While Snyder and Kick (1979) included 120 nations, my colleagues and I could only examine 86 in Nemeth and Smith (1985a) and 62 in Smith and White

(1992). These recent network analyses of world-system structure provide a more theoretically sound image of the entire system, but they contain too many missing cases (particularly among Third World countries) to be used in the analysis presented in this chapter.[6]

Urbanization and the World-System: Results

Table 2.1 presents values of the urban variables by world-system status and for various world geographical regions. The division by geographic regions follows the standard classification by international agencies and is familiar (with the exception of the region labeled DESERT—see the table note). The values presented in this table are simply descriptive statistics of the means of the untransformed variables—no inferential tests of significance appear here. To read the table, scan up and down for the differences between world-system positions or regions; read across rows for changes over time.

Basic Patterns

There is a great deal of information in this table. No attempt will be made to discuss all the details in the text, but two major themes do emerge. The first is that (reading down the columns) there are substantial differences between core and noncore, advanced regions and less developed countries on almost all the variables. The second is that (reading across rows), by and large, there is little evidence of convergence: Differences found at the earlier time point are also found at the later one. The gap between core and periphery seems to be particularly stable and even widens over time for the urban primacy and urban bias measures. The core scores lower on these variables, the gap between core and semiperiphery remains the same, and the core-periphery differences increase. The core (and advanced regions) also have higher levels of urbanization at both time points. But here, I can make a modest claim that some convergence has occurred (although some of this may be attributable to asymptotic effects of percentages approaching 100).

In summary, Table 2.1 shows substantial differences in urban patterns, with noncore and especially peripheral societies exhibiting more uneven urbanization. And the varying time lags built into the table show continuing divergent trajectories. So the comparison of variables before and after turns up little evidence for convergence. There is, therefore, little prima facie evidence to suggest that the international political economy view should be abandoned in favor of a return to developmentalism. On the contrary, the descriptive analysis shows that differences are correlated with world-system status. But does a country's role in the global system exert any *causal* influence on these divergent urban patterns? The regression analysis in the next section directly addresses this question.

A Causal Model

Most of the quantitative studies reviewed in Chapter 1 used panel regression analysis to explore world-system effects on urbanization (for example, Kentor, 1981; London, 1987). In a panel regression analysis, the dependent variable at a recent point in time is regressed on itself and the independent variable measured earlier. The result is an estimation of the effects of the predictor variables on *change* in the dependent variable. Using this technique ameliorates the problem of reciprocal causation that is endemic to cross-sectional analysis. Also, since the dependent variables at two points in time are usually very highly correlated to one another, panel analyses assign maximum explanatory power to the lagged dependent variable. Therefore, it is an extremely conservative test of the effects of the substantively important independent variables on change in the dependent variable (cf. Heise, 1970; Hannan, 1979). One of the limitations of this type of regression involves the statistical problem of heteroscedasticity (Jackman, 1980). The fine points of this issue (it has to do with nonindependent error terms) are irrelevant here. However, this problem can usually be avoided by logarithmic transformation of the dependent and logged dependent variables—which I have done in the following analysis.

Table 2.2 presents the results of five multiple regression equations. In each, the dependent variable for the earlier time point (i.e., the lagged dependent variable) is entered into the equation (so, for example, in the first column, LURB60 is the first predictor variable). As expected, a country's prior score on each urban variable is a strong predictor of that characteristic at a later time. The lagged dependent variable is highly significant (probability level over .05) in each equation (read across the top row of Table 2.2). The second independent variable is LGNP65—a logged measure of GNP per capita in 1965. This is a control variable consistent with the developmentalist assumption that the level of economic development should be the crucial determinant of urbanization. It is also a consistently significant predictor of the dependent variable (with one exception, noted later), although in the case of the overall level of urbanization in 1983, it is generally not quite as strong as the lagged dependent variable. The final two variables are the world-system position measures, which are the real variables of interest in this analysis. Following a conventional technique for regression with categorical independent variables, I assign the core as the reference category and create dummy variables for the periphery (PER) and semiperiphery (SEMIPER).

The causal efficacy of the world-system status varies across equations. The weakest effects are found in the GSECT equation, where the world-system effects are negligible. For this indicator of "urban bias," a very large proportion of the variance of the index in 1970 is accounted for by the lagged dependent variable and the overall level of economic development. The R^2 value of .85 is very large, suggesting that these parameters explain this measure of sectoral inequality very well indeed. For this particular variable, the divergence found in Table 2.1 (which was substantial) appears to be due to differences in early levels of economic development, not role in the world-system.

This is definitely not the case, however, for either lagged equations predicting the general level of urbanization or for the regression for urban primacy in 1980. A glance at these rows (first, second, and fourth) shows that the world-system effects are strong and statistically significant. In the first two panels, the global system variable is as significant as the initial level of development measure, with noncore countries exhibiting more rapid urban growth netting out the effects of initial level of economic development. (Moreover, entering LGNP65 into the equation assumes that it is completely independent of world-system status, which it almost certainly is not. This variable "dilutes" their effects, making the test of the international system variables even more conservative.) The explained variance in these equations, while slightly lower than that of GSECT, is quite high (68 percent, 79 percent, and 62 percent). The two equations predicting the later level of urbanization produce the most robust results, with both high R^2 and world-system variables (as well as LGNP65) that are significant at the .05 level. Predicting urban primacy in 1980 is more difficult—both the overall R^2 and the significant levels of the world-system dummy variables are lower; however, this is not too surprising since attempts to statistically account for outcomes on this variable often fail (see D. Smith 1984). One pattern that does not emerge across these equations is a lack of clear differences between the periphery and semiperiphery—"dependent urbanization" seems to suffice.[7] These results demonstrate not only that there are persisting differences between core and noncore on overall urban levels and urban primacy but also that the global system status variables seem to *explain* these differences, even when the lagged dependent variable and level of economic development are controlled.

The equation for urban primacy in 1990 produces the most inconsistent results. Here, only the lagged dependent variable (LPRIM90) is significant: neither the prior level of economic development nor the world-system status have clear effects (though the periphery category is significant at the .10 level, providing some evidence that peripheral countries are more prone to primacy controlling of the other variables). These weak results almost surely reflect problems created by missing cases (the N for this equation drops down to 43) rather than any recent changes in the underlying factors that generate urban primacy.

The results of the regression analysis provide strong evidence that two aspects of urbanization (percent urban and lead-city primacy) not only are different between core and noncore, but also show continuing trajectories that diverge based, at least in part, on world-system status. The differences in sectoral inequality appear to be more closely related to overall level of economic development.

Conclusion

This chapter presents a quantitative cross-national analysis of the effects of world-system status on urbanization. The pattern in the descriptive statistics is unambiguous: There are persisting differences between urban patterns across world-system strata; in every case, the periphery is most characterized by rapid growth and urban unevenness; and there is little evidence of convergence (except on the confounded overurbanization measure). The regression analysis bolsters confidence in a world-system explanation of these results. With its inherently conservative approach, the analysis offers strong evidence that world-system position is an important causal variable explaining lagged changes in two of the three measures of urban structure (percent urban and lead-city primacy).

These results provide clear empirical evidence that the international political economy approach to urbanization, with its emphasis on divergent trajectories, yields an accurate image of world patterns. The lack of convergence, between either world-system strata or global regions, warns of the inadequacy of the developmentalist "one urbanization" approach. While this analysis suggests that attempts to understand urban structure should begin with the international context, it does not necessarily mean that city growth is structurally determined by world-system factors alone. It would be unwarranted, for example, to conclude that this analysis suggests external world-system factors are more important than internal regional or historical effects on urbanization.

Indeed, I feel that posing the question of the relative importance of these broad factors affecting urban development obfuscates the complex interrelatedness of processes at various levels of the modern world-system. Instead, a truly adequate analysis of particular instances of city growth must include both international and intranational factors and examine the process in a historical-structural way (Nemeth and Smith, 1985b; Kennedy and Smith, 1989). One way to conceptualize this approach is to view international political economic factors as shaping and constraining various intranational factors that, in turn, are the more proximate causes of both patterns of urbanization and other structural transformations in noncore nations (London, 1987). This view suggests that, while cross-national research like that reported in this chapter can provide the broad-brush images of global patterns (or debunk general misconceptions about them), case analytic studies hold the key to a more complex understanding of the actors, processes, and mechanisms underlying specific urban outcomes. Filling in the details of these stories is the task of the remaining chapters of the volume.

3

The Logic of Comparative
Historical-Structural Analysis

Urbanization is a dynamic process. The student of the city necessarily studies social change. Analysts writing from vantage points all along the ideological, political, and theoretical spectrum show uncharacteristic consensus on one point—urbanization and societal development are irrevocably intertwined. From Marx and Weber through Manuel Castells and Amos Hawley, social theorists have consistently highlighted the profound social transformations that accompany the growth of cities. Castells (1977: IX) sees cities as foci for epochal forces and conflict that generate "increasingly explosive urban contradictions." Similarly, Hawley (1971: 3) argues, "Cities stand at the vortices of the currents and cross-currents of broad-scale change that alters and reconstitutes societies." Whether it is seen as a catalyst for innovation, opportunity, and political transformation (J. Friedmann, 1978: 87) or as a product of "broader socio-economic changes" (Roberts, 1978a: 9), the city—wherever and whenever it has been studied—has been viewed as a complex amalgam of phenomena in process. Whether conceived of as "generative" or "parasitic," in Bert Hoselitz's (1954) timeworn sense, the city has always been regarded by social scientists as a locus of social change. Examining the structure of cities in static terms provides us only the most rudimentary sketch of their true natures. Urban systems, like other social structures, are constantly in the process of becoming (Giddens, 1982: 14).

Thus, what is clearly called for is an analysis that will confront the issue of social change and address urbanization as an unfolding process. To really understand cities and urban systems, one must first comprehend the wider economic, political, and social contexts of their emergence and growth. As Castells (1977: 7) claims, "It is in this sense that the study of the history of the process of urbanization would seem to be the best approach to the urban question, for it brings us to the problematic of the development of societies."

Sociology Reaches for History

In the previous chapter, some generalizations were made about the relationship between role in the world economic system and urban configurations. The objective of that analysis was to highlight some broad patterns of urbanization on a world scale.

The remaining empirical analysis of this volume is devoted to intensive historical case studies. Analytically, this portion of the research focuses on the mechanisms determining urban patterns and processes in specific colonized areas or dependent nations. The goal is to show how particular historical dynamics in "local" areas produce the world pattern of urbanization that emerges from cross-national research.

This does not mean that the analysis involves "doing history" in the sense in which this expression is often understood (or misunderstood). There is a tendency to see a rough division of labor between historians and social scientists. Historians are viewed as chroniclers of particular idiographic events or sequences of events, while sociologists are thought to seek general nomothetic explanations of social change. Charles Tilly (1982: 5) adroitly portrays this common image: The division of labor, then, resembles the division between the mycologist and the mushroom collector, between the critic and the translator, between the political analyst and city hall reporter, between brains and brawn. History does transcription, sociology does analysis."

But Tilly (1982: 6) argues that such a division into "particularizing" and "generalizing" is really a mystification implying that history somehow is "failed sociology." Historians, however, usually do not just recount narratives—they address "master questions and relevant theories" that are "well defined" (Tilly, 1982: 26). The hallmark of the historical approach is not idiographic singularization. Instead, what demarcates any study as truly historical is the integration of time and place into the theoretical argument. In other words, "to the extent that when something happens matters, history is important" (Tilly, 1982: 12).

Tilly's intent in *As Sociology Meets History* is not to glorify the academic discipline of history. But he does try to show that sociological theories of change need to be historically grounded. Rather than viewing history as "failed sociology," he suggests that we are guilty of "failed history" (Tilly, 1982: 7). Nor is the problem entirely one of poor data. Tilly's own work demonstrates that social science history can be quantitative and use relatively sophisticated techniques of statistical analysis. The real problem that has caused sociologists to neglect or even denigrate historical analysis is theoretical. Simply put, mainstream sociological approaches to social change often minimized the influence of specific historical contexts. The developmentalist theories of macrostructural change emphasized ahistorical processes like differentiation and reintegration. Modernization theory also depicted a single, oft-repeated path or formula for economic growth and social advancement. The historical circumstances of social change were de-emphasized because they seemed to have little theoretical relevance.

As Tilly points out, all this has changed in recent years. In the 1970s and 1980s, sociologists began to take historical and comparative analysis seriously. The reasons, again, were primarily theoretical. During this period, sociology was undergoing something of a Kuhnian revolution. Modernization theory was replaced by approaches that emphasized dependency relationships, class struggle, and the uneven development of the capitalist world-system (see the introduction). These new theoretical perspectives on macrostructural change mandated historical research "because, in one way or another, they portrayed the current situation of the poor countries as the outcome of a long, slow historically specific process of conquest, exploitation and control" (Tilly, 1982: 39). Work by the major world-system analysts like Wallerstein epitomize this shift. The focus on a single master process—"the incorporation of peripheral areas into the expanding capitalist world-system" (Tilly, 1982: 40)—necessitates close attention to the details of where and when Western economic penetration actually took place.

Obviously, my research is also grounded in this theoretical tradition. The question of the timing of capitalist penetration and the changing role a society plays within the world economy are critical variables in my model (see Chapter 1). So the approach to the case studies will be "historical structural." In other words, basic notions about the way the world-economy works and how classes within it align themselves will guide the empirical study of historically situated cases (see O'Donnell, 1978: 5). A colonial area's initial role in the world-system may have led to the growth of certain types of cities. The manner in which urban patterns in these areas were either altered or maintained, as regional roles in the world-system changed, is explored in the subsequent analysis. A basic linkage, in this regard, is the relationship between structural positions in the world-economy and the functional role that the region's or the nation's urban system plays. As certain parts of the periphery experience "dependent development" and become semiperipheral, does their mobility affect regional or national urbanization patterns?

The analysis in the preceding chapter suggests that, in fact, structural role in the world economy may influence urban variables in systematic ways. But this analysis surveyed a short period of time and does not capture longer patterns of motion in the world-system. Unfortunately, comprehensive quantitative data on the key indicators are usually limited to the past twenty or thirty years. World-system theory predicts macrostructural changes to occur over very long periods of time. Efforts to gauge processes from the 1950s or 1960s to the present are bound to miss long-term cycles and secular trends.[1] Beyond this lack of dynamism, there is another shortcoming in the cross-national analysis: Although it does describe general patterns relating structural position in the world economy to urban patterns, it fails to get at the mechanisms and actors that create certain patterns in the various strata, regions, or nations.

To incorporate a long-term time dimension and to specify the political and economic processes that play out into particular urban patterns requires an historical approach.

Theoretical Methods for Comparative History

When most sociologists think of methodology and methodologists, they usually think of quantitative data and its collection, manipulation, and analysis. Indeed, the spectacular development of increasingly sophisticated techniques in statistical analysis is an outstanding achievement of North American social science. Until recently, however, interest in the methodology of comparative and historical research has been minimal. This may be attributable to a paucity of work in this field of research, as well as a tendency to see historical sociology as being both an artistic and a scientific endeavor (Nisbet, 1976).

Recently, this has begun to change. A number of sociologists and social historians have attempted to survey, critique, and refine the methodological principles used (often implicitly) by comparative and historical social scientists (Vallier, 1971; Smelser, 1976; Stinchcombe, 1978; Skocpol and Somers, 1980; Tilly, 1982). Two basic analytic approaches have emerged from this literature. One (Skocpol and Somers, 1980) argues for analytical strategies that test theories and lead to validation of "bounded generalizations." The other (Stinchcombe, 1978) sees good social history as doing something quite different from testing theories; instead, the real goal is to find significant types of "deep analogies" across historical contexts. My work incorporates aspects of both these approaches.

Actually, Theda Skocpol and Margaret Somers (1980: 175) isolate three distinct logics of inquiry in comparative history: (1) "parallel demonstration of theory," (2) "contrast of contexts," and (3) "macro-causal analysis." The first of these methodologies is rather simple but also quite limited. "Parallel demonstration of theory" involves elaborating a model or hypothesis and subsequently demonstrating that it fits for a series of relevant historical trajectories. While this approach can clarify and illustrate theoretical propositions and perhaps point to potential refinements, it can never validate any theory. The second logical approach, comparative history as a "contrast of contexts," emphasizes the differences between cases (Skocpol and Somers, 1980: 178–181). Essentially, this approach is the one taken by "historical particularists" (see Lenski, 1976), who argue for the historical integrity and uniqueness of each sociohistorical configuration. Again, this type of approach has very limited goals—its practitioners do not seek to arrive at any sort of historical generalization. Quite to the contrary, this type of study strives to place limits on overly generalized theories. If anything, researchers using this second methodology display a basic antipathy toward the whole social science endeavor of building generalizable theory.

The last type of methodology that Skocpol and Somers discuss is clearly the one they find most useful. This is the "macro-analytical" approach. By combining the "method of agreement" and "the method of difference" from John Stuart Mill, this approach synthesizes the type of analysis performed using the other two logics. The goal here is a familiar one. As in multivariate statistical analysis, effort is directed at adjudicating between various hypotheses. The comparative historian carefully picks and chooses his or her cases so that they vary and covary on the dimensions of interest in such a way that the rough equivalent of statistical "controls" are established. In order to reach "bounded generalizations," "cases are selected and case materials are manipulated according to the logic of the causal hypotheses being presented and tested (Skocpol and Somers, 1980: 194). This type of research logic is congruent with attempts to discover probabilistic "laws" of world-system development using a "comparative method" (Chase-Dunn, 1981a; see also Lenski, 1976). It seems to hold the most promise for advancing sociological theories of macrostructural change.

Although these three approaches are analytically distinct, Skocpol and Somers (1980) recognize that some empirical monographs employ more than one logic. They also suggest that in the process of theory building, refining, and dissecting, comparative researchers attacking a particular problem are likely to move through a methodological cycle. The strong emphasis on the way that the types of research strategies grow out of theoretical concerns is a key element of the Skocpol and Somers argument.

Arthur Stinchcombe's idea of what social historians should be trying to do is very different. Ironically given the title of his book—*Theoretical Methods in Social History*—he appears to be arguing entirely against using theories to guide historical work: "The question of how to apply social theory to historical materials, as it is usually posed, is ridiculous. One does not apply theory to history; rather one uses history to develop theory" (Stinchcombe, 1979: 1). The claim is that good social history does not depend on the theoretical apparatus (or baggage) that a researcher brings to a particular question. Thus, he contends, "the difference between Trotsky's Marxism, Smelser's functionalism and de Tocqueville's conservative despair makes hardly any difference to any important question of sociological theory" (Stinchcombe, 1979: 2). Instead, all good interpreters of social history essentially operate in the same way when it comes to thinking about historical facts.

What are these common methods? First of all, Stinchcombe is very clear about what they are not. In sharp contrast to Skocpol and Somers (1980), who advocate a macroanalytical method, he argues very strenuously against the notion that any form of hypothesis testing is essential to good comparative history. Instead, he says, the critical part of any historical inquiry is arranging the "loosely connected facts" of a narrative into a theory of "the phenomena under study." What are arrived at are "historically specific general ideas" (Stinchcombe, 1979: 4). The usefulness of these theoretical ideas can be seen in their "ability to analyze such narrative sequences" (Stinchcombe, 1979: 13).

How do we get beyond historical particularism by adopting such an approach? Stinchcombe's (1979: 7) answer is that the central operation for building theories of history is seeking causally significant analogies beyond instances." The common methodology of all comparative history, therefore, is the search for "deep analogies." How does an analogy become "deepened"? Stinchcombe (1979: 21) explains: "We would, in ordinary language, say that the analogy between A and D was a 'deep' analogy, if a great many statements true of A were also true of D." The way to do this is to pay close attention to the details and specifics of historical processes, while holding comparative cases in mind. For Stinchcombe (1979: 21–22), the biggest theoretical payoff comes not from highly general theoretical research but in studies that try to give "a causal interpretation to a particular case."

Stinchcombe's insistence on getting down to the details is totally consistent with the movement toward historically grounded explanations of social change. In his exegesis of some major works in comparative history, Stinchcombe deftly pulls out generalizable deep analogies dealing with authority structures and intergroup conflicts. He shows that despite their support for very different general theories, good social historians will point to similar historically specific general ideas. Stinchcombe clearly is on to something.

But what are we to make of the claim that general theoretical orientations are useless in comparative and historical research? If that is the case, Skocpol and Somers' (1980) analysis is reduced to meaninglessness (as is the lengthy discussion of the theoretical grounding of this project in Chapter 1). On this point, Stinchcombe appears to be vulnerable to criticism. Tilly (1982: 11), while on balance praising Stinchcombe's emphasis on "deep analogies, claims that the broad theories that Stinchcombe pans are, in fact, useful because they "contain instructions for the identification of deep analogies." All historical analysis, whether explicitly or implicitly, is guided by *some* theoretical notions about, at the very least, what types of events or sequences are important. The real problem with most general theories of social change—and the reason why Stinchcombe rejects them all as irrelevant—is that they simply are not very good theories (Tilly, 1982: 11). Still, even bad theory (Tilly points to functionalist approaches to the history of collective violence as an example) sensitizes the researcher to particular types of causal sequences. Good historically grounded theories, on the other hand, not only focus empirical studies but also suggest useful and verifiable deep analogies in history. Tilly (1982: 12) summarizes:

Whatever else they do, the social sciences serve as a giant warehouse of causal theories and of concepts involving causal analogies; the problem is to pick one's way through the junk to the solid merchandise. Stinchcombe rightly scores the "flaccidity" of our general theories of social change. He wrongly obscures the significance of good theory to effective historical analysis. Sociologists and historians alike, however, should be searching for theories that have adequate historical grounding.

The Logic of Regional and National Case Studies

In the subsequent chapters, I will try to assess the usefulness of the political economy of the world-system perspective on urbanization for specific historical cases of Third World development. In Chapter 1, a number of the basic hypotheses of this perspective were summarized. Some of the most salient bear on the overall research design for this historical-structural analysis.

At the most fundamental level, this model suggests that urban patterns and processes vary according to a nation's role in the world economy. The results of the world analysis in Chapter 2 support this general premise. Any macroanalytical approach to urbanization in the world economy must be sensitive to including countries from the various strata. In the subsequent analysis, the contrast between peripheral and semiperipheral nations is highlighted. An initial hypothesis is that the roles that nations play in the world economy affect the type of urbanization they experience. In an attempt to "control" for regional and cultural explanations of differing urban trajectories, two geographically distinct regions in the contemporary Third World are chosen for study.[2] Within each of these areas, nations hold different world-system positions.

Timing of incorporation and type of colonization are also theoretical variables of considerable significance. For the two noncore regions I have selected to study, there is variation on each factor. West Africa generally was penetrated and peripheralized at an earlier date than East Asia. *Within* the East Asian area, there is a considerable difference between Korea and Southeast Asia—with Korea undergoing incorporation and colonization at a much later date and a different phase of world economic expansion. Both of the nations chosen for the intensive case studies (Nigeria and South Korea) are members of the "strong" semiperiphery today. By selecting cases that control for some variables and differ on others, I believe my analysis potentially will point to bounded generalizations about urbanization in different strata, incorporated during different periods, and subject to different types of colonial and postcolonial "development" strategies.

A political economy perspective also suggests that certain types of elite structure and shifts toward particular types of industrialization are likely to lead to particular skewed patterns of urban development. Concomitant changes in labor force composition may also be of crucial importance. The growing need for cheap, informal sector labor and the political processes by which transportation infrastructures direct flows of resources to certain cities are two components integral to the uneven growth pattern I have called "dependent urbanization." To some extent, demonstrating that these processes are important in multiple cases involving Third World countries is one of my objectives. This type of approach roughly approximates what Skocpol and Somers (1980) have called the "parallel demonstration of theory" mode of inquiry. But Stinchcombe's notion of deep analogies really comes closer to what I am striving for. In explaining urban patterns and processes, I will try to trace out what Barrington Moore (1958, cited by Gutkind and Wallerstein, 1976: 7) has called "the chains of historical causation." Keeping comparative case studies firmly in mind, I hope to arrive at some deep analogies about the process of dependent urbanization. By its very nature, this process is an inextricably historical one. But by combining the macroanalytical technique and the methodology of deepening analogies, I aim to refine theoretical notions about dependent urbanization and, at the more global level, something about the nature of "the urban question" in general.

Organization of the Case Studies

The next four chapters will be devoted to the historical case studies. The analysis will move away from a focus on the world-system and zero in on urban patterns in broad Third World areas and, later, on the political economy of urbanization in two specific societies. In Chapter 4, I will describe the urban configurations of the countries of West Africa and explore some historical and contemporary processes that help to explain that general pattern. In Chapter 5, I will move into a more detailed look at Nigeria. Chapter 6 provides an overview of urban development in East Asia, and Chapter 7 follows up with a more intensive examination of South Korea. Throughout this section of the book, the emphasis will be on tracing the linkages between internal processes and changes in the world economic and political system.

4

Dependency, Development, and Urbanization in West Africa

West Africa: Uneven Urbanization and Inequality

West Africa was one of the last areas of the world to begin the urban transition.[1] Historically, despite a long tradition of indigenous towns in some parts of the region (see Gugler and Flanagan, 1978: chapter 1), the overall proportion of the population in urban areas was very small. Data for 1950 indicate that about 10 percent of all West Africans were city-dwellers (compared with well over 60 percent in North America and more than 40 percent in Latin America). Even in 1975, only 18.6 percent of West Africa's population was classified as urban, making this area one of the least urbanized in the world (all the preceding data are from United Nations, 1976: table 1.2, pp. 21–22).

But this is changing very rapidly. By 1990, 33.2 percent of the total population in Western Africa lived in cities (United Nations, 1993: table A-1). Only East Africa, among world regions, had fewer urban residents. Despite the small absolute share of people in cities and towns, however, West Africa does hold the dubious distinction of having experienced the most rapid urban growth between 1950 and 1970 of any of the twenty-two world regions (Davis, 1972: 200, cited by Gugler and Flanagan, 1977: 272). The area is also very close to the top in terms of projected rates for urban growth between 1990 and 2025 (United Nations, 1988: table A-4). Of twenty-three countries with urban growth rates above 3 percent between 1980 and 1985, six are from West Africa (Benin, Cape Verde, Guinea, Mauritania, Niger, and Togo) (United Nations, 1988: table 5).

Economic growth has not come with the rapid urban influx. West African countries ranked among the world's poorest, with 1970 gross domestic product per capita ranging from $53 for Mali to $347 for the Ivory Coast (United Nations data presented by Gugler and Flanagan, 1977: 275). The concatenation of rapid urban growth and relative economic stagnation prompts one observer (to describe the situation in West Africa and other parts of the continent as one of "exploding cities in unexploding economies" (Rosser, 1973: 31).

The relatively low level of urbanization and the rapid growth of cities and towns provide both a challenge and an opportunity to social scientists and policymakers. On the one hand, the pace of change and the varied national contexts of the West African urban transition make a comprehensive explanation difficult. The rapid change to an urban society makes this task all the more pressing as uniquely urban social problems confront these countries for the first time. Yet the relative lateness of city growth in West Africa may offer social scientists a better opportunity to understand the urbanization process and help to channel it in directions that will be truly generative in terms of national development, as both neo-Marxist (Walton, 1977: 15) and more traditional writers (Rosser, 1973: 2–5) have argued.

The evidence is beginning to suggest that the optimism of these latter views may be misplaced. Despite the continued predominantly rural character of West African societies, emerging urban patterns are beginning to display many of the familiar features of imbalance, inequality, and economic parasitism that urban researchers have noted in other areas of the Third World.

Urban Primacy

If the rapid growth rate for the total urban population in West Africa is staggering, the pace of urban concentration in the region's largest cities is truly mind-boggling. These huge cities are multifunctional. With a single exception, the most populated city in each West African nation is the capital.[2] And all of the capital cities in coastal countries are also seaports. Table 4.1 traces the demographic growth of the capitals between 1920 and 1976. In the 1920s, many of these places were no more than small towns with populations of only a few thousand; only Lagos exceeded 50,000 in total population. By the early 1970s, only four of these cities had populations below 100,000, and three of those were towns in the remote countries of the interior. By 1970, Lagos's size topped 2 million, making it the second largest city in all of Africa (United Nations, 1980: table 48). Between 1970 and 1985, the city grew at a staggering average annual rate of 7.08 percent, pushing the total population to over 5.8 million (United Nations, 1988: table 6). This made Lagos the twenty-seventh largest city in the world, and UN projections put its population at over 12 million people by the year 2000. Of the 100 largest urban agglomerations in the world, only 2 (Dacca, Bangladesh, and Medan, Indonesia) are growing more rapidly (United Nations, 1988: table 6).

Table 4.1 provides some idea of the speed of population concentration throughout the twentieth century. When examining these data, keep in mind that total population growth in West Africa in recent years has stood at "only" 2.3 percent annually (Mabogunje, 1974: 13) and that the average yearly urban growth

Table 4.1 Population of West African Capital Cities, 1920–1976

City	1920s year	source[a]	population (thousands)	1930s year	source[a]	population (thousands)	1940s year	source[a]	population (thousands)	1950s year	source[a]	population (thousands)	1960s year	source[a]	population (thousands)	1970s year	source[a]	population (thousands)	Average annual growth 1950s to 1970s	Two-city index[b] year	ratio
Nouakchott													1961	C	6	1972	E	55[c]		1972	2.3
Dakar	1921	V	34	1931	V	54	1945	V	132[c]	1955	C	231[c]	1961	S	375[c]	1976	C	799	6%	1972	6.8
Banjul	1921	C	9	1931	C	14	1944	C	21	1951	C	20	1963	C	28	1973	C	39	3%	1973	4.2
Bamako	1926	C	16	1936	E	21	1945	E	36	1958	C	76	1965/6	C	168	1972	E	225	8%	1969	5.6
Bissau										1950	C	18	1960	L	22	1970	C	71	7%	19%	9.2
Conakry	1921	L	9	1934	L	9	1943	L	26	1958	C	76[c]	1960	C	112[c]	1972	C	526[c]	15%	1972	8.8
Freetown	1921	C	44	1931	C	55	1944	C	99[c]				1963	C	160[c]	1974	C	274	5%[d]	1974	3.6
Monrovia	1920	G	5	1934	G	10	1945	G	18	1956	C	42	1962	C	81	1974	C	164	8%	1974	6.6
Abidjan	1921	L	5	1931	L	10	1942	L	36	1955	C	126	1963	S	242	1970	E	555	10%	1970	4.8
Ouagadougou	1926	V	12	1933	V	12	1945	V	18	1957	V	47	1961/2	C	59[c]	1975	C	170	8%	1975	1.5
Accra	1921	C	44	1931	C	61	1948	C	124	1958	C	69	1960	C	388[c]	1970	C	636[c]	8%[e]	1970	1.8
Lomé	1923	C	6	1931	C	7	1944	C	38	1950	C	41	1964	S	116	1970	C	193	8%	1970	6.6
Porto-Novo	1921	L	20	1938	A	24	1943	L	29	1950	L	9	1961	S	64	1970	E	87	4%	1973	1.1[f]
Niamey	1926	L	3	1931	A	2	1943	L	6				1960	A	79	1972	S	108	12%	1973	3.7
Lagos	1921	C	100	1931	A	126				1952	C	333[c]	1963	C	1,090[c]	1976	E	2,500[c]	9%	1971	1.3

[a]abbreviations indicate the following types of data: administrative census (A), census enumeration (C), calculated estimate (E), guesstimate (G), secondary source (L), sample survey (S), evaluated secondary source (V).

[b]The two-city index of urban primacy is based on the ratio of the populations of the largest and second largest city.

[c]Population in the urban agglomeration.

[d]Average annual growth for Freetown is for 1963 to 1974.

[e]Average annual growth for Accra is for 1948 to 1970.

[f]The largest city in Benin is Cotonou, not the capital city.

Source: Peter K. Mitchell, director of the Demographic Documentation Project, Centre of West African Studies, University of Birmingham; column 7 calculated from columns 4 and 6, unless indicated otherwise.

Adapted from J. Gugler and W. Flanagan, 1978. *Urbanization and Social Change in West Africa* (New York: Cambridge University Press, 1978).

for all of Africa is 4.4 percent (United Nations, 1980: 41). Between 1970 and 1985, the capital cities of Conakry, Abidjan, and Niamey more than tripled in size (United Nations, 1988: table A-10). In the late 1960s, the two largest cities in the region, Lagos and Accra, fell just short of double-digit growth percentages. Throughout the region, the population growth rates of the largest cities doubled or trebled in recent years (United Nations, 1988: table A-10).

The rapid growth of these cities is also reflected, in most instances, in the two-city primacy indexes that appear in Table 4.1. Most of the smaller coastal countries exhibit relatively high primacy ratios, ranging from 3.6 for Freetown in Sierra Leone to 9.2 for Bissau in Guinea-Bissau. Two of the larger coastal nations, Ghana and Nigeria, exhibit low degrees of primacy, indicating a more evenly distributed urban population. John Clarke (1972: 449), who studied these urban hierarchies in some detail, notes that the extremely even rank-size distribution of Nigeria is unique in all of Africa. He also claims that Ghana's urban hierarchy approximates the lognormal pattern expected by models proposed by urban geographers. The areal-extensive interior countries also show low but rising primacy ratios. In twelve of the fifteen nations, the primacy of the capital city increased between the 1960s and the early 1970s.

Two of points about the statistical measure of primacy need to be made. First, to be meaningful, the primacy ratios for West Africa need to be placed in a comparative context. In this regard, it is important to note that West African urban systems do not approach the extremely primate patterns of some countries. Bangkok, the epitome of a primate city, was 33.4 times larger than the second largest Thai city in 1970 (London, 1980: 28). Clarke (1972) lists nine other Third World countries, including six in Latin America, that top all West African primacy ratios. But Clarke also points out that an index above 2.0 indicates an imbalanced urban hierarchy in terms of the rank-size rule. He also suggests that if current trends continue, African primacy ratios are very likely to rise.

The second point about primacy ratios takes the form of a general caution about the limitations of the measure itself. Obviously, for all the demographic data reported thus far, accuracy is a serious concern. Demographic information for Third World countries and particularly for Africa is notoriously bad (Rosser, 1973: 6). Even if the information is accurate, problems of data comparability arise because estimation procedures, years of enumeration, and definitions of urban places vary widely between the nations (see United Nations, 1980: annex 1). Beyond the reliability and comparability issues, one should keep in mind that aggregate population data may not accurately capture what some writers mean by the term *urban primacy* and the dominance relationship that it implies (see London, 1980: 5-8). The spatial distribution of the populations may be only a rough indicator of functional primacy. It is important that the inferential limitations of "formal spatio-demographic analysis" are clear (Slater, 1978: 27).

Therefore, to augment the demographic measures already presented, some other indicators of primacy should be mentioned. Since functional primacy involves the unequal distribution of political and economic power and control over other parts of the national system (London, 1980: 6), it is reasonable to conceptualize the unequal concentration of resources in the largest cities as a measure of primacy.

Data on measures of such resource imbalances are available for only a few countries. William Hance (1970) reports that Dakar, with only 16 percent of the Senegalese population, consumes 95 percent of the country's electricity and employs 70 percent of all commercial workers and 80 percent of all manufacturing labor in the nation. Lagos, although not a primate city based on demographic rank-size criteria, also exerts a great deal of urban dominance as Nigeria's capital, largest city, and busiest port. Despite having only 1 percent of the nation's huge total population, Lagos has 38 percent of all registered vehicles, consumes 46 percent of all electricity, has 56 percent of all telephones, and publishes 90 percent of all periodicals in Nigeria. Clearly, these cities exert a great deal of functional dominance over the urban hierarchies they head. Hance (1970: 210) claims, however, that "the dominance of a single city is even more marked in some [other] countries," including Conakry in Guinea, Abidjan in Ivory Coast, and Lomé in Togo. Gugler and Flanagan (1977: 281) give a vivid description of what this unequal allocation means: "The growth of the national capital and its ever more impressive skyline are a source of pride to some. But whoever ventures beyond to the vast expanses of West Africa is stunned by the disparity between the concentration of resources in the capital cities and the neglect that is the fate of much of their hinterlands."

Intra-Urban Inequality

Actually, as Gugler and Flanagan (1977, 1978: chapter 2) take great pains to illustrate, one need not leave the confines of the city to see inequality. The urban areas of West Africa follow the pattern found in other regions of the underdeveloped world: The distribution of income, amenities, and life chances is very skewed.

As in the case of functional primacy, systematic data on urban inequality are sparse. For most of the cities of West Africa, comprehensive information on inequality and poverty is conspicuously absent.[3] To some extent, qualitative accounts must suffice to document these phenomena.

Perhaps the best description of the distribution of urban resources and the stratification system of a city is found in Cohen's (1974) study of Abidjan. Michael Cohen presents both quantitative and qualitative information to describe the skewed distribution of five key urban resources: land, housing, education, jobs, and social services (Cohen, 1974: chapter 3). The pattern that emerges is a very regular one.

A small group of government-connected officials control land concessions, send their children to advanced schools, live in luxurious villas, and receive disproportionate shares of material wealth in terms of both income and public benefits (Cohen, 1974: chapter 3). Without getting bogged down in the details of Cohen's case, I would note that housing and income seem to be particularly important indexes of urban resource distribution. A discussion of inequality in these areas will allow comparison between Abidjan and some other large West African cities.

Housing is one of the more obvious manifestations of material inequality in cities in Africa and throughout the Third World. The tall buildings of capital cities often cast their long shadows on slums and squatter settlements. Table 4.2 shows that Abidjan is fairly typical of West African cities in this regard. About 60 percent of the residents live in areas that can be described as "low-income settlements" or "spontaneous settlements" (for a discussion of the terminology, see Salau, 1979b: 330–332). Of the cities covered by the surveys, Dakar, Lomé, and Ibadan all showed equally high or higher percentages of population in this type of housing. In his study of Abidjan, Cohen focuses on a number of different classes of housing. In 1969, a year in which 375,000 residents of the city lived in slums and bidonvilles, the top government officials were living in European-style villas with rents close to $1,000 per month (Cohen, 1974: 47–48).[4] Cohen claims that these homes and another group of "smaller but very luxurious homes" house an elite group of fewer than 500 families. In addition, several thousand middle-class and business families live in modern, relatively expensive apartments. There is a yawning gap in housing standards separating these fortunate few from the city's masses.

Similarly rich data on upper-class housing for elites in other West African cities do not appear to be readily available. Gugler and Flanagan (1977: 286), however, seem to believe that great inequality is the norm: "The wide gap separating a tiny elite and the majority of the urban population is conspicuously demonstrated in housing. The contrast between the mansions of the rich and the overcrowded tenements and shacks impresses itself on the most superficial observer."

Perhaps the most obvious indicators of inequality within cities are the differences in intra-urban income and employment status. In Abidjan, Cohen describes a three-tiered occupational stratification structure. High-ranking government cadres, making up about 5 percent of the population, earn between $124 and $385 per month. Some 13 percent of the population earn middle-level salaries, ranging from $62 to $124 monthly. Eighty-two percent of the city's residents comprise the bottom tier of workers, who earn less than $62 per month. A good percentage of these masses are under- or unemployed. Data in Table 4.3

Table 4.2 Slums and Squatter Settlements in Some West African Cities

City	Year	Percent of Total Population Living in Slums and Squatter Settlements
Accra	1968	53
Abidjan	1964	60
Monrovia	1970	50
Ibadan	1971	75
Dakar	1971	60
Lomé	1970	75
Ouagadougou	1966	52

Sources: United Nations, *World Housing Survey* (New York: United Nations, 1973), pp. 44–45; ECA, *Human Settlements in Africa* (Addis Ababa: ECA), p. 18; Ademoula Salau, "The Political Economy of Cities in Tropical Africa," adapted from his article in *Civilizations* 28: 281–290.

Table 4.3   Reported Unemployment in Select West African Urban Areas

Country	Year	Town(s)	Proportion Reported Unemployed	Population	Source of Data
Sierra Leone	1967	capital city	15%	persons over age 14	survey
Ivory Coast	1963	capital city	15%	adult males	survey
Ghana	1960	large towns	12%	persons over age 14	census
	1970	two largest cities	9%	men over age 14	census
Benin	1968	urban areas	13%	men aged 15–60	computation
Nigeria	1963	27 towns	14%	persons over age 14	survey
	1966–1967	urban areas	8%	labor force age 15–55	survey

Source: Adapted from J. Gugler, and W. Flanagan, "On the Political Economy of Urbanization in the Third World: The Case of West Africa." *International Journal of Urban and Regional Research* 1, no. 2 (1977): 272–292.

indicate that about 15 percent of all adult males in Abidjan are unemployed. The table also shows fairly comparable unemployment rates in other West African urban areas. A study of Liberia's capital reports even worse employment conditions there: "Some 23-27 percent of the labor force is estimated to be without jobs in Monrovia. The average migrant to Monrovia stays there for 2 to 4 years before obtaining work" (Hasselman, 1981, quoted by Rondinelli, 1988: 304). Perhaps the largest share of the working urban masses in Abidjan and other West African cities find jobs outside of the "formal sector" of the economy in "small-scale" or "petty commodity" production (Riddell, 1978: 244). S.V. Sethuraman (1977) estimates that as many as 60 to 70 percent of all African urban workers are employed in this sector. The debate over the function and viability of this so-called informal sector of the economy, which I will discuss, need not concern us now. The critical point here is that work in the petty production sector involves low levels of pay, long hours of labor, and little job security for individual workers, and it leads to an increasingly uneven distribution of resources within cities (Riddell, 1978: 250, 1980: 72; for West African case studies, see Hart, 1973; Gerry, 1978). Inequality between the elite and the masses in West African urban areas is as sharp in terms of income and employment opportunities as it is in terms of housing.

Overurbanization

West African cities and urban systems exhibit a great deal of imbalance and inequality. What effect does this pattern of urbanization have for economic growth and development in West Africa?

Several authors (Riddell, 1978, 1980; Gugler and Flanagan, 1977, 1978, chapter 2) argue that West Africa is overurbanized. In advancing this claim, they are reviving an old argument about the generative versus parasitic nature of large cities in underdeveloped countries (Hoselitz, 1954; Keyfitz, 1965; Durand and Palaez, 1969; see London, 1980). Apart from any consideration of the a priori desirability of equity in the distribution of resources, the argument made by these authors is that rapid urban growth promotes economic inefficiency. Despite the low proportion of the population residing in cities in West Africa, Gugler (1982: 173) argues that these societies may be conceived of as overurbanized because rapid city growth (1) "leads to less than optimal allocation of labor between rural and urban sectors," and (2) "increases the cost of providing for a country's growing population."

This argument is based on the recognition that city growth in West Africa is primarily the result of massive rural-to-urban migration (Caldwell, 1968: 139; Rosser, 1973: 26; Gugler and Flanagan, 1977: 274; Riddell, 1978: 241). This migration creates a misallocation of labor at both the sending and receiving ends. According to the argument (Gugler and Flanagan, 1977: 276), since there is currently little population pressure on the land (rural areas in West Africa are *not* overpopulated), migration drains valuable labor from the rural sector and lowers agricultural output. Meanwhile, in urban areas, there is not enough work to go around. This results in large-scale under-, mis-, and unemployment (Riddell, 1978: 243; Gugler, 1982). Another dysfunction caused by this migration involves the cost of providing for swelling city populations, which is purportedly much higher than that in rural areas. One assumption of this argument is that population concentration brings with it diseconomies of scale in the provision of services such as housing, transport, sewerage, fuel, and food (Gugler and Flanagan, 1977: 277). The high cost allegedly arises from the distorted and inequitable form of urban growth. This proposition is based on the evidence that urban-based elites have vociferous appetites for the conspicuous consumption of modern amenities—elegant buildings, broad avenues, well-kept parks—all of which are unnecessary and wasteful drains on meager national resources.

Generic overurbanization arguments have been widely criticized from a variety of perspectives (for example, see Hawley, 1971: 279–282; Castells, 1977: 41–42). Nevertheless, the effects that the speed and patterning of city growth have on the attainment of national development goals deserve careful consideration by policymakers. Advocates of the overurbanization thesis at least raise some relevant issues.

Summary: Uneven Urbanization

In this section, I try to provide an overview of the urbanization process in West Africa. The picture that emerges is merely a sketch, but one characteristic that clearly stands out is the uneven nature of urban growth in terms of both spatial and demographic imbalances and material inequality. In the previous discussion, some tentative causes of these patterns emerged. Now it is time to turn toward an explicit effort to explain and ultimately diagnose these problems.

Research on West African urbanization is, itself, quite uneven. Much of the descriptive work has been carried out by scholars operating from the urban and regional planning tradition. Some of this work is very good and analytically useful. One problem with this literature, however, is that it tends to be very descriptive, and theoretical development is often weak or nonexistent.[5] Writers who bother to discuss theoretical issues at all frequently opt for a vague form of modernization theory (El-Shakhs, 1974) or advocate an open eclecticism (Walter, 1974). The predominance of "stage theory" thinking and the wholesale import of techniques and concepts from Western planners may explain why these researchers shy away from attempts to theoretically ground their studies. Despite the fact that modernization theory approaches have come under increasing attack by students of Third World development (see Portes, 1976), this remains the predominant school of thought among African planners. Rejecting a similar developmentalist model,

Amin (1974: 8) comments, "Eclecticism is the inevitable price paid for this false theorizing."

Several authors addressing the process of rapid urbanization in West Africa lament the lack of solid theoretical grounding upon which to base their studies (Ayeni, 1978; Salau, 1979a). The purpose of the subsequent discussion is to move toward a comprehensive approach to urbanization in West Africa.

Politics, Power, and the Form of Urban Growth

In the late 1970s, sociologist Bruce London (1979: 485) observed, "A new generation of comparative urbanists is creating a more 'political' comparative urban sociology. This trend involves a movement toward the analysis of intergroup power relationships in the urbanization and development process."

More recent West African research has joined this trend. Rejecting traditional approaches that claimed that urbanization is mechanistically determined by the introduction of modern culture, technology, or markets, several writers systematically demonstrate the crucial impact that the distribution of power within societies has on the development of cities and urban systems. They focus attention on elites and the policies they pursue that, in turn, shape cities and settlement hierarchies.

According to this view, the powerful in societies, like most other people, tend to be economically rational: They generally act to further their own class interests and economic well-being. Policies formulated on this self-interest basis need not and often will not coincide with development goals congruent with the needs of the general population. West African elites, like those in other parts of the contemporary Third World, tend to be city-dwellers. Urban policies are likely to create cities or systems of cities that fit the needs of the powerful. These policies may take many forms: explicit or implicit, national or local, active or passive.[6] Therefore, rather than being a generative process, urbanization can be a structural change that is parasitic to the interest of genuine national development.

This type of analysis explains the phenomenon of overurbanization (see the previous discussion). It begins with the recognition of a large gap in life chances between the urban and rural sectors (Gugler and Flanagan, 1977: 273). This imbalance is of interest not merely because of equity considerations. The urban-rural differential is also the overriding factor in rural-to-urban migration. How can one account for these rural-urban imbalances? Riddell (1978: 256) claims,

> To explain them is to enter the realm of political economy; it is to understand that elements of the "colonial situation" still exist despite political independence. It is even more important to recognize "internal colonialism," the fact that throughout West Africa there is an urban core and a rural periphery, and that the

former draws part of its subsistence from the latter. It does this by economic
means, supported by reinforcing laws, regulations, and policies.

Policies that emanate from the cities contain an urban bias because "cities are the
centers of power and privilege" (Gugler, 1982: 188). The clearest examples of this
are the primate cities of West Africa. It is no coincidence that all but one of the
largest cities in each nation is also the national capital (see Table 4.1). The
functional primacy that was described earlier is evidence of the concentration of
resources in these large cities. Writers like Gugler, Flanagan, and Riddell stress that
the reason for urban concentration is primarily political. They further argue that the
crucial axis of power is primarily urban versus rural. In the words of Michael
Lipton (1977: 13, cited by Riddell, 1978: 257, and Gugler, 1982: 188): "The most
important class conflict in the poor countries of the world today is not between
labor and capital. Nor is it between foreign and national interests. It is between the
rural classes and the urban classes.

How does this political process of rural exploitation work? Essentially, the
urban elites (along with their allies among middle-class bureaucrats, merchants,
managers, and professionals) exert their power through the state. The governments
of the independent West African nations control the disposition of economic
surpluses, which under colonial rule were drained abroad by private interests
(Gugler, 1982). Surpluses from the entire country—the metropolis, small towns,
and rural areas—accrue directly to the national capital in the form of taxation and
trade duties. Public expenditures usually disproportionately benefit the capital city:
"A large part of this surplus goes into public works that are allocated to a hierarchy
of places in which the capital city frequently receives the lion's share while rural
areas face neglect" (Gugler, 1982: 189). These public works often consist of
conspicuous investments designed to create a "modern" aura in the capital city: such
things as "airports, four lane highways to whisk visiting dignitaries to magnificent
conference halls, and skyscrapers to house the offices of the bureaucracy" (Gugler
and Flanagan, 1977: 285). Equally important are more indirect and subtle
mechanisms by which these governments facilitate resource flows to the cities.
These include manipulations of monetary policies and the setting of urban wages
and prices on agricultural commodities (Riddell, 1978: 257).

The argument that government bias favors urban areas (and particularly the
national capitals) provides a straightforward explanation for urban-rural inequality
and the functional primacy of the largest cities. By extension, it may also explain
the demographic imbalances within West African urban hierarchies and the large
flows of migrants to primate cities. This thesis suggests that people move where the
resources and opportunities are concentrated. This type of explanation may
overstress "pull" over "push" factors, but its general claim seems to fit the empirical
pattern of migration. Given the already low population concentrations in rural areas
of West Africa, it follows that the loss of labor in the countryside may damage

potential agricultural output (Gugler and Flanagan, 1977: 276). In this manner, the notion of urban bias begins to account for the misallocation of labor and resources that supposedly characterizes the process of overurbanization.

But what about intra-urban inequality and the misallocation of labor *within* the city? Obviously, this dimension is ignored when writers like Lipton claim that the essential conflict in the Third World is between town and countryside. At this point, the political economy approach of Gugler, Flanagan, and Riddell becomes murky. These authors are well aware of the great degrees of inequality, poverty, and unemployment in West African cities (Gugler and Flanagan, 1977: 286–288; Riddell, 1978: 242). They also point out that various elite-backed policies exacerbate the degree of inequality between groups within cities (Gugler and Flanagan, 1977: 287). But while there still is a vague political component in this analysis ("elites" versus "the urban masses"), that component seems to fade into the background. When they are explaining internal inequality and urban labor structures within West Africa's large cities, these self-proclaimed political economists lapse into language reminiscent of functional equilibrium theories.

The gist of their overurbanization thesis is that massive flows of migrants create demographically bloated, "exploding" cities. The result of this process, which itself was caused by politically created rural-urban differentials, is an urban economic and social system in which "something is basically out of kilter" (Riddell, 1978: 242). The social disorganization created by this massive influx of people creates all sorts of urban problems. In the large cities, "the numbers far exceed the absorptive capacity of towns and cities, both as regards housing and work" (Riddell, 1978: 243). Spontaneous settlements testify to this failure in housing. Similarly, "unemployment," "underemployment," and "misemployment" are clear evidence of excess labor (Gugler, 1982: 174–179). Gugler (1982: 176–177) claims that the informal sector in West African cities can be included in the latter two categories: Labor in these cases is "underutilized" or "contributes little to social welfare." He places domestic help and scavengers in the misemployed category, claiming they are totally unproductive and literally "live on the crumbs from the rich man's table" (Gugler, 1982: 178). Riddell (1978: 250) seems to agree that the informal sector is a manifestation of social pathology that is characterized by poverty and that "linkages to the rest of the economy are weak."

In addition to mentioning poverty and lack of productive employment, Gugler and Flanagan (1977: 287) note that numerous urban residents lack basic services such as transport, water, and sewerage. The result is severe deprivation and disease for many urban residents. Part of the problem, these authors claim, is that "emulation of some of the consumption patterns for the national elite, resident foreigners, and tourists does not leave enough money for the basic necessities of life" (Gugler and Flanagan, 1977: 288). This argument, tinged with a hint of blaming-the-victim logic, implies the problems' roots lie in demographic concentration: The cities simply have received more migrants than they can handle.

Why does this argument seem to depart from a political economic analysis at this point? One basic problem involves the way in which these writers conceive of the origin and nature of political power. It is correct and potentially very useful to focus on how West African "governments act as a form of exchange mechanism for the society and economy which they represent" (Riddell, 1978: 256). Because of the legacy of colonialism and the manner in which foreign rule came to an end, a great deal of conflict in these societies is mediated by the state. In other words, there is a certain "primacy of public authority" setting rulers apart from and in opposition to the masses (Cohen, 1974: 5). Kwame Nkrumah's exhortation to "seek ye first the political kingdom, and all things will be added unto you" accurately reflects the arena of conflict (quoted in Cohen, 1974: 7). Government administrators and political functionaries are often able to parlay their positions into great wealth and personal gain (Cohen, 1974: chapter 3; Gugler and Flanagan, 1978: 154–162).

But a vague description of an entrenched "urban elite" working to maintain its "own narrow interests" is of very limited explanatory power, unless we know what those interests might be. Without a clear conception of the position of the elites in local and international class structures, these writers must focus on governmental leaders' locational biases in favor of capital cities. These biases are real and are critically important in terms of their effects on urban-rural differentials. A more specific analysis of the elites' intracity policy (especially vis-à-vis the urban masses), however, is only possible if the national elites are located in reference to wider political economic forces.

Gugler, Flanagan, Riddell, and Cohen fail to do this in a systematic way. Instead, they see the present political elite as arising out of the particular exigencies of the transition to independence (Cohen, 1974: 6; Gugler and Flanagan, 1978: 151–155). Cohen's argument is an extreme example of this type of thinking. Asserting that "political power . . . is the dynamic principle of social stratification in African states," he disavows any economic basis for the rise of the new elites and "challenges the applicability of Marxist theory to the internal dynamics of the new states" (Cohen, 1974: 6). Analyses by Gugler and Flanagan (1977, 1978) and Riddell (1978) place a similar emphasis on the primacy of politics, while only hinting at the relationship between political power and decisionmaking and the wider context of the national and world economies.

This weakness in these authors' approaches influences the policy recommendations they provide. By focusing on the internal political causes of uneven urbanization and ignoring the effects of external linkages, they leave the overly optimistic impression that internal political reforms are sufficient to ameliorate urban imbalances. Riddell (1978: 257) expresses this view particularly well:

> Thus, the political leaders of West Africa today have in their hands the tools by which some of the colonial legacies can be removed; specifically, they can alter a situation whereby in the past and continuing today, their rural, agricultural economies are "exploited" by those who live elsewhere—in urban centers and in other countries. . . . In other words, should the governments of West Africa wish to reduce the urban-rural differentials in many aspects of life, they can do so.

Although this statement suggests that West African states enjoy a great deal of relative autonomy (in regard to both national and international class structures) and that political decisions are based largely on voluntaristic choices by leaders, Riddell, himself, realizes it is not that simple. For instance, he lists several possible constraints on government policy, including "the dependent position of West Africa vis-à-vis the world economic system." He also notes, after detailing several policy options designed to establish "a new rural-urban equilibrium," that implementation of his proposals would be very unlikely: "[It] is doubtful that the existing political regimes in West Africa will introduce the necessary changes; they are too concerned with maintaining their economic position, and that of the groups which they represent, to upset the *status quo*" (Riddell, 1978: 259).

The problem with Riddell's analysis (and that of the other authors reviewed in this section) is that it fails to come to grips with the issue of who these regimes *do* represent. By moving the discussion of West Africa's position in the world economy and the issue of dependency relationships to the center of this discussion, the resolution of this and other issues is made easier. In the following section, I propose a more adequate political economy of urbanization in West Africa.

Dependent Urbanization in West Africa

The literature discussed in the previous section emphasized the importance of the political component in the patterns of growth, distribution, and internal structuring of cities in the region. The explicitly political focus of Gugler and Flanagan, Riddell, and Cohen is a step toward a better understanding of the urbanization process. But these writers fail to provide a solid theoretical framework for comprehending the wider economic and class structures that underpin politics in West Africa, and this weakens the explanatory power of their work. Development of a political economy approach to urbanization in West Africa, linking this process to the structure of exchanges and the class dynamics of the capitalist world economy, provides a more adequate theoretical foundation.

A suggestive (but not very well-developed) article by Ademola Salau (1978) offers a useful starting point. In his article, Salau addresses some of the same problems of African urbanization confronted by the writers already discussed:

urban-rural differentials, rapid growth, and the demographic and functional primacy of the largest cities. But he recognizes the need for "a new perspective on the role of cities in Africa" to address the uneven pattern of urban development (Salau, 1978: 286). Hinting at the basis of this new approach, he points to the relevancy of dependency/world-system analysis:

> There is now a large literature on an alternative perspective of urbanization. Instead of debating the positive or the negative influence of urbanization, the focus taken by these scholars is based on the idea that contemporary urban development in developing nations results primarily from international capitalism or of what Wallerstein terms the "modern world-system." . . . According to this school of thought, Africa, like other developing areas, fulfills certain definite functions in the "world economy" or world market, and the domestic development is limited or conditioned by the needs of the dominant economies within that world market. The international world-system affects internal development indirectly by generating an infrastructure of dependency. The process of urbanization is a critical part of this infrastructure (Salau, 1978: 286–287).

Unfortunately, while staunchly advocating the use of this theoretical approach, Salau leaves the systematic development of its implications for African urbanization to others. The subsequent discussion demonstrates, briefly and in a preliminary manner, how this perspective can be applied to the processes and problems of urbanization in West Africa. I focus on four specific issues:

1. The historical context of the origins and changes in the form of West African cities and urban systems;
2. The role of politics and the state in the dynamics of urbanization;
3. Intracity inequalities and the nature of the urban informal sector;
4. The overurbanization issue.

The Historical Context of Urban Growth

Twentieth-century urbanization in West Africa was a dramatic, sweeping transformation. Indeed, this change continues to unfold today. But its roots reach deep into the past, and is necessary to trace out chains of historical causation. A political economy approach emphasizing West Africa's role in the expanding capitalist world economy provides a theoretical guide for this endeavor.

There are a number of scholarly discussions of the history of West African cities. Although the coverage varies, several writers concerned with present urban patterns provide synoptic histories of West African urbanism that run well back into ancient times (Hance, 1970; Rayfield, 1974; Gugler and Flanagan, 1978; Salau, 1979a). One major theme in these treatments is the antiquity of trading center towns in West Africa. Another is the long-established tradition of town living in some areas, particularly Yorubaland (see Gugler and Flanagan, 1978). These descriptions of urbanism's long history and continuity are of interest because they challenge Western ethnocentric assumptions equating urbanism with modernity and European contact.

The clearest theme, however, and the one most germane to the present discussion focuses on the critical impact of European contact and colonization. West African urban history is often presented as occurring in a series of phases: an early stage characterized by intracontinental trade (pre-1600), a middle stage during which the European powers set up outposts to conduct the slave trade (1600–1850), and the colonizing period in which European influence permeated the region (from 1850 onward) (Rayfield, 1974; Salau, 1979a). Gugler and Flanagan (1978: 26) describe a similar progression: "West African urbanization took a new direction in the seventeenth century with the development of maritime trade. The commercial function of the seaports was complemented in the nineteenth century by the implantation of the colonial structure, first on the coast and then gradually inland."

Despite some disagreement about the dates and titles of the stages, scholars agree on the importance of understanding the gradual incorporation of West Africa into the modern world-system. I will systematically relate these stages of urban growth directly to the changing needs and imperatives of capitalist accumulation on a world scale.

Two attempts to link broad stages of Africa's developing linkages to the world economy are found in Samir Amin (1973) and Immanuel Wallerstein (1976a, 1989). The stages of urbanization that Rayfield and Salau suggest closely correspond to Amin's "pre-mercantilist," "mercantilist," and "full integration" periodization, as well as to the description Wallerstein gives of Africa's changing status in the world-system over the same period (moving from an "external arena" to a "peripheral" position). This notion of peripheralization is particularly important (for the best general discussion of the terminology and its specific application to West Africa, see Wallerstein, 1989: chapter 3).[7] The beginnings of the decline of British hegemony, coupled with the rising demand for raw materials during the "second Industrial Revolution" in the late nineteenth century, triggered a scramble for African colonies (Wallerstein, 1976a: 39). In this context,

> the colonial city developed . . . as a centre of commerce and administration, rather than industrial production. It originated as a means whereby the metropolitan rulers established a base for the administration of the countryside, and the exploitation of its resources, and consequently the transfer of the surplus extracted from the countryside to the metropolis. At the same time, the city itself engaged in the parasitical extractions of a surplus from the countryside (Williams, 1970: 236, quoted by Gugler and Flanagan, 1978: 26).

Without going into this matter in greater detail, it seems safe to say that the pattern of colonial urban growth was tightly linked to West Africa's changing role in the developing world-economy. The importance of capitalist penetration and incorporation seems to be at least implicit in most historical accounts.

Discussions of the present urban patterns almost invariably refer to the legacy of a colonial past (for examples, see Mabogunje, 1974; Gugler and Flanagan, 1978; Salau, 1979a). Gugler and Flanagan (1978: 26) express a common view: "The present patterns and conditions of urbanization owe much to the colonial past. This is true not only of the atmosphere and location of the towns, but also with regards to the nature of the roles these towns have played in the economic development of states."

Yet ironically, these same authors (and others) pay little attention to the recent world-economy context. Instead, there is a tendency to stress the historical discontinuity that takes place with the end of colonialism and the rise of new indigenous government bureaucracies and local urban elites (Cohen, 1974: 6; Gugler and Flanagan, 1977: 285, 1978: 31, 151–155). This argument about the rise of home rule is invoked to explain the rapid growth of primate cities in the mid-twentieth century. With national independence, however, the bonds of dependency clearly were not broken; West Africa has remained a peripheral area in the world economy throughout this period (Wallerstein, 1976a: 38–49).[8] The internal political power structure, which generates the rapid growth of capital cities, itself developed within limits imposed by this relation of dependency. Rayfield (1974), O'Brien (1979), and Salau (1979a) argue for the essential *continuity* between pre- and postcolonial periods. Old "colonial rulers" were replaced by new "native elites," but "the modern African city is essentially a colonial city still, just as the cities of the previous phases were" (Rayfield, 1974: 182). West African cities throughout the twentieth century have been examples of "dependent urbanism" (Salau, 1978: 288).

This is not to say that these cities and urban systems have not undergone major structural changes in recent years. The demographic trends in Table 4.1 alone are enough to demonstrate this. But an alternative approach to one that explains these changes strictly in terms of internal politics and an end to colonialism is possible. Changing urban patterns in West Africa are linked to the changing nature of dependency itself. Latin American dependency theorists have gone to great lengths to document the various phases of dependency that countries in their region experienced (see Sunkel, 1973; Cardoso and Faletto, 1979). After World War II, the capitalist countries in the core of the world-system began to gear their economies toward the production of expensive consumer products that relied on high rates of technological innovation (Roberts, 1978: 76). In this type of advanced capitalism, huge transnational corporations had the competitive edge. It became profitable for these corporations to transfer some of their production activities to underdeveloped countries. This marked the rise of a period of import substitution industrialization in many Third World countries (Cardoso and Faletto, 1979: introduction). Governments of underdeveloped nations often encouraged the growth of import substitution industries. Ostensibly, the indigenous manufacturing of consumer goods would decrease dependency on foreign imports and help meet foreign exchange/trade deficit problems. But this new economic direction, adopted to varying degrees by the countries of West Africa (see Coquery-Vidrovitch, 1977, summarized in O'Brien, 1979), required both the availability of a small but highly trained and disciplined labor force and the existence of a concentrated consumer market.

The key aspect of the ISI strategy for this discussion is its impact on the urbanization process. Bryan Roberts (1978: 81) claims that the general drift in many Third World countries toward capital-intensive import substitution has important ramifications for urbanization:

> The concentration of middle- and high-income populations in a few urban centers makes investments in capital-intensive consumer goods attractive. These industries are located in, or close to, the centers of population and contribute to the attraction of large cities for rural migrants. Improvements in urban infrastructure such as roads, lighting, sanitation and housing are part of the dynamics of this industrialization.

In other words, ISI tends to be tied to urban primacy and intra-urban inequality.

In fact, as Gugler and Flanagan (1978) note, the growth of import substitution industries that did occur in West Africa in the 1950s and 1960s was heavily concentrated in the major cities. This pattern of industrialization, brought about by worldwide changes in the organization of capitalist production, doubtlessly contributed to and/or reinforced political processes that were biased toward patterns of more spatially concentrated population and wealth.

Politics and the State

A *leitmotif* running throughout this book is the importance of politics and the state in shaping urban growth. It is through the governmental apparatus of West African nations that the policies affecting city and urban system structures are made and implemented. But the existing political economy approaches to urbanization in the region fail to grasp the important relationship between national politics and the international system.

Gugler and Flanagan (1977, 1978) provide clear descriptions of the urban elite that rose to national prominence after the withdrawal of the colonial powers. They also note that this powerful group has implemented an urban bias in the political process. There seems to be a tendency for these elites to coalesce in single-party authoritarian states in the countries of the region (Gugler and Flanagan, 1977:

279–280; see also Cohen, 1974: chapter 7). Two important questions come to mind. First, what is the relationship between this indigenous political elite in West African states and the dominant classes in the core capitalist countries? Second, what is the nature of the state and political domination in this situation?

To move toward general answers to these questions, the discussion must move back to the post-World War II period, when current West African governments emerged at the end of formal European colonial rule. Cohen (1974) is correct when he points out that the new African elites that assumed power at this time were not members of an identifiable class in the orthodox Marxian sense. They could hardly be considered members of the propertied bourgeoisie (Cohen, 1974: 6). But as their direct colonial administration was coming to an end, "the British and French were eager to hand their power to elites who would keep the African states safe for capitalism, above all their own capitalism" (Davidson, 1966: 206, quoted by Magubane, 1976: 186). The leaders that came to the fore often were nationalists whose ideologies called for self-determination and liberal democracy (Ake, 1976: 200–204). However, as Roger Murray (1963: 85, quoted by Magubane, 1976: 186) points out:

> After independence, the state becomes a major economic force in the absence of an entrepreneurial class, occupying a key role in economic development. State functionaries . . . handle large contracts and negotiate the future of the country with representatives of overseas concerns: corruption and the enjoyment of unrecorded prerequisites abound.

Preindependence ideologies gave way to economic rationality. The indigenous elites acted "to maintain the exploitative relations and a stratification system that they dominated" and "to firmly discourage demands for redistribution of wealth and for mass participation" (Ake, 1976: 205). The emphasis on order and stability that these states have come to represent reflects the economic interests of the new elites in maintaining their societies' close linkages with the capitalist world economy.

The result of this process is the rise of an elite with have clear class interests. Richard Sklar (1979: 544) claims that to the extent that these African elites have consolidated into "dominant classes in those societies that maintain markets and allow capitalist accumulation as a consequence of private property in the means of production," it is meaningful to speak of "bourgeoisie class domination in Africa." But this emergent bourgeoisie is quite different from the dominant capitalist class that developed under different historical circumstances in the Western countries. Given the important role of the state in capitalist development in Africa, this class is usually identified as a "bureaucratic," "administrative," "managerial," or "state" bourgeoisie (see Sklar, 1979: 544–547). Regardless of specific nomenclature, a critical point is that this is a transnational class:

The managerial bourgeoisie has a pronounced tendency to coalesce with bourgeois elements at comparable levels of control in foreign countries. Coalescence of the managerial bourgeoisie (domestic section) with the corporate international bourgeoisie means that class action has taken a historically significant form of transnational class formation (Sklar, 1979: 547). Evans's (1979b: 11) description of Brazilian elite formation fits these cases as well: "The end result of the incorporation of the periphery into the international capitalist system, as far as the elite is concerned, is to create a complex alliance between elite local capital, international capital, and state capital, which I have called the 'triple alliance.'"

An implication of this form of class domination is that the state begins to "act as a form of exchange mechanism" (Riddell, 1978: 256). But instead of operating "to meld the interests of the several groups within the its population," the nation-state will attempt, as its major goal, to balance and coordinate the interests of the local, state, and international bourgeoisie groups. The policies pursued by the West African elites, while not necessarily *determined* by external relationships in the world economy, nevertheless at least take the elites' transnational class alliances into account (Sklar, 1979).

Urban policies viewed in this context represent more than a simple pattern of urban bias. They are likely to reflect strategies for facilitating and subsidizing the profitmaking activities of the administrative elite and their partners, particularly transnational enterprises. The state is likely to promote patterns of urbanization, migration, and structured inequality that are functional for this powerful alliance and that work to maintain peripheral capitalism. Infrastructural development and wage and tax legislation promoting ISI can be interpreted in this way. They result in both increased affluence for the indigenous elites and higher profit remissions for multinational corporations. Thus, the concentration of amenities in the capital cities or major ports not only provides for the material comfort of the political elites of the "state bourgeoisie," but also subsidizes the lifestyles of employees of the transnational enterprises with offices in these cities. Policies (or the lack of policies) addressing intra-urban inequality also result from decisions (or nondecisions) based on transnational class considerations, as will be shown.

Intraurban Inequality and the Informal Sector

A comprehensive political economy approach to West African urbanization should be able to explain the internal structure of cities as well as the broader demographic shifts (i.e., from rural to urban areas or between parts of the national urban system). Within West African cities, there is a huge disparity in material wealth between a small group of elites and the urban masses. Large numbers of urban dwellers reside in illegal, makeshift housing referred to as "shantytowns" or "bidonvilles." They eke out their subsistence in the petty commodity or informal sector of the economy. Some attempts to explain this inequality, poverty, and marginal employment see this situation as the ultimate negative consequence of massive rural-to-urban migration. In other words, it is a by-product of overurbanization (see the prior discussion of this subject). This section presents a different interpretation that focuses on the way in which intra-urban inequality and the informal sector may play a functional role in peripheral capitalist formations linked to the world economy.

One component of this argument was already alluded to: the link between the rise of ISI and urban concentration. ISI manufacturing requires an internal market of consumers, preferably clustered together in urban areas, who are sufficiently wealthy to purchase the final products (Roberts, 1978a: 81). Poverty, in and of itself, tends to retard this sort of industrial growth. Given the aggregate poverty of the West African nations, however, the skewed income distribution in the large cities concentrates income sufficiently to create some consumer demand for the products of import substitution industrialization.

But what of the urban informal sector or urban petty commodity production?[9] How are they linked to capitalism at the local or international level? Gugler (1982, 1988) and Riddell (1978) voice the widely accepted view that "the so-called informal sector" is marginal and isolated, a relatively nonproductive artifact of old, traditional ways of life. Workers in this type of employment are labeled as "under-" or "misemployed" by Gugler (1982: 175–176). "Casual work" in temporary jobs, street vending, and work in family enterprises are characterized by "the underutilization of labor" and represent "underemployment," while "misemployment" is work done in socially useless jobs. Begging and prostitution are placed in this category, but according to Gugler, the category also includes service people who clean houses and streets and scavengers who recycle the refuse of the more affluent.

Recent research on Third World cities suggests that viewing the informal sector as nonproductive is inaccurate. Begging and prostitution, of course, generate little in the way of material output, but each of the other types of apparent underemployment and misemployment can be conceptualized as socially useful but very inexpensive work. Two attributes of informal sector enterprises stand out: "First, they are labor intensive. Second, they avoid formal state supervision and regulation" (Portes, 1985a: 57). As a result, laborers work long hours, utilize the work of friends and family, and avoid all tax, wage, and social security regulation; this, in turn, makes the cost of labor in the informal sector much lower than that in formally regulated businesses. Lower wage costs mean that goods and services produced in the informal sector can be purchased by formal sector workers and businesses for less. This then lowers labor and material costs for these formal capitalist enterprises, allowing the manufacturers of the underdeveloped country to be highly competitive in the world market.

All of the workers that Gugler (1982) identifies as underutilized fit into the productive informal sector in this sense. "Misemployed" domestic servants and maintenance people also perform necessary labor very cheaply. Even the scavengers whom Gugler claims are a "vivid portrayal" of totally unproductive labor often provide cheap inputs to industry, as well as eking out a subsistence for themselves. In his study of the "vultures" of the Cali garbage dump, Chris Birkbeck argues that by recycling discarded material at very little reclamation cost, these informal sector workers are providing a direct subsidy to Colombian industry. He suggests that "rather than view the garbage picker as a vagrant who should really be working in a factory, we should see him as a worker who is already part of an industrial system" (Birkbeck, 1978: 161). Sethuraman (1977) notes that the recycling of discarded materials through the informal sector is also widespread in urban Africa, providing, for example, low-cost inputs to the Ghanian aluminum industry.

Gavin Williams and Emmanuel Tumusiime-Mutebile (1978: 1103), writing on Nigeria, summarize the role that this sector plays in West Africa:

> Petty commodity producers provide inputs which the capitalist firms are unable to produce profitably. These include cheap food and consumer goods for the employees of capitalist firms and the state which serves them, thus reducing wage costs—and inflating the salaries of the managerial staff. They maintain "the reserve army of labor," which limits the bargaining power of organized labor, thus reducing wage costs, and ensures a flexible supply of labour to capitalist employment. They provide an opportunity for additional earnings, and the possibility of establishing themselves as independent men to employers, thus both subsidizing and encouraging wage employment. They provide the protected market for the product of capitalist firms. Far from being displaced by capitalism, petty commodity production . . . is essential to capitalist production.

The key point of these arguments is that informal sector economic activities are integrated closely with the formal economy found in peripheral capitalist societies. The informal sector is subordinate to and exploited by the formal sector in ways that may be somewhat analogous to international dependency relationships. This is one of Chris Gerry's (1978: 1152) arguments in his article about Dakar: "The subordinate situation of the petty producer vis-à-vis capitalism can be seen as a specific aspect of the generalized subordination of the Sengalese economy to the international capitalist system." Portes (1983, 1985a) sees the informal sector as playing a basic role in the entire world economy. Providing an explanation of how low wages in the Third World are maintained, he notes that

> The informal sector—a vast network of activities articulated with, but not limited to remaining subsistence enclaves—has implications that go beyond the peripheral countries. Direct subsidies to consumption provided by informal to

formal sector workers within a particular peripheral country are also indirect subsidies to core-nation workers and, hence, means to maintain the rate of profit. Thus, through a series of mechanisms well-hidden from public view, the apparently isolated labor of shantytown workers can be registered in the financial houses of New York and London (Portes, 1985a: 61–62).

In West Africa, urban inequality, poverty, squatter settlements, and informal economies may, indeed, be signs of social pathology and the misallocation of labor. But it follows from the argument presented earlier that the problems' true roots lie in much more global circumstances than the rapid growth of urban population alone.

The Issue of Overurbanization

Despite the small absolute percentage of all West Africans who are urban residents, it has been argued that the region suffers from overurbanization. Briefly repeating the general theme, I will note here that: overurbanization is the purported condition of Third World societies whose rapid urban growth has promoted economic inefficiencies. The clearest recent defense of this position is advanced by Gugler (1982, 1988).[10]

Some of the problems with Gugler's defense of the overurbanization argument involve the logical and empirical grounds on which the argument is based. For instance, Gugler (1982: 181–182) forcefully contends that "diseconomies of scale" increase the cost of basic services (such as housing, transport, sewerage, food, and fuel) in urban areas. But he ignores the relative decrease in costs that might accrue to the urban populations through "economies of scale" for these or other services. Discussing rural-urban differences, he cites material describing the *historical* differences between town and country costs for the currently *developed* countries. But it is not at all clear how this material can be related to very dissimilar conditions found today in West Africa (or in other underdeveloped areas of the contemporary world).

A more basic weakness in Gugler's defense of the overurbanization thesis is his failure, discussed earlier, to comprehend the functional importance of the urban informal sector. He views it as unproductive and marginal, which leads to an odd inconsistency in the entire argument. While dismissing urban family enterprise and street vendors as examples of the underutilization of labor, he emphasizes the high potential productivity of rural family craft and trading operations during the agricultural off-season. Why rural petty commodity production is a productive use of labor while its counterpart in the city is not is left unexplained.

Casting aside this specific criticism, I believe the overurbanization thesis has more fundamental problems. One has to do with the criterion of evaluation. Overurbanization is supposedly manifest when the demographic concentration in cities lowers economic efficiency and reduces national productivity. One immediate difficulty in determining whether this condition is present or absent involves constructing an instrument to measure relative "efficiency." Gugler assumes that such an index could measure efficiency in an objective way (although he does not explore this measure in his discussion). Further, he assumes that the increase in productivity that efficiency could bring would be desirable. But any serious consideration of these questions leads one to ask, "Efficiency and increased productivity for whom?"

Gugler's argument seems to advocate reforms that would increase the efficiency of the nations' economies and presumably better the living conditions for the masses of citizens. For instance, he notes that in sub-Saharan Africa, loss of rural labor is inefficient because, given already the low rural demographic density, an additional drain results in less extensive and intensive cultivation of arable land. But his assumption that increases in agricultural output would be used to meet the food needs within these countries is open to debate. A more likely scenario for increased agricultural output is the growth of large-scale corporate or state-controlled farms that produce primarily or even exclusively for the export market. In fact, there is evidence that this is precisely what has happened recently in the African Sahel area (Murdoch, 1980). Agribusiness would be a more efficient vehicle for profitmaking. Its main beneficiaries would be the "triple alliance" of local, state, and international capitalists. But whether any great advantages from such increases in efficiency would ever reach the masses is very much an open question. Scholars point to a paradoxical result of Africa's agriculture production for the world market: "*A continent unable to produce sufficient food to provide a majority of its citizens with even a barely minimal diet has been able to record sharp increases in its annual production of agricultural goods destined for external markets*" (Lofchie, 1976: 554, quoted, with emphasis added, in Murdoch, 1980: 162–163). And there is yet another irony. Since large-scale agriculture is often mechanized and capital intensive, it will almost always result in rural population displacement—and increased urban migration.

The informal sector and urban inequality also present a version of the "efficiency for whom" paradox. These structures are efficient from the standpoint of the local formal sector and its allies in the state and internationally. Gugler may be absolutely correct when he claims that there are too many street vendors or casual workers to be "optimally" employed. Perhaps their labor would be more socially useful growing crops or working in manufacturing. But by reducing the costs of goods and services for capitalist firms and their workers, these informal sector workers, by their sheer numbers, are functional for the peripheral capitalist economic structures of Third World countries.

Although I have offered a rather strong critique of the overurbanization thesis, I still believe it holds a certain seduction. It seems to contain an adequate, if somewhat oversimplified, description of the situation in the countries of West Africa and elsewhere in the underdeveloped world. These nations do exhibit uneven patterns of urban growth at both the city and urban system levels. These patterns appear to be associated with poverty and inequality. Intuitively, it is tempting to locate the source of the problems in rapid urban growth and increasing demographic and functional primacy.

Walton (1977: 12) describes the pattern of population concentration in Africa and Latin America and concludes: "This results in what has been misleadingly termed 'overurbanization,' i.e., the inability of the economy to absorb the expanded population. What is specious in the term, of course, is that it is not urbanization per se that produces this unabsorbative condition, but those forces of accumulation which simultaneously produce both conditions." West Africa's insertion into and continued participation in the capitalist world economy as a peripheral area is a critical factor in its urban inequality and poverty, its massive rural-to-urban migration, and the urban bias of the societal elites. Overurbanization is one result.

The importance of this discussion goes beyond mere academic debate. African policymakers, believing that overurbanization lies at the root of their national economic woes, proposed and adopted programs designed to restrict cityward migration and provide incentives to keep rural residents on the land (for a discussion, see Riddell, 1978: 246–249). These policies faced political and economic obstacles (including massive unrest and a coup d'état in Upper Volta in 1966 as a direct response to the implementation of one such policy) and failed to provide lasting solutions to problems of rapid city growth or urban unemployment. Yet despite the attention that Riddell (1978) and Gugler and Flanagan (1978) give to the political forces that shape urban patterns in West Africa and despite the warnings about the elite's vested interest in the status quo, the policy recommendations that these scholars propose focus on demographic solutions. They do not address the need for changes in external dependency relationships, internal power structure, or the interlock between the two. These strategies only buffer one of the symptoms of underdevelopment in West Africa; meanwhile, the causes of the disease tend to be ignored.

Conclusion

West Africa is a crucible of urban change occurring within the context of underdevelopment. The rapid growth of cities, concomitant with economic stagnation and abject poverty, is a strong indictment of simplistic modernization theory/developmentalist assumptions about urbanization and societal transformation. In this chapter, I have shown how a political economy of the world-system perspective helps to explain the uneven urbanization characteristic of most West African countries. By and large, these nations are prime examples of peripheral urbanization.

In the next chapter, I will examine the case of Nigeria. Like the rest of the region, it was thoroughly peripheralized through colonial penetration. But in recent years, this gigantic country has been cited as something of an exception in West Africa. It may even be an example of semiperipheral "dependent development" (Evans, 1979b). Can Nigeria be classified as semiperipheral? If so, what implications does this have for urbanization? These questions will be addressed in Chapter 5.

5

Nigerian Urbanization:
A Semiperipheral Case?

The crucial insight of the dependency/world-system approach is that a process like urbanization can only be understood as part of the historical expansion of the world economy. To understand this process as it actually unfolds, it is necessary to focus on specific countries or circumscribed smaller regions. To move beyond historical particularism, it is useful to compare the case studies analyzed against other historical trajectories.

Does a country's differential or changing role within the world economy affect the urban patterns that develop within it? Of course, I have already given a tentative affirmative answer to that question in Chapter 2. Now, my interest shifts to specifying how urbanization occurs in particular countries. The selection of countries to be examined is linked to the quantitative analysis discussed previously. Fortunately, the results of network analysis point to an obvious deviant case in West Africa. The blockmodeling of international trade data indicated that Nigeria is a member of the "strong" semiperiphery of the world economy (Nemeth and Smith, 1985a).

This statistical analysis can be backed up by qualitative arguments suggesting that Nigeria plays a role in the world economy distinct from that of its peripheral neighbors. In a seminal article on the contemporary semiperiphery, Wallerstein (1976b: 465) identifies Nigeria as one of a geographically diverse group of countries fitting into that category. Similarly, in his monograph on world-system dynamics, Daniel Chirot classifies Nigeria as one of a group of countries that "are potentially major economic and political powers" in "the new semiperiphery" (Chirot, 1977: 213). In perhaps the most complete discussion of Nigeria's role in the world economy, Evans (1979a: 308–314) suggests that the process of "dependent development" has begun in Nigeria, pulling the country toward semiperipheral status. Evans's assessment is somewhat tentative, conceding that the "deepening" of industrialization in Nigeria is only beginning. But he claims that the class structure and the role of the state and the multinational corporations suggest that Nigeria is entering the early stages of "the Brazilian model of development." Of course, this is *not* a negation of dependence. Semiperipheral countries, while in a position to reach economic development levels beyond the reach of the periphery, are still constrained by their subordinate position relative to "core" nations. But the dependent development of the semiperiphery contrasts sharply with the more severe stagnation and underdevelopment in the periphery. The possible implications that the shift to a semiperipheral role may have for urbanization are not so clear, but they are worth exploring.

Chapter 4 provided some hints that the urbanization process in Nigeria diverges from the regional pattern. For example, Nigeria's urban system exhibits a relatively even distribution of city sizes. Although Lagos may not be greatly different from other large West African cities in its internal structure, its demographic primacy ratio is considerably lower than that of any of the other seaport capitals (see Table 4.1).

Furthermore, Amin (1974: 80–81) argues that "the pattern of migrations in Nigeria is totally different from that which characterized all the other countries to the west of its borders." Unlike the one-way floods of people from northern hinterland to southern metropolises typical of the rest of West Africa, Nigerian cityward migration "appears to be far better balanced" (Amin, 1974: 82). The interior is not emptied into a swollen primate city; rather, migrants in this very large nation tend to gravitate toward regional urban centers. Taking both population and skilled labor into account, Amin (1974: 83) claims that migration flows have pushed the country toward an interregional equilibrium. This pattern is very uncharacteristic for West Africa and, if dependency arguments are valid, very different from the imbalanced migration patterns we would anticipate in a peripheral area.

A more focused study also points to Nigeria's divergent experience of urbanization. Lubeck's (1977) case study of Kano, Nigeria's second largest city, demonstrates that only some of the general characteristics of "dependent urbanization" are present in this old northern city. Relatively moderate population increase, a predominance of local and national investment in growing industrial production, and an apparent absence of the sprawling shantytowns all differentiate Kano from other cities in "dependent countries."

Lubeck's (1977) article ends with a hypothetical explanation for why Nigerian urban patterns may differ from those in other parts of the Third World. He claims: "The prior development of a city and the manner in which an urban area is incorporated into the world-system provide important sources of variation" (Lubeck, 1977: 289). Although my focus will be on the urban system (rather than "a city") and on the entire region that became Nigeria (rather than "an urban area"),

Lubeck's statement represents the working hypothesis that will be used in the following historical-structural analysis.

Indigenous Urbanization: Towns and Trade

One basic assumption that many Western social scientists make about urbanization in Africa is that it is a very recent phenomenon, originating after European contact. Colin Rosser's (1973: 18) comment is typical: "The experience of urbanization in Tropical Africa is essentially a twentieth-century phenomenon and . . . a product of Africa's colonial history.

While it is doubtlessly true that *most* urban areas in tropical Africa trace their emergence to European colonialism and incorporation into the capitalist world economy, this is not the entire story. Africa was not an undifferentiated mass prior to colonialism; substantial variations existed in its level of indigenous development. Prior development must be considered, even in an explanation of urbanization that stresses the importance of incorporation and subsequent role in the world-system.

The stereotypic image of "the Dark Continent" tends to obscure the early development of cities and other forms of complex social organization in parts of Africa. Long before European mariners dared to venture down West Africa's coast, indigenous urban areas in the region had developed. These ancient cities were often the centers of fairly large political and economic empires (see Rayfield, 1974; Gugler and Flanagan, 1978: chapter 1). A number of these urban centers were located in what was to become northern and central Nigeria.

Akin Mabogunje (1968) provides the most detailed account of Nigerian urban history. In a discussion of "medieval urbanism" in northern Nigeria, he points to the vitality of long-distance trade across the Sahara Desert. Cities grew at the edge of the desert as trade entrepôts, much as ocean ports would grow during more recent times (see also Gugler and Flanagan, 1978: 6). These urban areas were both politically and economically important, serving as administrative nodes for a succession of extensive empires, the largest and most famous of which was the vast Songhai Empire of the fifteenth and sixteenth centuries. But their major and enduring role was commercial. Mabogunje's choice of the term *medieval* is quite deliberate. However different their later paths of development might have been, the clear emphasis is on the *similarity* of function that Mabogunje claims for the African trade centers and feudal cities in Europe. He sees a world historical rise of international trade as the common *raison d'être* for the growth of cities in Africa *and* Europe.

Nigerian cities such as Kano, Katina, and Sokoto emerged in the agriculturally rich grassland that formed the ecological buffer zone between the camel trade of the desert and the more difficultly traversed tropical forests. With the decline of the great empires in the seventeenth and eighteenth centuries, a number of city-states emerged that were administered from these and other trade centers. During this period, these small territorial units formed an economic and political federation that became known as the Hausa States, centered in what is now the northern third of Nigeria. Early European visitors at the beginning of the eighteenth century not only reported extremely lucrative trading and extensive craft production but also estimated fairly large populations. Several of these cities apparently had populations of 30,000 to 50,000 during this period, and one traveler visiting Sokoto in the 1820s claimed that the city contained well over 100,000 people (Mabogunje, 1968: 64, table 3).

The large sizes of these cities, their commercial function, and their high levels of stratification and heterogeneity leave little doubt that they did, indeed, fit the *urban* definition. Furthermore, Mabogunje (1968: 68–71) claims that an urban *system* had developed in the area, with massive Sokoto at the apex and smaller centers knit together in a network of trade and craft production. The existence of this "traditional" system of cities in Hausaland has had major implications for urbanization patterns in Nigeria up to the present since a number of these trading cities have remained large and important urban areas in the twentieth century.

Northern Nigeria is not the only region of the country to have experienced high levels of pre-European city growth. Large urban centers also developed in a portion of the central forest belt in an area known as Yorubaland (Mabogunje, 1968: chapter 4; Rayfield, 1974; Gugler and Flanagan, 1978: 16–22). The exact origins of these towns are something of a mystery. Mabogunje (1968: 74–79) argues that urban settlements in Yoruba originated as "colonial settlements" imposed on the area by a more advanced civilization from farther north. Other authors are not so sure of the origins of Yoruba towns (Gugler and Flanagan, 1978: 16).

Regardless of what the original impetus for the rise of towns in Yorubaland might have been, these towns once again comprised a number of relatively large, thriving trade centers well before the British arrived. Like the Sudanic towns of Hausaland, Yoruba urban areas were centers of administration, commerce, and craft production (see Mabogunje, 1968: chapter 4). Trading connections linked these towns to one another as well as to the Hausa and trans-Saharan trade. Despite a decline in many craft activities after the introduction of cheap European manufacturers, Mabogunje (1968: 82–85) argues that the reports of early travelers to Yoruba indicated that a number of centers had begun to take on regionwide craft specialization. These nineteenth-century travelers also provided estimates of the sizes of Yoruba towns. At midcentury, six of these centers reportedly had populations of well over 40,000 persons. Ibadan and Abeokuta, both in central Yoruba and on major north-south trade routes, were the largest urban areas: Both contained populations estimated at over 100,000 (population figures are from Mabogunje, 1968: 91).

In the early nineteenth century, some Western travelers visited a very small and rather isolated Hausa settlment located on an island where the Oguh River met the

Atlantic Ocean. At that time, few residents or visitors to Lagos would have guessed that it would soon be a gigantic world-renown city. That growth was to begin later, as a direct result of Nigeria's colonial incorporation into the capitalist world economy.

There is little doubt that Nigeria had developed a venerable and vital urban heritage before British colonialism. Cities tied together by webs of trade dominated two large regions of what later became Nigeria. It is obviously true that colonialism and the manner in which the area was integrated into world production and exchange networks became overriding determinants of urban growth and change in the twentieth century. But the prior development of two fairly extensive regional city systems was clearly part of the social landscape confronting the colonizing power, and it had a major impact on the urban system that developed subsequently. Colonial powers in many parts of the world faced essentially nonurbanized people with very simple levels of social organization, but this was clearly *not* the case when Britain colonized Nigeria at the end of the nineteenth century.

Colonial Urbanization and Peripheralization:
A Drift Toward Primacy

The Slave Trade

Equating the incorporation of Nigeria and the rest of West Africa into the capitalist world economy with formal European intervention would, of course, be a basic error. The area actually became a key component of the modern world-system much earlier, with the rise of the Atlantic slave trade. The effects of this incursion on African societies is the object of a great deal of discussion and debate (see Amin, 1973; Wallerstein, 1976a, 1989: chapter 3; Inikori, 1982). It seems clear that the "forced migration" of millions of Africans during the seventeenth and eighteenth centuries produced serious negative impacts in West Africa on both demographic and social structures (Williams, 1976; Inikori, 1982: introduction). The opening of a market for African slaves in the New World did more than depopulate West Africa and other source areas: The new economic value of slaves provided incentives for slave-raiding and increased levels of intertribal warfare. In Wallerstein's terminology, the rise of the slave trade marked the beginning of West Africa's "incorporation" into global "commodity chains" that eventually led to a more thoroughgoing "peripheralization" of the region (Wallerstein, 1989: 130).[1]

The social and political dislocations of the slave trade probably affected the location and growth of Nigerian towns and cities during the eighteenth and nineteenth centuries. Mabogunje (1968) reports widespread strife in Yorubaland in the early 1800s. Slave-raiding and related warfare resulted in the destruction of many small towns and large-scale migration to the major ones (Mabogunje,

1968: 90–93). Mabogunje (1968: 93) summarizes the situation: "All in all, the nineteenth century was a period of town coalescence and growth in response to the need of defense and security." Yet despite the intrusion of the capitalist world economy in the form of the slave trade, the overall pattern of urbanization in Nigeria remained basically unchanged. Although a few large cities experienced short-term growth, even they retained essentially the same economic and political functions they had previously performed.

The slave trade also signaled the rising importance of the Atlantic ports. Anthony Hopkins (1973: 110) points to the dual role of these ports: "Besides organizing the sale and shipment of slaves, the coastal entrepôts also supervised the storage and distribution of goods received in exchange." Two of the most important slave ports in what became Nigeria were Bonny on the Niger River delta and Calabar at the mouth of the Cross River (Mabogunje, 1968: 108–109; Hopkins, 1973: 106; Inikori, 1982: 22–23). Both towns were located far to the east of Yorubaland in an area populated by Ibo people with no "ancient tradition of urbanism" (Mabogunje, 1968: 108). The rise of these and a few other relatively isolated ports in Iboland can be directly traced to the world economy's need for coerced labor.

By virtue of its location as an excellent natural port, Lagos also became involved with the slave trade. But through the eighteenth century, the town was very small: Mabogunje (1968: 239) cites an estimated population in 1,800 of 5,000. The number of slaves passing through Lagos was insignificant, especially compared to the huge human cargoes shipped from Bonny and Calabar (see relevant data in Inikori, 1982: 23). Ironically, however, British and French bans on slave-trading at the beginning of the nineteenth century catapulted Lagos into preeminence as the major exporter of slaves for its channels provided a much safer hideout for slave ships attempting to avoid French and British naval attacks (Mabogunje, 1968: 239–240). While the slave trade was effectively thwarted where it had formerly thrived, Lagos's protected location, coupled with intensified internal strife in central Yorubaland, elevated the port into a major center for the slavers. Lagos's increasing share of the slave trade, in turn, stimulated growth; by 1850, the town was estimated to be approaching the 20,000 population mark. Nevertheless, Mabogunje (1968: 241) argues that compared to other Yoruba towns, "Lagos was a very small town occupying a small part of a small island" during this period.

Despite its modest size, Lagos's success in the slave-exchange business was drawing a good deal of attention. In fact, the Lagos slave trade was to be the proximate cause (or at least the public rationale) for the first overt British military intervention in Nigeria. In December 1851, a British squadron sailed into Lagos's lagoon and bombarded the city. Although this attack reduced almost half of the town to rubble, it did effectively bring the West African slave trade to an end (Mabogunje, 1968: 107–241). Many residents of the city fled, and when Lagos came under British power, it was a town in ruins. Mabogunje (1968: 241) notes that for months after the bombardment, British authorities found it "necessary to appeal to people to return to the island." Yet British imperial policy, which had initially destroyed Lagos, was later to set into motion a pattern of urbanization and development that would concentrate growth at this port.

Formal Colonization

The political economy of the world-system approach suggests that colonization is usually motivated by a direct economic payoff. To an extent, the imposition of formal British colonial power in West Africa in the late nineteenth century seems to contradict this proposition. At the time, the British still exhibited great strength, if no longer absolute hegemony, in the world-economy (Chase-Dunn, 1979; Bousquet, 1980). Normally, a core power in a hegemonic position would be expected to reject colonization and continue to rely on the advantages that accrue to it by free trade (Bergesen, ed., 1983). Yet Britain decided to formally colonize Nigeria in the late nineteenth century, seemingly in direct contradiction to its own economic interest in a more laissez-faire situation.

There are two explanations for this apparent paradox. One focuses on the political economy internal to Nigeria and other parts of West Africa; the other centers on patterns of international competition in the world-system.

By the mid-1800s, the economy of the area that was to become Nigeria had largely made the transition to legitimate commerce (as opposed to the old slave-trade base). Cash-crop production was on the rise, further transforming the rural economy (Wallerstein, 1989: 147). Palm oil was in great demand in Europe for use in the production of soaps, lubricants, and candles (Hopkins, 1973: 129), and large numbers of foreign traders established themselves at Lagos to deal in this lucrative trade (Mabogunje, 1968: 106, 242). But these traders were frustrated to some extent by political instability, high local travel tolls, and poor transportation in the interior, which disrupted the flow of export products like palm oil (Hopkins, 1973: 156). The post-1750 political situation saw "a number of strong, largely slave-selling states" in violent competition with each other throughout the region "where 'anarchy' made pacific trade impossible" (Wallerstein, 1989: 187). Therefore, merchants began to pressure European governments to take a more active role in regulating and rationalizing West African economies. These traders called for foreign intervention to "control the vagaries of the market," which was a crucial step in the gradual capitalist penetration and peripheralization of West Africa (Wallerstein, 1976a: 37). Formal colonization was the end point of a long-term process of incorporation, and it represented a response to the needs of European commercial interests.

Wallerstein (1976a, 1989) claims that other forces were at work as well. He argues that by the last quarter of the nineteenth century, British hegemony was beginning to be challenged by Britain's colonial rivals. Germany and France, particularly, were challenging British merchants for control of West African trade. In 1879, French troops moved into West Africa pushing eastward from Senegal, claiming territory as they penetrated the interior (Hopkins, 1973: 162). In the mid-1880s, Germany moved into Dahomey and the Cameroons, on either side of territory the British later established as Nigeria. The British, who already controlled a small coastal area near Lagos, sent troops up the Niger River to protect the trade areas controlled by British firms—particularly the large, powerful Royal Niger Company, which had swallowed up most of its commercial competitors but now faced the threat of French and German military power (Hopkins, 1973: 163). Rather than entering the fray because formal colonialism directly served its national economic interests, Great Britain colonized Nigeria (and also the Gold Coast) to avoid having its access cut off by other countries' colonial control. Wallerstein (1976a) labels the British move on Nigeria as an example of "preemptive colonization."

Lagos and "The Open Economy"

Britain formally established its dominion over Nigeria on the first day of the twentieth century. But the form of its colonial rule was very different from the coercive, tightly controlled colonialism displayed by other powers at other times. Britain's policies regarding the "dual mandate" and its encouragement of "indirect rule" (Mabogunje, 1968: 111; Hopkins, 1973: 189–192) eliminated much of the direct government control associated with earlier Spanish colonialism or even concurrent policies of less powerful early-twentieth-century colonizers such as the Japanese (see Chapter 7 for a discussion of Japanese imperialism).

The colonial strategies of the British and other core powers in West Africa, at first glance, appeared rather benign. The major goal was to "rationalize" the African export economies in order to create larger "free trade" areas within which goods and people would move relatively unhindered (Munro, 1976: 89–90). The emphasis was on the creation of an "open economy" (Hopkins, 1973: 168–169). Open economies, according to Hopkins, are heavily dependent on the export of primary products in exchange for consumer manufactures, are dominated by expatriate interests, and have low tariff barriers (especially on the products of the dominant nation). Governmental and financial arrangements are set up to minimize the obligation and risk incurred by the metropolitan power. Obviously, the extent to which a colonial area approximates this ideal-typical pattern corresponds rather directly with the degree to which it can be described as a dependent "enclave" economy (Chirot, 1977: chapter 2; Cardoso and Faletto, 1979: XIX).

A key economic function in this type of development is the growth of a point to serve as the "headlink" through which metropolitan and colonial goods can flow. The port of Lagos was to serve that function. It would experience the same type of rapid urban growth as that experienced by similar nodes in the interstate system, particularly the primate cities of the export-based economies of nineteenth- and early-twentieth-century Latin America (Frank, 1969; McGreevey, 1971; Hardoy, ed., 1975) and the Philippines (Nemeth and Smith, 1985a). British interest in facilitating a free flow of products such as palm oil and later groundnuts and cotton out of Nigeria and a constant counterstream of English manufactures into the colony gave rise to policies that tended to concentrate people and resources in Lagos.

One key to the city's growth was the early concentration of European merchants at Lagos. Within a few months of the naval bombardment and British occupation, agents from the United Kingdom, continental Europe, and the United States began arriving and setting up business in the newly established British protectorate (Mabogunje, 1968: 242). The major motivation for gradually bringing the surrounding coastal areas in the city's immediate hinterland under the Crown's control was to establish "stable political conditions" for these traders (Mabogunje, 1968: 244). The relatively early consolidation of British power over a narrow band of coastal territory gave merchants based in Lagos an important commercial advantage (Hopkins, 1973: map 10, p. 163).

Lagos's political advantages and its consequent rise as a base of operations for foreign traders helps to explain why it became more important in world commerce than other older and more established ports to the east, such as Calabar and Bonny (Home, 1976). Both of these ports were extremely important during the slave trade, and their commerce had remained largely in the hands of indigenous traders. But the transition to legitimate exports such as palm oil proved difficult for these entrepôts. The changing basis of trade created a "crisis of the aristocracy" in nineteenth-century West Africa—a political crisis stemming from "a contradiction between past and present relations of production" (Hopkins, 1973: 143). Old traders faced stiff new competition from a new generation of Africans eager to share in the profits of commerce. The result was a great deal of political and economic instability in and around the Niger Delta ports (Hopkins, 1973: 146–147). The internal problems of these other entrepôts were compounded by the growing importance of the foreign merchants, who held a key advantage over indigenous merchants through their control of oceanic shipping.

It may have been this latter factor that tipped the balance decisively in Lagos's favor in the late nineteenth century. A technological change was taking place in the 1870s that was to forever alter the pattern of maritime trade along the West African coast: Faster and more predictable steamships were rapidly replacing sailing ships as the primary carriers (Hopkins, 1973: 148). One of the results of this change was the growing commercial importance of a single Nigerian port—Lagos. Besides being faster and more cost-efficient, steamers "concentrated competition at the ports of call, in contrast to the days of sail, when ships could adapt their schedules to meet varying market conditions. Evidence of increasing concentration was to be seen in the expansion of a few favoured centres, such as Dakar, Freetown and Lagos, and, ultimately, in the decline of [other] well known trading stations" (Hopkins, 1973: 151).

Infrastructural Development

Other more deliberate policy decisions further concentrated international trade at Lagos. The relative lack of British government involvement and investment in the Nigerian economy was already noted. Indicative of official British policy toward the imperial role in colonial economic development is the emphasis on administrative financial self-sufficiency in West African colonies. Government spending was stringently tied to custom duties and a few other tax receipts, and very little was allowed for any type of colonial development efforts (Hopkins, 1973: 188–192). There was, however, an important exception that would have a major impact on the development of Nigeria's urban system and spatial economy.

The one ambitious development project that the British *did* take up was the creation of a transportation-communication infrastructure, particularly the building and/or improving of railways and port facilities (Mabogunje, 1968: 142–149; Hopkins, 1973: 192–198; Munro, 1976: 90–95). Hopkins cites a top British colonial official: "The material development of Africa may be summed up in one word—Transport."[2] In Nigeria, transport development funneled increasing amounts of trade toward Lagos.

The port facility at Lagos was the object of a number of improvement projects undertaken by the British administration. The first, proposed in 1892 and finished in 1917, involved three huge stone moles to protect the harbor entrance, built at the cost of near 800,000 pounds sterling (Mabogunje, 1968: 248–249). Continuous upgrading of the harbor, wharves, and transit sheds occurred throughout the period of colonial rule. These improvements bolstered Lagos's position as Nigeria's primary international port. Even the development of another new modern facility in the 1920s at Port Harcourt (Hopkins, 1973: 195) provided little challenge. Mabogunje (1968: 252) emphasizes Lagos's huge trade volume: "In fact, if Dakar's trade in bunker oil was excluded, Lagos by 1954 had become the most important West African port both by value of trade and by tonnage handled."

Of course, links to the interior were equally important in making Lagos a great trade center. Railroad and port developments proceeded together. The original impetus for the construction of the rail line lay, in part, in reaching inland quarries where stone for the harbor project was available. But the railroad pushed on much farther into the interior. By 1901, the line had reached the huge trading city of Ibadan (Mabogunje, 1968: 194). Pushing on through Yorubaland, the railroad's connections to Ilorin were complete in 1908, and by 1911, a link was established with the Hausa metropolis of Kano, a distance of 711 miles from Lagos (Hopkins, 1973: 195). This railroad net solidified Lagos's claim to administrative and commercial preeminence, paved the way for the political amalgamation of northern and southern Nigeria (1914), and spurred a dramatic increase of export agriculture in the Kano region (Mabogunje, 1968: 144–145, 249). Lagos became the magnet that drew the products of an entire vast developing nation to its wharves. An eastern rail line to Kano through Port Harcourt was only completed in 1926, too late to be much of a threat to the metropolis's commercial dominance.

This preeminence was further reinforced by the underlying logic of British railway construction. The emerging rail system was designed to further lubricate the movement of goods in the open economy. Underpinning British strategy were diverse motives and a number of powerful elites—merchants, shipping companies, administrators, speculators—who saw the development of rail lines to the interior as forwarding their own particular interests (Munro, 1976: 91–92). But like other colonial efforts, the overarching rationale behind British railroad construction "was to concentrate on what they [the British] could profitably exploit and export from the country in the hope that this would have some incidental benefit on internal change (Mabogunje, 1968: 143).

As a result, the railroad system reinforced a "dendritic" pattern of exchange (C. Smith, ed., 1976).[3] Even with the completion of the eastern rail line in the 1920s, genuine national integration of the spatial economy was very incomplete. Hopkins (1973: 198) explains: "Communications were designed mainly to evacuate exports. There were few lateral or inter-colonial links, and little attempt was made to use railways and roads as a stimulus to internal exchange." Mabogunje (1968: 143–144) points out that this British-imposed transportation system often seemed "entirely arbitrary" from the viewpoint of contemporary Nigerians for the railroads were laid so that they often bypassed important indigenous cities and trading centers. Obviously, this pattern benefited Lagos and diminished the important trade functions of many of the old and existing urban centers (Mabogunje, 1968: 149).

Dependent Urbanization and Incipient Primacy

A major result of the concentration of commerce in Lagos was growing economic, political and demographic dominance. This was directly attributable to the strategy of developing an open economy, which was imposed by Britain. Geographer Cesar Vapnarsky (1966: 10) argues: "The lower degree of closure, i.e., the more the system is inherently dependent on other systems to maintain its ecological stability, the higher can be expected the degree of primacy of the city (or cities) which establishes the link between the given area and the external world" (quoted in Owen and Witton, 1973: 326).

Mabogunje (1968) documents the incredible growth of Lagos in the twentieth century. Between 1900 and 1950, the city's population grew more than fivefold, with over 230,000 in residence at the end of that period. Population growth was related to increased economic and political power. Lagos attracted a flood of migrants because of the promise of well-paying jobs. The city had the overwhelming majority of wage and salaried jobs; its workers enjoyed the highest average annual earnings in Nigeria. Many of the most sought-after jobs were high-paid, secure, administrative jobs in government. After Lagos became the capital of a unified Nigeria in 1914, the bureaucracy grew steadily in size and influence. Lagos's commercial control grew beyond that of a simple trade center when the Central Bank of Nigeria, as well as European and U.S. financial institutions, were established there.

Despite Lagos's unprecedented growth in the first half of this century, Mabogunje (1968) emphasizes that the real "metropolitan explosion" did not begin until after 1950. Between that date and 1963, the population within the juridical boundaries of the city tripled and reached over 1 million in the metropolitan area (Gugler and Flanagan, 1978: 38). By 1976, the metropolitan population was estimated at 2.5 million (Gugler and Flanagan, 1978: 41). In 1985, a staggering 5.84 million people lived in Lagos, which had become the world's twenty-seventh largest city (United Nations, 1988: table 6), and by 1990, it had grown by (an almost unbelievable!) 2 million more people to 7.74 million (United Nations, 1993: table A.11).

Much of this astounding growth can be linked to independence and preliminary efforts to promote true internal development. To gain control of the open economy and to counter increasing negative balances of trade, Nigerian officials began to encourage and actively promote import substitution industrialization. In 1948, the government started buying land near the capital to be offered to foreign and domestically owned businesses for industrial development. By 1964 the number of industrial establishments had risen to 300, compared to only 15 in 1951 (Mabogunje, 1968: 255–256).

This type of development strategy is a familiar one, which a number of less developed countries attempted in the mid-twentieth century (Cardoso and Faletto, 1979; Frank, 1981b). Writing with particular reference to Latin America, Cardoso and Faletto (1979) point to ISI's popularity during the 1950s. The expectation was that indigenous manufacturing of consumer goods would decrease dependency on imports and help meet foreign exchange/trade deficit problems (Cardoso and Faletto, 1979: chapter 5).

As noted in Chapter 4, ISI had important implications for the pattern of urban development wherever it was attempted. Its appetite for labor and markets meshed with the growth of large cities, high intracity inequality, and sizable numbers of wealthy consumers. Metropolitan Lagos fit this pattern well. Mabogunje (1968: 267) attributes the swelling size of Lagos to the economic opportunities attendant to industrialization. He also documents, in an anecdotal way, the growth of a small-scale or informal sector. Consistent with the mainstream perspective of the 1960s, Mabogunje (1968: chapter 11) emphasizes the "twin-centred" nature of the urban economy with a declining "traditional" marketing system contraposed to "modern" businesses. He also notes the presence of large slums and "unplanned" settlements. Predictably, Mabogunje (1968: chapter 12) attributes these dysfunctional aspects of urban growth to "overurbanization." He points to "the paradoxical situation that it is in the growing centres that unemployment is most pronounced" (Mabogunje, 1968: 317).

In Chapter 4, I presented an alternative theoretical explanation for some of the characteristics Mabogunje associates with overurbanization. The gist of that argument was that informal sector activities (and, by extension, inequality and large numbers of urban-dwellers lacking formal jobs) are functional in peripheral capitalist economies.

The key point here is that, by and large, the pattern of historical growth in Lagos followed a trajectory rather typical of dependent cities. Lagos seems to be representative of the rise of a huge, inegalitarian Third World capital city. Mabogunje (1968: 319–322) even goes so far as to discuss the dilemma faced in Lagos as "the problem of the primate city." Yet here is another paradox: Despite its functional dominance in a number of ways, Lagos is *not* a primate city in the demographic sense. In fact, it was not even the largest city in Nigeria until the 1960s! In the following section, I will emphasize how Lagos deviates from the typical dependent primate city model.

Indigenous Regional Centers and "Counter-Primacy"

Lagos has not become a national primate city because Nigeria contains other very large, growing urban areas as well. In fact, only by the time of the 1963 Nigerian census did Lagos move ahead of the old Yoruba city of Ibadan in terms of population (Mabogunje, 1968: 319). Despite Lagos's rapid growth, Nigeria's Davis Index score on urban primacy in 1970 was still just under 1.0, lower than that of most core nations.[4] By 1970, Ibadan's population was approaching 750,000, while population figures in another Yoruba city, Ogbomosho, and in the Hausa metropolis of Kano both hovered around the 350,000 mark. Indeed, the tenth-largest city in the nation had just under 200,000 residents.[5]

Explaining this pattern requires a closer examination of these cities. Not including Lagos, seven of the top ten cities are located in Yorubaland. Port Harcourt, the eastern port and railroad termimus, is the only Ibo city on this list. All the cities except Lagos and Port Harcourt were major urban centers by the mid-eighteenth century (see Mabogunje, 1968: chapters 3 and 4). It is clear that the level of urbanization and development in the Hausa and Yoruba regions before the colonial period had a lasting impact on the Nigerian urban structure.

In effect, the pattern that has developed is an amalgamation of a number of pre-European regionally primate systems. The preindustrial cities of Ibadan and Kano clearly show this pattern. Kano is a very ancient city that was a key entrepôt in the trans-Saharan trade and, as Lubeck (1977: 284) points out, the primate city of Hausaland in the nineteenth century. Similarly, Ibadan dominated an extensive political and economic empire in northern and eastern Yorubaland in the late nineteenth century. Even in this area of many towns, Ibadan's 1891 estimated population of about 120,000 was very large—this city was clearly both demographically and functionally dominant in its region. It is likely that a number of the smaller preindustrial cities in Yorubaland dominated more circumscribed areas of farms and small towns in patterns of regional primacy, too. These dominance relationships are predictable given the type of agrarian surplus extraction upon which preindustrial cities relied (Sjoberg, 1965).

There has been a good deal of debate over the "boundary" problem when analyzing urban systems (C. Smith, 1982a; Walters, 1985). Some researchers argue that national primacy ratios that suggest lognormal city-size distributions for large, less developed countries may mask regional primacy, where the region is often the more relevant unit of analysis (Berry, 1971).

Given Nigeria's large size and distinctive patterns of indigenous regional development, Berry's argument may initially seem to apply. Clearly, at least two primate regional urban systems existed in precolonial times. With British colonialism and the gradual integration of the open economy, however, this idea of regional primacy became less tenable. A key element in the process, of course, was the development of the transportation system. The completion of the rail line to Kano in 1911 made it increasingly meaningful to speak of a Nigerian *national* urban system. In fact, Hopkins (1973: 197) argues that the railroad's arrival in Kano "was an event of great significance in African commercial history. It marked the final decline of the old, north-facing, trans-Saharan trade, the reorientation of the markets of the interior towards coastal ports, and the coalescence of two centres of exchange which, in previous centuries, had been only in sporadic contact with each other. Most of the other major old centers that remain large and important today were also brought into contact by this rail line. Of the ten largest Nigerian urban areas in 1970, six are located along the railroad line between Lagos and Kano. By 1911, all of these cities were involved in an exchange system oriented toward Lagos and the centers of world capitalism beyond (see also Home, 1976).

With this new integration and orientation, the pattern of urbanization might have been expected to change to fit the pattern of an externally oriented peripheral nation. The explosive growth of Lagos has demonstrated that this dynamic is not entirely absent. But in the face of such pressure, some of the older indigenous centers have shown a surprising dynamism and propensity to grow. It is not satisfactory to ascribe this to some vague social momentum whereby large cities, ceteris paribus, will continue to grow. An adequate explanation of such phenomena requires specifying the mechanisms involved.

Two somewhat distinct yet intertwined explanations come to mind. The first draws on Carole Smith's (1985) "class relations theory of urban primacy" (see above, chapter 1). Unlike the situation in Guatemala, the class structures that developed in Nigeria's big indigenous trading centers (such as Kano and Ibadan) were conducive to local economic innovation and expansion. The second line of argument involves the timing and nature of British colonialism, which had an interest in preserving and even expanding economic activities in the preexisting metropolitan area.

Lubeck's (1977) article on Kano buttresses the first type of explanation. Emphasizing the importance of "indigenous institutional development" prior to British conquest, Lubeck claims that much of the economic vitality of the city, particularly early in the twentieth century, was initiated by indigenous African entrepreneurs. In fact, local merchants in the Kano area were sufficiently strong and resourceful to actually develop a thriving small-producer export economy based on groundnuts at a time when the British colonial authorities were promoting cotton-growing. Hopkins (1973: 219) agrees "that changes within the agricultural system had little or nothing to do with external influences." He also credits the initiative and business acumen of the Hausa traders with producing a bonanza around Kano. Despite its relatively simple technology, this business is still extremely productive, and it brings export earnings to Kano's African merchants even today. Lubeck (1977) notes that Kano's "local entrepreneurial capital" continues to survive in at least a relatively autonomous manner in the contemporary period. Under the leadership of these entreprenuers (and with help from Nigeria's increasingly developmental-oriented state), Kano should remain a growing, economically vital Nigerian city, perhaps gradually moving into manufacturing activities such as food- and agricultural-processing.

The picture Mabogunje (1968: chapters 8 and 9) paints of Ibadan's economic prospect is not quite so bright. He constantly contrasts this "traditional" metropolis with "modern" Lagos, noting that Ibadan has not been able to achieve the commercial success of the capital. But he admits that the city continued to grow, if not as quickly as Lagos: "Ibadan as an important commercial centre was attracting an increasing number of immigrants" (Mabogunje, 1968: 199). Industry had also begun to develop in Ibadan, primarily on a small-scale entrepreneurial basis. Mabogunje (1968: 201) reports 2,000 small businesses in the city. He argues that this "poor industrial base" underlies Ibadan's "slow" growth rate of "only" 2.8 percent per annum between 1952 and 1963 (Mabogunje, 1968: 202). Unlike Lubeck's upbeat description of Kano, the theme here is one of growing population with insufficient formal employment opportunities. Mabogunje sees this as a pathological situation, but from the global perspective presented here, it is a rather normal pattern of growth for a dependent city.

Mabogunje's (1968) description of recent impetuses to growth also illustrates the second line of argument. He notes that a number of expatriate firms located in Ibadan immediately after railroad connections were established. One of the objectives of these enterprises was to garner the produce of the land around the city. But consistent with British intentions, these firms were also interested in developing a market in this large city, already populated by a number of wealthy merchants. Mabogunje (1968: 194) relates that "a major concern was the search for a profitable commodity of trade in order to raise the purchasing power of the populace for buying imported goods from Europe." Discussing postindependence changes, including the location of a regional capital at Ibadan, he points out that the "remarkable concentration of purchasing power in the city stimulated rapid growth in commerce and employment opportunities. Numerous new firms were established and many older ones expanded" (Mabogunje, 1968: 200). Obviously, Ibadan's large size made it an attractive place to promote elite consumption. Despite Mabogunje's claim that there were few industrial enterprises in 1963, it would appear that the conditions were right for the deployment of ISI, which would stimulate further peripheral capitalist development and urban population growth.

Lubeck (1977) sees parallel developments in Kano's future, but a better theoretic grasp of the world economy causes him to evaluate such development much more cautiously. Writing after the discovery of large Nigerian oil reserves, he describes "the hasty arrival in Kano of multinational enterprises, anxious to recycle petro dollars" (Lubeck, 1977: 289). Despite his concerns, Lubeck believes that this infusion of capital will lead to growth, if not of a kind he would endorse.

In summary, the factors promoting "counter-primacy" revolve around the continued viability of old, large indigenous cities as loci for both production and consumption. Yoruba and Hausa urban merchants adapted well to the demands of the export economy. They were aided by a British policy that stressed little direct colonial economic intervention, which allowed economic activities in cities like Kano and Ibadan to expand. In turn, the prior concentration of population and income made these cities favorable places for capital investment and business growth. The result was mixed: A relatively even, nonprimate distribution for the national urban hierarchy combined with the rapid urban population growth, bloated tertiary sector, and gross levels of intra-urban inequality usually associated with peripheral development. This structure of urban development is best understood as the result of a conjuncture of forces dominated by the changes produced by Nigeria's incorporation into the world economy. But it was affected as well by the indigenous heritage of the region.

Present and Future: Semiperipheral Urbanization?

Will this hybrid pattern of low urban primacy but rapid growth and high inequality continue? And how will Nigeria's changing role in the world economy affect future urban patterns?

As I suggested at the beginning of this chapter, a number of scholars claim that Nigeria's role in the world-system may be changing. The emergence of Nigeria as a key oil-producer and exporter in the early 1970s (see Kirk-Greene and Rimmer, 1981: chapter 7) is one element in this change. Equally important is the Nigerian state's response to this development. Variously described as an attempt at "negotiated dependency" (Lubeck, 1977) or a "triple alliance" of state, national, and multinational capital (Evans, 1979b: 308-314), recent policy directions pursued by the Nigerian government can be seen as attempts to gain more national control over the direction of economic growth. Evans (1979b) admits that a portrayal of Nigeria as the "Brazil of Africa" would be overdrawn. But he argues that important steps (such as "indigenization") have been taken to limit foreign control of an economy that fell just short of South Africa's in terms of total gross national product (GNP) in the late 1970s. This transition to more national control of an increasingly closed economy (see Hopkins, 1973: 171–172), at least raises the possibility of economic and political policies more conducive to the internal development of the Nigerian economy. The transition to semiperipheral status hardly implies an end to uneven development; Evans (1979b: 311) describes Nigeria as "a country groping out of classic dependence." But it may have some implications for the future growth of the Nigerian urban system.

First, it is plausible that the process of dependent development in the semiperiphery mitigates against growing urban primacy. I have claimed that Lagos's rapid growth was due to its role in an open economy, oriented first toward the evacuation of exports and later toward a policy of import substitution industrialization. While both Lagos's export function and its concentration of consumers will doubtlessly continue to be important (and promote further demographic growth), other changes are occurring that promote urban development in other centers.

In an economy increasingly geared to internal growth and moving toward more manufacturing, there are economic incentives for capital and people to move close to the factors of production. The location of mineral resources could become influential in determining patterns of urban growth. In this regard, it is crucial to note that the oilfields are located in eastern Nigeria, an area of very low urbanization before, during, or after the colonial period (Kirk-Greene and Rimmer 1981: chapter 7). Oil-related development already includes a major ocean terminal at Bonny and three new refineries at Port Harcourt, Warri in Bendel state, and Kaduna in northern Nigeria. Extensive tin deposits discovered and exploited much earlier prompted the British creation of the town of Jos in the 1920s (Mabogunje,

1968: 145), and this area could also become a prime site for industrialization. In the early 1980s, Anthony Kirk-Greene and Douglas Rimmer (1981: 90) reported that "enormous deposits of natural gas have been discovered in the Niger delta." These authors describe a huge development project, financed by the Nigerian government and several oil multinationals, aimed at developing a natural gas liquefaction plant at Bonny. In an economy moving toward manufacturing and with growing indigenous control, all these areas of low urban development but rich resource endowment could give rise to new, large-scale urban areas.

More directly related to the politics of Nigeria as a rising semiperipheral state are national development policies explicitly designed to bring about more-balanced regional growth (see Kirk-Greene and Rimmer, 1981: chapter 12). Since the 1960s, the government has adopted explicit national plans that are developmentalist and committed to increased geographic equity (Dudley, 1982: chapter 7; Kirk-Greene and Rimmer, 1981: 146–149). The results of these plans have not always corresponded well to their goals, because of both the constraints of dependence and the corruption of the Nigerian elite (see Evans, 1979b: 313, for a brief description of the "cement scandal" in 1975–1976). Kirk-Greene and Rimmer (1981: 148) claim that some dimensions of uneven development are more effectively dealt with than others: "It is doubtful that equity policies conducted on this dimension do very much to reduce inter-household inequality in Nigeria. But they may be quite effective, continued long enough, in diminishing disparities among regions of the country and among communities within regions." Equalizing resources to various urban areas is likely to promote a more even distribution of economic opportunity between cities for potential in-migrants. This would reduce Lagos's disproportionate attraction to migrants and weigh against increased national urban primacy.

But Kirk-Greene and Rimmer quote suggests that the other aspect of dependent urbanization, intra-urban inequality, may not change. This brings us to a dilemma of dependent development in the semiperiphery, as both a theoretical and a practical issue. A key element (as discussed in Chapter 4) of the pervasiveness of urban inequality and poverty is the ubiquity of the urban informal sector. What is the relationship between dependent development (or, put differently, national mobility into the semiperiphery) for this aspect of uneven urbanization?

A political economy of the world-system approach does not propose any theoretically a priori answer to this question. Up to this point, the coincidence of urban primacy and imbalanced urban systems, on the one hand, and intra-urban inequality and the informal sector, on the other hand, have been stressed. Often they *do* appear in tandem. This seems to suggest that just as dependent development or semiperipheralization leads to decreases in urban primacy, so, too, should it lower the internal characteristics of dependent urbanization. But the Nigerian example provides evidence to the contrary. Lubeck (1977) and

Mabogunje (1968) agree that a large, relatively poor urban informal sector continues to thrive. Perhaps some generally high level of inequality should be expected in the semiperiphery. Chirot (1977) and others state that economic growth in the semiperiphery has often brought about heightened rather than reduced income inequality (Chapter 7; see also Barnet and Mueller, 1974). But this is not always true. In Chapter 7, the case of a semiperipheral country with relatively low intra-urban inequality and a much smaller urban informal sector is discussed.

Why do we obtain different outcomes between countries of the same world economic strata? Portes (1983) suggests an answer. Consistent with his previous writings, he claims that the informal sector's function is "to alleviate, from the point of view of firms, consequences of the proletarianization process" (Portes, 1983: 163). In other words, these activities allow noncore countries to provide cheap labor to formal capitalist enterprises. Discussing a number of Latin American countries conventionally labeled "semiperipheral," Portes (1983) notes dissimilar degrees of informal sector development between them. His argument is that these differences are attributable to historical differences between the role of the state and the nature of class conflict (Portes, 1983: 164–168). Thus, despite having *common* world economic roles and governments committed to economic growth and the type of "good business climates" conducive to large-scale capital investment, these states developed *different* strategies for controlling and exploiting cheap labor. While the less obvious control on wages and labor costs represented by a large informal sector is present in some of these countries (i.e., those of the Southern Cone), others (e.g., Brazil) have succeeded in these same objectives using more direct political repression of the labor movement. Where authoritarian regimes succeed in keeping wages low through open repression the urban informal sector may actually decline (Portes, 1983: 167).[6]

Economically, Nigeria is currently just at the beginning of the process of dependent development. Politically, the country's post-colonial experience has been characterized by conflict and instability. While the current military rulers' proclaimed commitment to democracy was exposed as a sham when an opposition leader, Mashood Abiola, won the 1993 presidential election—and was promptly arrested—it is not at all obvious that the Nigerian state is developing into the type of rigidly repressive system characteristic of the "deepening" stages of dependent development in South Korea or Brazil. Instead, we see the emergence of what Peter Evans (1995: chapter 3) calls a "predatory state" (he uses the Mobutu regime in Zaire as the prime example). These states are "weak" in the sense that they have little capacity to bring about economic or social transformation (cf. Migdal, 1988). A recent journalistic account (Coll and Shiner, 1994) found the Nigerian military government "riddled with corruption, pinched for funds and absorbed by domestic turmoil" (1) and unable to provide even basic services, much less direct development efforts. So, while the Nigerian state is in no sense democratic, it also lacks the organization and efficacy of other bureaucratic authoritarian industrializing regimes; despite political dictatorship, the power of the government to plan economic, social, demographic policies is quite weak.

Given the lack of a state willing and/or able to mobilize and repress labor in an industrializing development project, Portes's argument about alternative proletarianization processes suggests that there should be a growing urban informal sector of poor, underemployed people and an expansion of associated phenomena, such as shantytowns and rapid urban population increases, in Nigeria in the near future. Changes in Nigeria's world economic role weighing against increased urban primacy are not likely to mitigate against continued rates of intra-urban inequality.

Concluding Note on Conjunctural Causation

The Nigerian pattern suggests an important theme stressed by various dependency/world-system writers. There is no reason to expect that everything worth explaining can be mechanistically derived from a nation's "external" status in the world-system. The analysis in this chapter has suggested that both the indigenous preincorporation urban heritage of Nigeria and the developing role of the state and class conflict are important in explaining the process of urbanization.

A complete analysis needs to take into account both internal and external forces, as well as the articulation between them (see pertinent discussions in Braudel, 1977: chapter 3; Cardoso and Faletto, 1979: introduction; Frank, 1979: chapter 1). No analysis of urbanization in Nigeria (or elsewhere in the Third World) can hope to explain this process without considering the world-systemic effects. Noncore countries in situations of relative dependency face critical constraints on their patterns of development. But operating within the parameters established by world-system development, internal processes determine the patterns of social structural change. The noncore Third World is not an undifferentiated mass. Factors other than a nation's world-system status must be analyzed to understand processes such as urbanization. But these factors should not be seen as alternative explanations. Instead, as in so many of the complex processes of macrostructural change that comparative sociologist study, it is the conjuctural effects that become important (see Ragin, 1987). In this case study of Nigerian urbanization, the level of indigenous development and the nature of state-class relations appear to affect urban outcomes, *given Nigeria's role in the world economy*. But to study them in isolation from the pervasive effects of the country's status in the international system would make little sense.

6

Urban Diversity in East Asia: Toward a Political Economy Approach

East Asia: Divergent Urban Trajectories

Ideally, this chapter would begin by succinctly summarizing the general pattern of urbanization for East Asia.[1] But this is very difficult since East Asian urbanization has taken varied paths. Unlike West Africa, there is no one typical form of urban trajectory.

The aggregate statistics for the entire region suggest a pattern that is very close to the average for "less developed areas." Combined data for 1990 show that 33.2 percent of the total population resided in urban areas (United Nations, 1988: calculated from tables A-1 and A-3). The mean level for all "less developed regions" was 31.5 percent in 1985. East Asia remains one of the least urbanized world regions, recently falling slighty behind West Africa (see Chapter 4) and far less urbanized than Latin America or the advanced countries (United Nations, 1988: table A-3). Aggregate data on urban increase since 1950 reveal fairly high annual rates—between 3 and 5 percent—through 1975, dipping to just under 3 percent in the 1975–1985 period. While these rates are much higher than growth in the "more developed regions," they are fairly typical of Third World nations.

But these combined statistics are more the result of balance between the extremely different urban configurations of the area than indicative of a general type. Several rather distinctive subregional patterns are present that merit separate discussion.

Japan

Examination of the same data at a lower level of aggregation shows that the most striking variation occurs in Japan. Even in 1950, over half of the Japanese people were classified as city-dwellers. By 1970, the percent of urban residents had risen to over 71 percent, which is considerably higher than the average level of all "more developed regions." Not surprisingly, recent Japanese yearly urban growth rates have been much lower and steadily declining, following a pattern typical of other core countries. Ivan Light (1983) notes that much of the urban population growth in recent years has been concentrated in the nation's largest cities. Yet in spite of this tendency, "Japan does not experience urban primacy" (Light, 1983: 161), another sharp contrast with many of the urban systems in peripheral East Asia. Japan's urban pattern, like other aspects of its social and economic development, stands out as a deviant case in East Asia and, in fact, in the entire non-Western world.

Because of its uniqueness, Japan's urbanization has come under the same type of close scrutiny that has been directed at other facets of social change in this nation. A number of writers have attempted to describe and explain this anomolous trajectory of city growth (Yazaki, 1968; Kornhauser, 1982; Light, 1983: chapter 7; for a collection of articles, see Association of Japanese Geographers, 1970).

One clear theme that emerges from this work is the importance of early indigenous Japanese cities in accounting for contemporary patterns. By 1700, Japan possessed a fairly extensive network of urban centers (Yazaki, 1968: chapter 5; Kornhauser, 1982: 70–71; Light, 1983: 156–158). The scale of some of these cities was truly astounding for a preindustrial society. Kornhauser (1982: 71) reports that according to estimates based on Tokugawa records of rice allotments, "Edo is calculated to have a population of well over 1 million in the latter part of the eighteenth century, and this would have made it the largest city of the world of that day." Light (1983) argues that many other urban centers also grew during this period. He cites another historical study (Rozman, 1973) that claims 10 percent of Japan's population lived in cities of 10,000 or more, arguably the highest overall level of urbanization ever achieved by a preindustrial society (Light, 1983: 156). Obviously, Japan's "traditional" pattern of urbanization conditioned later growth.

But consistent with the argument presented thus far, Japanese urbanization has also been affected by the nation's economic development and industrialization. The issue of why Japan is the sole representative of the non-Western world to become an advanced, more developed core nation is an old and contentious one in comparative social science. No attempt can be made here to fully discuss this subject. But it is worth noting that the Japanese case has long been cited as a prime example of the importance of endogenous nation-specific cultural factors as the driving forces behind macrostructural change. In particular, modernization theory proponents have argued that Japan's development has been very different from China's because of major differences in indigenous cultures (see, for example, Levy, 1955, 1962, or Holt and Turner, 1966).

Frances Moulder (1977), however, directly has confronted these "traditional society theories" of Japan's industrial development. Arguing from a world economy perspective, she argues that Japanese society, while not being initially so different from China, managed to reach a high level of economic development because Japan avoided early European conquest and colonization. Japan "remained relatively autonomous within the world-system whereas China was incorporated as a dependent satellite" (Moulder, 1977: 199). Rather than being subjected to the colonial or neocolonial pressures felt by China, the rest of East Asia, and much of the present Third World, Japan actually developed into a "subimperial" power in its own right (see also Chirot, 1977, and Chapter 7 in this volume).

Light (1983: 155–156) correctly points out that Moulder's argument, in and of itself, is not an entirely satisfactory explanation of Japan's rapid twentieth-century urbanization. Too much emphasis on external world economic forces makes it easy to overlook the indigenous level of urban development in Japan. Once again, the concatenation of world-systemic and national and local forces must be considered.

China

An examination of the statistics for overall levels of urbanization show China lagging behind the rest of East Asia. In 1950, only 11 percent of the total population was classified as urban. By 1970, that proportion had almost doubled and was slightly higher than the comparable score for Southeast Asia, the other subregion that is relatively nonurban (see United Nations, 1980: table 8). China also fits the "underdeveloped" profile for urbanization when the urban growth rate from 1950 to 1960 is examined. Its huge 6.84 percent annual urban growth rate for that decade ranks close to the highest reported by the United Nations for any region over a similar time period during the second half of the twentieth century (see United Nations, 1980: Table 5).

But China's distinctiveness begins to show itself in the post-1960 urban growth rates. These rates reveal considerable declines from the previous decade, to slightly above 3 percent per annum. This pattern stands in sharp relief to the initially lower but rising urban growth rates in the rest of non-Japanese East Asia.

China's low urbanization level and rapid growth rate in the 1950s present an interesting contrast with those in Japan, and they further support a political economy of the world-system argument. The Chinese pattern seems to fit into the general configuration associated with what has been referred to as "dependent urbanization." One apparent deviation from this pattern is the absence of primacy. China, in fact, appears to have a "concave" city-size distribution. Its score on the standard primacy index for 1970 is -4.7. The negative signing indicates that secondary cities are *larger* than they would be relative to the largest city if the rank-size rule held.

As in the case of Japan, this urban system has roots that stretch deep into the nation's history. Like Japan, China was a preindustrial society with many cities, including some of incredible scale. In fact, the accounts given of the extent of Chinese urbanization suggest a pattern strikingly similar to that of Tokugawa Japan.

"Something like ten percent of late-traditional China's immense population lived in cities . . .. Cities large and small are nothing new to China; Sian, Kaifeng, Hangchow, Nanking and Peking have each in its time been the largest cities in the world, with populations as large as one million as long as a thousand years ago" (Murphey, 1980: 18).

Of course, the imperial structure of China was undeniably quite different from the political economy of Japan. Just in terms of the scale and sophistication of the two nations' early *urban* systems, however, there seems to be a great deal of similarity. This fact lends credence to Moulder's (1977) assertion that China's later openness to colonization led to its divergent development trajectory relative to Japan. The rough comparability of Japan's and China's eighteenth-century levels of urbanization, at minimum, mutes the power of Light's (1983) critique. It also suggests that later changes brought about by the contrasting world economic statuses of the two countries may be crucial in accounting for very dissimilar contemporary urban patterns.

Although the relatively high level of urban development in preindustrial China was not to foreshadow rapid urban growth in the twentieth century, it can be directly linked to the lack of national urban primacy in the contemporary era. William Skinner (1977) points out that late imperial China had several *regional* city systems rather than one national urban hierarchy. The massive Chinese empire, while politically unified, was only loosely integrated, economically or commercially. If we look at nineteenth-century regional patterns, which Skinner (1977: 236–243) argues are the *only* appropriate urban systems to analyze, we discover that cities like Canton or Beijing were regional primate cities. Other areas had roughly rank-normal regional distributions of city sizes. The concave city-size distribution for the entire nation (indicating many very large secondary cities) continues to be the result of combining several historically separate urban systems. This pattern of multiple regionally based urban hierarchies in China's past helps explain the current low primacy ratios.

But again, China's changing status in the world-system may have powerfully reinforced and perpetuated an older indigenous pattern. Since the consolidation of Mao Tse-tung's revolution in the 1950s, China's role in the world-economy has been transformed. Some analysts see China as becoming part of a "communist world system" (Chirot, 1977: chapter 8); others assert that it is a semiperipheral nation within one overarching capitalist world economy (Frank, 1977; Chase-Dunn, 1981b; for a summary of this controversy, see Steiber, 1979). Regardless of the resolution of this debate, most researchers would agree that one result of the Chinese revolution was a development strategy premised on some degree of withdrawl from the capitalist world economy and the establishment of greater Chinese autarky and economic self-determination.

The end (or at least loosening) of dependency relations with the West and the rise of a strong autocratic government committed to planned decentralized development significantly affected China's population growth and urban patterns. Fertility during the Mao era declines in China were the most widely publicized aspect of the government's demographic policies (see, for instance, Heilbroner, 1980: 61–62). Equally impressive were the successes of programs designed to slow the growth of large cities and directly confront problems of overurbanization or uneven urbanization (see Mingione, 1981, esp. pp. 172–179). Some authors point out that not all the effects of this strategy were desirable (Murphey, 1980: chapter 3). Others emphasize the rigid control needed for the successful implementation of this national urban policy (Kronholz, 1983). The crucial point for this discussion is that the dynamics of the urban process were very different in China from those in areas that are located in the periphery or the semiperiphery of the capitalist world-system.[2]

Of course, China has undergone massive change in the last decade. The Deng economic "reforms" of the 1980s are likely to lead to major changes in both the overall trajectory of Chinese socio-economic development and later urban patterns. They seem to signal a return to much closer integration with the capitalist world-economy, with China taking on a standard semiperipheral role and moving to emulate the dependent development of East Asian NICs such as South Korea and Taiwan. In the 1990s, China's international trade has skyrocketed, and the country has become a magnet for foreign investment. What impact does this have on the urbanization in China? Scholarly research and popular press reports suggest an erosion of city-ward migration controls. As Chinese cities become flooded with "floating" populations of "urban transients" (see Solinger 1995), a more typical pattern of peripheral uneven urbanization may be increasingly evident. Indeed, this would truly be yet another manifestation of the fading of the Maoist vision.

An East Asian Semiperiphery

The United Nations (1980) data show a third variation on the urban theme. These countries are much more urbanized than China or countries in Southeast Asia, but they remain far behind Japan in terms of the percent of the total population living in cities (see United Nations, 1980: table 8). Average annual urban growth rates since 1950, however, have been consistently high (hovering around 5 percent). By the early 1970s, these nations' populations were more than 50 percent urban. The United Nations classifies these countries as "Other East Asian." Although the tiny city-states of Hong Kong and Macao, as well as sparsely populated Mongolia, are included in this classification, 89 percent of the total population included in this category is in North or South Korea. Almost three-quarters of all Koreans live in the Republic of Korea (South Korea).

South Korea's population was 43 percent urban in 1970 and more than 50 percent urban by 1975 (Mills and Song, 1979: 8). Despite rapid city growth, however, South Korea experienced neither dramatically increased primacy nor widening intracity inequality.

Using the standard primacy index, South Korea showed a slightly convex city-size distribution of 5.15. The Davis Index score for that year was 1.51. Edwin Mills and Byung-Nak Song (1979: 48, 52) comment on this measure:

> The 1975 [primacy rate] for Korea is slightly above the 1960 worldwide average of 1.42, but well below its value for such countries as Argentina, France, Hungary, and Mexico. Japan's primacy index was 1.62 in 1960. Thus, despite the concentration of people in Seoul, Korea is not a highly primate country by worldwide standards . . .. The conclusion is that Korea is only slightly more primate than the average country and shows no tendency to become still more primate. The size distribution of cities has shown remarkable stability during the last quarter of a century. Almost all Korean cities have grown rapidly, but there is no tendency for Seoul, or any other city, to become increasingly dominant.

The internal growth of South Korea's cities has also been relatively free of the degree of inequality and poverty that has characterized dependent urbanization in other parts of the Third World. The high rates of un- and underemployment present in so many peripheral cities are not as obvious here since "rapid economic growth has enabled cities to absorb migrants into the urban labor force" (Mills and Song, 1979: 29). Estimates from the early 1970s indicated that illegal housing was on the decline; about 8 percent of the urban population nationwide and up to 16 percent of Seoul's residents lived in such settlements in 1973. More recent data on urban poverty and illegal housing are a bit less unequivocal, showing at least small increases in each category in the 1980s (see Chapter 7). But *comparatively*, South Korea clearly does deviate from the extreme pattern of intra-urban inequality that I reviewed in earlier chapters.

South Korea is not alone in this pattern of urban development. Taiwan has followed a similar path. Taiwan's urban hierarchy resembles South Korea's; its 1975 standard primacy index was 5.84 (Davis Index = 1.43). Urban growth has been fast paced, and as a result, by 1975, 51 percent of Taiwan's people lived in cities with populations over 20,000 (Republic of China, 1982). As in South Korea, this pattern of growth apparently bucks the trend for rapidly urbanizing and industrializing Third World countries in that it apparently has not been accompanied by increasing income inequality (Barrett and Whyte, 1982: 1065–1066). Two other "countries" in East Asia, Hong Kong and Singapore, also molded economic prosperity with rapid urban growth. Particularly, these city-states succeeded in controlling spontaneous housing (Gilbert and Gugler, 1982: 102) and in improving general standards of living (Spates and Macionis, 1983: 304–307).

At first, this collection of nations seems to present an anomaly, a glaring exception to the pattern of dependent urbanization. Despite dependency, these countries managed to avoid the excesses of uneven urban development. Concurrently, they have enjoyed a sustained, relatively equitable pattern of economic growth.[3] How can a political economy of the world-system approach explain this?

Some claim that it cannot. Richard Barrett and Martin Whyte (1982) argue that the experiences of these East Asian countries point to basic "flaws" in dependency/world-system theory. Unfortunately, these critics engage in the time-honored intellectual exercise of setting up and knocking over a straw man in their argument. Their basic strategy is to take a dependency hypothesis from one of the early studies in this tradition (A. G. Frank's polemical 1969 article is their favorite), remove it from its original context, simplify it, and, finally, "test" it using the Taiwanese case. Given the rather transparent intentions of the authors to "disprove" dependency/world-system theory, it is hardly surprising that none of their eleven "hypotheses" fit for Taiwan. Having dismissed dependency theory, Barrett and Whyte suggest that a "mix of factors" (including the island's "sinic culture") contributed to its economic growth. A more recent version of this same argument (Barrett and Chin, 1987) rehashes the same points—but is even more inexcusable, due to the stubborn refusal of the authors to consider the elaborations of the international political economy approach during the 1980s.

Despite the dubious methodology and eclectic conclusions of these authors, their articles serve to reaffirm a basic point. Simplistic versions of the world-system approach—versions that look merely at core-periphery exploitation as a zero-sum game, that can only see the "malevolent mechanisms," or that propogate a "stagnationist" version of dependency—simply will not do. Fortunately, the world-system paradigm has moved considerably beyond such conceptions. Barrett and Whyte's (1982: 1070) contention that "most dependency writers assume that the various forms of dependency have similar effects" is ridiculous in light of the debate following the English translation of Cardoso and Faletto's classic book (1979). Similarly, Barrett and Whyte's argument that world-system theorists consign dependent nations to eternal economic stagnation is incredible in light of the current overriding concern with the semiperiphery and the prospects for mobility in the international system through dependent development (see Evans 1979a, 1979b). Significantly, several of the "factors" that Barrett and Whyte (1982) see as critical in Taiwan's successful development—such as a strong state bureaucracy able to pursue a policy of "negotiated dependency"—are also essential components of world-system definitions of semiperipherality and dependent development. In fact, the strong interventionist state that they claim as evidence *against* world-system expectations is *precisely* the political form we would anticipate in an upwardly mobile semiperiphery.[4]

The real issue, then, is to determine why these countries became semiperipheral (in contrast to the more pervasive pattern of peripheralization in East Asia and elsewhere in the Third World) and to explore the mechanisms by which this dependent development affected urban patterns.

This subject is important enough to set aside in its own chapter; consequently, Chapter 7 addresses the political economy of urbanization in South Korea. The next section and the remainder of this chapter will focus on a region that has followed a very different path: Southeast Asia.

Southeast Asia

The data for this region fit the pattern of dependent urbanization very well. Southease Asia's overall level of urbanization is very low. Just over one-fifth of the population lived in cities in 1970—only Eastern Africa and the Indian subcontinent are less urban (United Nations, 1988: table A-3). However, Southeast Asian cities are experiencing rapid growth rates; these rates have remained close to 4 percent per annum since 1950, placing the region slightly above the average growth level for all "less developed regions." This rapid growth is centered on the largest cities. McGee (1976: 23) points out:

> Not only is Southeast Asia one of the least urbanized of the Third World regions, but it also has one of the highest proportions of urban populations concentrated in these large cities. Thus, of the urban population resident in centres of over 20,000, the percentage who are concentrated in large cities exceeding 100,000 is 70 per cent in Thailand, 73 per cent in the Philippines and over 60 per cent in Malaya and Singapore.

With this rapid growth of the "great cities" comes the uneven urban hierarchy present in so many underdeveloped countries. "In Burma, Thailand, Cambodia, South Vietnam, and the Philippines the largest urban concentration is at least five times as large as its nearest rival . . . the dominance of the 'primate city' is unquestionably the most important feature of urban structure" (McGee, 1967: 23–24). Between 1950 and 1970, all of these nations plus Malaysia and Indonesia exhibited a tendency to become more primate as measured by the standard primacy index.

Uneven growth is also manifest *within* the cities. McGee (1967: 27) claims that Southeast Asian urban centers share the same problems of rapid city growth "experienced by other cities of the Third World; the economic problems of unemployment, unbalanced occupational structures, poverty and inequality of incomes."

As in West Africa, housing is one of clearest indicators of material inequality in Southeast Asian cities. The "built environment" puts the affluence of the elites and the poverty of the masses in sharp relief. While lamenting the lack ofcomprehensive data, McGee (1967: 157) reports that

> in 1961 there [were] an estimated 750,000 squatters in Djakarta (25 per cent), 100,000 in Kuala Lumpur (25 per cent); in 1963 some 320,000 in Manila city (23 per cent) and in Singapore from 200,00 to 250,000 (approximately 26 per cent). When it is realized that these estimates only record the squatter populations within city boundaries and that there's a sizeable squatter population living outside the city, it can be seen that the total population of squatters in Southeast Asian cities is very large indeed.

It seems very likely that income and employment opportunity are also very unequally distributed. Data on income distribution are difficult to come by. McGee (1967: 95) cites a Philippine government study that indicates that within the metropolitan Manila area, 37.5 percent of the total family income is shared by only 8.7 percent of the households. He clearly does not believe that the Philippines are unique in this pattern. To the contrary, he argues that the existence of an extremely wealthy but numerically small group of upper-class urban elites is the rule in Southeast Asian cities.

Once again, this discussion of uneven urbanization leads us back to the issue of overurbanization. In Chapter 4, a case was presented that argued against some of the simplistic versions of the overurbanization thesis. Third World cities are not parasitic and economically dysfunctional purely because of demographic and political urban bias (see Gugler, 1982, for a counterargument). Still, the concept of overurbanization retains some utility if it merely refers to an empirical pattern of urban development that appears to impede the universal goal of national development.

Obviously, overurbanization is not applicable to Southeast Asia if it refers merely to high urban-to-rural population ratios. Data have been presented that show a low percentage of the population in cities. But demographers stress that these urban-rural proportions have been depressed by very rapid population growth in the countryside, not by slow city growth (Goldstein, 1978; Hackenberg, 1980). If more meaningful criteria for overurbanization, focusing on the economic dysfunctions of large, rapidly growing cities, were used, Southeast Asia would likely qualify. McGee's (1967) description of "excessive" numbers of street hawkers and teeming masses of unemployed and underemployed people living in "shared poverty" clearly fits within Gugler's (1982) definition of overurbanization. Michael Timberlake's operationalization of the same concept is very close to what McGee (1967: 17–21) means by "pseudo-urbanization"—city growth without industrial development. The urbanization that has taken place in Southeast Asia appears to have failed to produce cities that generate national development.

This empirical pattern of city growth in Southeast Asia should seem familiar. In West Africa, the same traits characterized urban development: urban primacy, intracity inequality, and urbanization without economic development (see Chapter 4). These two regions are separated by thousands of miles, peopled by dissimilar racial groups and steeped in distinct cultural traditions, yet they exhibit strikingly similar patterns of urbanization and development. Throughout the balance of this chapter, as explanations for the Southeast Asian urban configuration are discussed, I will also explore this regional analogy. The similarities between these two areas will help in the formulation of a theory of dependent urbanization that is fully cognizant of the linkages between the international economy and intrasocietal forces affecting the urban process.

Southeast Asian Cities: The Search for a Theory

Not surprisingly, analogous social and demographic trends sometimes are associated with parallel forms of social science research and intellectual debate. A surge of interest in comparative studies in the 1960s resulted in projects exploring Southeast Asian demography, development, and urban patterns. Like their counterparts studying social change in other parts of the Third World, researchers investigating Southeast Asia employed the basic assumptions of the then-dominant modernization theory perspective in their work. Their model of development was implicitly or explicitly based on North American and European historical experiences. Students of urbanization emphasized the long-term generative effects the process would have on economic, social, and political development.

Unfortunately, the empirical reality in Southeast Asian countries has provided little evidence to support these views. Instead, researchers like McGee (1967) report high levels of primacy, burgeoning squatter settlements, growing unemployment, and heightened inequality.

Perhaps the most sophisticated attempt to reconcile the pattern of urban growth with the developmentalist model is an early essay by Keyfitz (1965). Focusing on urban-rural inequality, Keyfitz argues that the current imbalanced and apparently parasitic situation of the primate cities is a necessary step in the long-term process of capital accumulation. This progression, he argues, had previously taken place in Western industrial societies and is an essential (if unpleasant and perhaps unfair) element in the modernization of societies. While Keyfitz's article epitomizes the developmentalism of the era, it is not at all dogmatic, and it calls for further research to empirically determine, for instance, if rapid cityward migration is becoming dysfunctional to national development.

Subsequent defenses of the orthodox perspective on urbanization and modernization, however, are more superficial and strident. The major theme of these articles is that despite a number of urban problems, Southeast Asian cities will ultimately be the driving force behind economic growth and societal advancement

(Bose, 1971; Berry, 1971; Fryer, 1972; Ginsburg, 1972). Ashish Bose (1971) and Donald Fryer (1972) provide tabular data on rising primacy and rapid urban migration and discuss the resultant problems of unemployment, chronic housing shortages, and growing poverty. But Fryer (1972: 42), nevertheless, concludes that "the city is the fundamental agent in the modernization process" and blames poor city administration for the problems. Similarly, Bose (1971) dismisses overurbanization arguments as "flimsy generalizations" (despite "unexpected trends" that appeared in the data). He provides a textbook statement of a modernization theory approach in his introductory remarks: "urbanization is an essential element in the process of economic growth and social change in South and Southeast Asia in the transformation of rural, agricultural economics into industrial urban economics, and in the transition from tradition to modernity" (Bose, 1971: 81).

Berry's (1971) article, despite an antiseptic title and pages of diagrams and equations, is one last passionate defense of the old belief in the ultimately beneficial nature of Southeast Asia's primate city growth. Berry (1971: 166) claims that despite the apparently divergent trajectories of development in Southeast Asia and the West, the major difference between these areas is the slow pace of the "urban revolution" in Asia as compared with that in the West. Claiming that critics of modernization theory have used "value-laden" terminology (he cites *primate cities* and *dual economies* as examples), Berry (1972: 137) proceeds to present an obviously one-sided caricature of the theory's detractors as radical, antigrowth "traditionalists" (his hardly "value-free" term!).

It is questionable whether this sort of "analysis" really contributes much to our understanding of social change. Polemics are useful when they refine theory; theory is strongest when it helps to explain facts. Regardless of the cleverness or sheer vehemence of the arguments advanced by its remaining adherents, the modernization theory approach could not explain many aspects of urbanization in mid-twentieth century Southeast Asia. Researchers using this perspective collected a great deal of data and helped to define many issues that demanded investigation. Moreover, some of their perceptive observations foreshadowed later theoretical refinements. For example, both Fryer and Berry argue that urban primacy is closely linked to "incorporation into the world economy" (Fryer, 1972: 36) and "external trade dependency" (Berry, 1971: 139). But there clearly was a need for a theoretical reformulation that would incorporate some of the unexpected results of research and try to make them comprehensible. T. G. McGee, the leading expert on Southeast Asian cities, was a leader in the long search for a theory of urbanization in Southeast Asia and the Third World.

The Paradox of the "Proto-Proletariat"

Interestingly, McGee's first call for a reconceptualization of theoretical ideas about Southeast Asian urbanization appears in the same edited volume as Berry's polemic. Addressing the same general issue of generative versus parasitic cities, McGee (1971: 177) dispassionately notes, "Clearly at this stage of Asian development one cannot argue that all Asian cities are contributing to national development." He cites Mabogunje's (1968) argument that a city form will follow its unique economic function and dismisses models that would lead us to expect that Southeast Asian cities "will play identical roles and functions to those of the West" (McGee, 1971: 178).

As a geographer, McGee (1967: chapters 1 and 5) clearly sees spatial imbalances and urban primacy as ways in which Southeast Asian urban patterns are fundamentally different from city growth in the West. But his primary focus is on these cities' internal structures. In particular, McGee is interested in the dual economies of Southeast Asian cities.

McGee's (1971: 166–171) "socioeconomic model of the Asian primate city" begins with Clifford Geertz's distinction between "firm-centered" and "bazaar" economies in urban Indonesia (see Geertz, 1963). McGee claims that Asian cities continue to be dominated by the labor-intensive, family-run businesses of the traditional markets; the firm-type, capital-intensive, large-scale economy affects a much smaller proportion of the labor force. Unlike Western cities historically, this modern industrial sector is unable to absorb much of the labor of new urban migrants. As a result, the pervasive bazaar economy, despite being "basically a symptom of economic underdevelopment," has continued to soak up excess labor. He states: "In economic terms the existence of large bazaar sectors in these cities, it can be argued, is inhibitive to economic growth, for they are characterized by under-employment and low productivity, but in social and political terms they perform important functions as absorbers of labor which would otherwise be unemployed and a much greater burden—one would be tempted to say *threat*—to the State" (McGee, 1971: 173).

McGee's response to the overurbanization thesis is subtle. On the one hand, he is highlighting the functional aspects of the bazaar economy. But on the other, he is also painfully aware of its human costs in terms of poverty, squatter settlements, and widening inequality (see McGee, 1967: chapters 7 and 9). Nor does he see any real positive input into national economic development coming from this backward and inefficient sector.

McGee also makes strides toward locating the Southeast Asian city in its international context. He points out, "Cities are part of a total social and economic system which is not only national but international" (McGee, 1971: 160). He believes that the underlying cause of the dualistic structure of Southeast Asian cities can be traced back to colonial exploitation and relative economic underdevelopment in relation to the West. McGee is also aware of the reciprocal interactions between the capitalist and bazaar sectors. But even McGee does not abandon the assumptions of modernization theory yet. In this early article, he professes his faith in the ultimate demise of the "traditional" sector. McGee had not yet discovered the way the bazaar economy, through linkages to the firm economy, subsidizes international capitalism in an *economic* way.

In later writing, McGee further develops some of his notions about the structure and effects of dual economies in Southeast Asian cities (McGee, 1973, 1976; see also Yeung, 1975). In his 1973 article, he argues that a proper understanding of the economic structure—not the retention of some ill-defined "rural culture"—explains the paradox of "peasants" in Third World cities. This analysis of the urban economic structure, while basically agreeing with his earlier papers, uses the imagery of two distinct but interpenetrating circuits drawn from work by Milton Santos (see Santos, 1979). McGee is careful in this presentation to clearly delineate the contrasts between the two circuits, stressing the labor-intensive, family-oriented nature of the "urban peasants" in the lower circuit (see McGee, 1973: table 1, p. 138). He also suggests (correctly) that an expression such as the "protoproletariat" would perhaps be more appropriate.

McGee continues to refine and sharpen his theoretical model in an article published in 1976. While his general theme is the same, there are important variations that suggest he is moving even closer to what would later be called the political economy of the world-system approach. One shift is a much heavier emphasis on the likelihood of long-term persistence (or perhaps even growth) of the proto-proletariat. His previous view that the growth of this class of producers is a transitional step in the development process is altered in light of empirical evidence of the classes's persistence. His assessment of the economic productivity of the informal sector (another terminological switch) is different, too. Here, he claims that "in many Third World cities informal sector activities are operating efficiently" (McGee, 1976: 23). Furthermore, McGee pays much closer attention here to the interpenetration and reciprocal relationships between formal and informal sectors. He reiterates his contention that the existence of this dualistic economic structure is directly tied to "the dependency of peripheral economies upon the metropolis within the international system" (McGee, 1976: 9). But despite drawing together nearly all of the important elements, McGee fails to fully solve the "paradox of peasants in the cities." The missing linkage is between the urban informal sector and the role that it plays in the *world-economy*, beyond the local and national economies. A comprehensive explanation of the persistence of the proto-proletariat stresses the key role the informal sector plays as a mechanism of surplus extraction in the entire global system (Portes, 1983).

Parasitism, Primacy, and Politics

Bruce London is also interested in the parasitic versus generative city debate. But unlike McGee, London's primary unit of analysis is the national system of cities. He focuses on urban primacy and its effects in Thailand.

As London points out, Bangkok is *the* primate city par excellence. In demographic terms, it dwarfs all other urban places in Thailand. In 1970, the capital was thirty-three times more populous than the country's next largest city (London, 1980: 28). And Bangkok's demographic primacy is matched by its functional primacy for political power and economic resources are disproportionately concentrated in the city. Drawing on Walton's (1975) discussion of "internal colonialism," London links the "parasitic" primate city to the "exploitation" and "neglect" of the hinterlands. To properly understand this relationship, though, we must take care not to rectify the concept of primacy. Echoing an argument presented by James Lincoln (1977), London (1979: 486) warns that since cities are not actors, "it is not possible for a city to 'exploit' or 'neglect.' The real focus of studies of urban primacy and the resulting inequalities should not be on "the impersonal, competitive market and institutional mechanisms" (a la Keyfitz)(London, 1979: 485). Instead, such studies must analyze intergroup political relationships and the process of elite decisionmaking.

London's empirical analysis (1979 and 1980) focuses on a political history of Thailand over the last 125 years or so. Since his theoretical approach attempts to synthesize the political economy and human ecology approaches, a section of the analysis is centered on policymaking affecting transportation. He argues that national elites centered in Bangkok governed Thailand in a manner that led to neglect and even outright exploitation of the outlying provinces. To understand the reason for this parasitic relationship, we need to look to the narrow self-interests of the small group of urban elites who ruled the country. London's emphasis on the political elites' decisions as the cause of policies allows him to suggest that intrametropolitan inequalities need to be studied in the same way: "Clearly, the primate metropolis dominates the hinterland and hence the nation. Just as clearly, however, a small elite dominates the metropolis" (London, 1979: 505). Though his research does not probe inequalities within the primate city, London's analytical framework *does* make the connection between these two aspects of uneven urbanization.

London's call for a more political emphasis in analyzing urban development is a step in the right direction. His critique of conventional "institutional analysis" is convincing. The view that ecological and political economic perspectives are potentially complementary opens up fertile new theoretical ground (which I have explored throughout this book). But the model London develops is lacking in several ways and fails to fulfill its potential as a theory of uneven urban development.[5]

The first conceptual problem in London's analysis is his insistence on augmenting the materialist emphases of both human ecology and political economy with a "cultural component." He argues that without an explicit attempt to factor in "normative" and "social-psychological" variables "human ecology is *not* a synthetic, macroscopic theoretical perspective on the total process of social organization" (London, 1980: 12). Human ecologists have omitted the normative aspect from their theoretical models because that aspect tends to reduce to rather nebulous, unoperationalizable concepts about individual values or cultural predispositions. Inclusion of these "cultural" variables adds little to the empirical analysis (Berry and Kasarda, 1977: chapter 1). Instead of providing a clear theoretical focus, the culturalist arguments cause London's historical analysis to meander through seemingly irrelevant material that is supposed to demonstrate the evolution of modernizing "political values" or illustrate the distinct "cultural identities" of differing regional groups. It would seem that many of the same changes might be explained more parsimoniously by referring to the material interests of various actors and groups. To London's credit, the emphasis on the normative component, while prominent in his dissertation/monograph (1980), does not reappear in his other work.

Two other criticisms can be leveled against London's formulation of a political economy approach. The first has to do with his heavy emphasis on "power elite theory" (London, 1980: 43–49). Regrettably, London's interpretation of this theory is not very clear on the relationship between economic and political power. The result is a confusing array of "political," "symbolic," and "economic" elites with competing interests and influence (London, 1980: 54). The group that most of the analysis focuses on is the "political elite" whose policies lead to regional inequality. Members of this group act in a self-interested way to survive politically, but London's conceptualization obfuscates the ways in which elite policy may be linked to individual or class economic needs.

A related problem with the model is the way in which it links Thailand to the international system. There is no appreciation of distinct international class alliances affecting elite decisionmaking. Instead, the effect of the world-system is conceptualized vaguely as international pressure threatening Thai sovereignty. The Bangkok elites' actions are interpreted as an adaptive response to impinging imperialism. Nation-building is an act of elite self-preservation prompting heightened parasitism vis-à-vis the hinterland (see esp. London, 1979: 508–511). Yet it is at least possible that some elite decisionmaking is not motivated solely by a desire to maintain internal social control. Some policies might conceivably be more directly linked to the *economic* role that the Thai economy and the elite class played in the international system (see Elliot, 1978; Bell, 1978, discussed later). So while breaking in some key ways with old developmentalist assumptions, London's analysis still fails to provide an adequate treatment of economic dependency and how it conditioned elite policymaking.

Summary

In many ways, London's political economy approach is strikingly similar to the perspectives of Gugler and Flanagan, Riddell, and Cohen on West African urbanization (see Chapter 4). All of these authors recognize the key role of politics in the process I have referred to as uneven urbanization. But they continue to focus too narrowly on the political economy of the nation-state without locating this system in its international context.

McGee is closer to developing a more comprehensive political economy approach. He is cognizant of the importance of the dependent city's location in the world economy. Thus, his model foreshadows world-system approaches to dependent urbanism. Additionally, his discussions of the proto-proletariat are clearly moving closer to the conception of the informal sector found in the contemporary international political economy approach. One could argue that, over time, his own theoretical formulations have converged with that perspective. If McGee's analysis has a fault, it is that he underplays the importance of elite power and decisionmaking. This tends to minimize the importance of class conflict and the relationship between state policies and the patterns of urban growth.

A comprehensive world-system analysis of Southeast Asian urbanization needs to mold the insights of McGee and London together, connecting primacy and the proto-proletariat, urban economic function and urban elite policymaking, interregional imbalance and intraurban inequality. It also must fully explore the linkages between local and national processes and dynamics in the international system.

Dependent Urbanization in Southeast Asia

In this section, I will attempt to apply the political economy of the world-system approach to Southeast Asian urbanization. Paralleling Chapter 4, the following material is divided into four broad topics: (1) the historical context, (2) politics and the state, (3) intracity economies and the informal sector, and (4) the overurbanization issue. My purpose is to sketch broad patterns and suggest further research.

The Historical Context of Urban Growth

One obvious fact, which can be ascertained from statistical data (see the earlier discussion), is that Southeast Asia has undergone a major urban revolution in the second half of the twentieth century. Like West African societies, Southeast Asian societies were predominantly agrarian for many centuries. Rapid urbanization is a relatively recent phenomenon. But as in other parts of the Third World, urban forms have existed for millennia. Cities played leading roles in ancient societies in the area as far back as the first century A.D. Indigenous patterns of urbanization were in some cases subsumed and in other cases superceded with the incorporation of Southeast Asia into Western-dominated world trade. The history of early city growth and the effects of the expanding capitalist world economy need to be explored to understand contemporary urban patterns in Southeast Asia. Throughout this section, McGee's 1967 survey will be the main guide.

Societies in Southeast Asia were a varied lot in the years prior to European exploration (Catley, 1976). Some reached relatively advanced levels of civilization—witness, for instance, the magnificent architecture of Angor Wat, capital of the ninth-century Khmer Empire (McGee, 1967: 32). Other parts of the region remained very primitive; when the Spaniards arrived in the Philippines in the early sixteenth century, they found a society barely advanced beyond the hunting-and-gathering stage (Reed, 1972).

Early urban development followed a similarly diverse pattern. In mainland Southeast Asia, many agrarian-based city-states had risen and fallen by the first millennium A.D. The earliest and most persistent of these cities were seaports, and they adopted "market" functions at an early date. The importance of trade in the eastern Indian Ocean and South China Sea region led to a string of such cities down the Malay Peninsula and on the islands of Sumatra and Java by about 1,000 A.D. (McGee, 1967: 29–36). More distant parts of insular Southeast Asia, including the Philippines (Reed, 1972) and New Guinea (Amarshi, Good, and Mortimer, 1979), never developed settlements larger than villages before European colonization.

The large indigenous cities that did develop combined the surplus extraction function common to most preindustrial cities (Sjoberg, 1965) with the trading function. McGee emphasizes that this indigenous regional commerce should not be underestimated. For instance, he describes the Malayan city of Malacca, established in the 1300s, as "a city that was made for merchandise." This port's entire economic base depended on maritime trade (McGee, 1967: 39–41).

The European colonial powers first arrived on the scene to control this lucrative oriental trade. Typical of the early phase of European domination were the Portuguese seizures of Malacca (McGee, 1967: 42). At this point, the general strategy was to create bases at already established ports. Until the nineteenth century, Europeans were content to skim off profits from already lucrative commerce rather than attempt to economically transform either these cities or their hinterlands (McGee, 1967: 47); Wallerstein (1974a: 335–336) describes this as an "enclave" form of imperialism in East Asia. This policy contrasted with the much more thoroughgoing colonization efforts that created such radical changes in the Americas. Wallerstein explains the differing approach in terms of the much higher cost-to-benefit ratio for colonizing Asia. Especially critical was the tremendous friction of distance between Europe and Southeast Asia, given the primitive level of shipping technology.

Because of the form of initial contact with the West, "the effect of imperial penetration on the social structure of Southeast Asia was limited" (Catley, 1976: 57). Areas of indigenous urban settlement did not undergo radical changes. In most cases, the Europeans used the preindustrial cities to their own advantage but changed them little. Dualistic patterns emerged as Europeans set up garrison towns incorporating elements transplanted from the West. But outside the walls of their forts, the colonists had little effect on the organization of either the large cities or the smaller settlements. Perhaps the main effect of the early phases of imperialism was to reinforce the importance of cities where the Westerners had major trading bases.

The Philippines are an exception to this pattern (McGee, 1967: 43). The lack of any prior large-scale urbanization required the Spaniards to create their own cities there. Manila was established at the site of a small fishing village to serve as Spain's main military and maritime base in the region (Reed, 1972, 1977). The city became Spain's gateway to the Orient, the end point of the trans-Pacific trade route that remained under Hispanic control for nearly 300 profitable years (Schurz, 1939). But like other European outposts, Manila was considered important for its commercial functions, and little effort was made to exploit the resources of surrounding areas (Reed, 1972; Wernstedt and Spencer, 1967). Beyond central Luzon, life in the Philippine archipelago was not greatly altered. As in areas of indigenous urbanization, the main effect on later patterns was to initiate a process favorable to increased urban primacy.

The situation was to change during the eighteenth century. The Industrial Revolution's effects were felt far beyond England, transforming the global economy. McGee (1967: 52) explains: "The need for markets and raw materials for the rapidly industrializing nations of western Europe and the inability of the West Indies to supply enough tropical produce were prime factors in encouraging a shift in colonial emphasis to the tropical lands of Southeast Asia." A gradual process of territorial division among the major colonial powers left all of Southeast Asia under European or U.S. rule by the end of the first decade of the twentieth century. Only Thailand retained political independence, and even that country's development efforts fell under the control of Western advisers (McGee, 1967: 52). Thai history during this period has been likened to "colonization by treaty" (Elliott, 1978: 23–27). Despite being less dramatic than the swift partition of Africa, the colonization of Southeast Asia led to equivalent results. Imperial domination and the deep penetration of the world market's effects into the countryside brought to a basic transformation of entire societies (Catley, 1976: 59–60).

City growth was radically altered, too. The more intensive form of colonialism required the growth of the large, multifunctional port town to serve as "an economic intermediary—a middleman—between the metropolitan power and the colony" (McGee, 1967: 58). "The most prominent function of these cities was economic; the colonial city was the 'nerve center' of colonial exploitation. Concentrated here were the institutions through which capitalism extended its control over the colonial economy—the banks, the agency houses, trading companies, the shipping companies and the insurance companies (McGee, 1967: 56).

The result was the two linked dimensions of uneven city growth characteristic of dependent urbanism. Perhaps most visible (and certainly easiest to quantify) was the rise of the primate cities. "In the nineteenth century urban growth was dominated by colonial ports. Singapore, Manila, Rangoon, Batavia and even Bangkok tripled their populations with the enlargement of their commercial and political functions" (McGee, 1967: 54). In the early twentieth century, the demographic growth rates of these cities *accelerated* (see McGee, 1967: tables 6 and 8). Intra-urban inequality also was exacerbated. Data for the early twentieth century show that the tertiary sector was already disproportionately large and that unemployment and underemployment were on the rise (McGee, 1967: 58). McGee's general theme is that the basic patterns of the early twentieth century emerged during this period of formal colonialism. But unlike some students of West African urbanization, McGee realizes that "formal colonialism" is not the crucial variable: Economic subordination and dependency are even more critical. The historical experience of Thailand illustrates the point that even continuous local "sovereignty" had little effect on the country's pattern of development (Bell, 1978; Elliott, 1978). More critical was "the economic integration of the country into the world capitalist economy" (Elliot, 1978: 27). Bell (1978: 56) explains the nation's role in this international system:

> From 1870 to roughly the 1930s, Thailand served the needs of British capital accumulation by supplying cheap rice to her colonies. Through an alliance with the Thai ruling classes and Chinese merchant classes, the British sought to strengthen the agrarian basis of the society and, in the 20th century, exercised a form of neo-colonial influence by controlling the pattern of economic and social development, including the disposition of State revenue, foreign reserves and financial policy. . . . The informal nature of British colonialism served as a brake on anti-colonial sentiments. . . . It also fostered the myth of an independent country as a "land of the free" (literal meaning of *Thailand*, which was adopted . . . in 1939, replacing the name Siam).

Despite its formal national sovereignty, Thailand was just as affected by its dependent position in the world economy as its Southeast Asian neighbors were. This became even clearer in the twentieth century. The presence of indigenous kings or premiers has little effect on fluctuating international prices for rice or rubber.

While noting Thailand's political independence as an anomaly, McGee argues that this country follows essentially the same pattern of urban growth as the rest of Southeast Asia (and, of course, Bangkok's primacy ratio exceeds that of all other national capitals). London's (1979, 1980) emphasis on Thai sovereignty is misplaced. As in other Southeast Asia countries, the economy and social structure in Thailand has been transformed to meet the needs of core interests. Neocolonialism, which London (1980: 60–61) discusses in regard to rural underdevelopment, also shapes urban processes. Far from disproving the world-system perspective argument, the Thai case highlights the importance of an internationally stratified economic system.

The end of formal colonialism reinforces this point. Despite new national governments, urban imbalances have increased (McGee, 1967 on urban primacy, pp. 80–81; on growing intra-urban inequality, chapters 7, 8, and 9). McGee's explanation of this pattern emphasizes the basically unchanged distribution of wealth and power. While it is true that the Europeans and Americans who ran both the colonial administration and major commercial enterprises have either departed or now exert reduced political clout, the overall stratification system is little changed (McGee, 1967: 95–105). And even if the individual incumbents are Asian, the structure of economic and political power remains the same. The new indigenous elites have not done much better than their foreign predecessors in redressing either rural-urban inequality of urban under- and unemployment (McGee, 1967: 95–96 and chapter 10).

A partial explanation for this stagnation may lie in an analysis of the material interests of Southeast Asian elites. Elliott (1978: 45) claims, "The present ruling class is inextricably tied to the transnational structure of imperialism." Problems such as inequality and imbalance in urban system development are not just the products of a past era of intrusive colonialism. External dependency vis-à-vis the world economy continues to be reflected and reinforced by elites whose class interests coincide more closely with fractions of international capital than with balanced national development. Paraphrasing Bell (1978: 70), the influence of international dependencies has become interwoven into the whole fabric of Southeast Asian societies, primarily through the development of a class structure typical of subordinate capitalism. The patterns of urban development are a manifestation of this in a very visible, "spatiodemographic" manner. Like West Africa's primate cities, the huge metropolises of Southeast Asia are examples of dependent urbanism.

But, as mentioned in Chapter 4, it is important to note that continued dependency does not imply a static situation. Given the speed of urban demographic growth alone, it is clear that a static explanation will *not* do. We can link recent urban patterns to dependency by reiterating the degree to which the nature and mechanisms of dependency themself change. The colonial relationship emphasizing monoculture and the export of raw materials gave way to a newer form of the global division of labor. Large-scale, technologically sophisticated multinational corporations have become increasingly important (see, for example, Chirot, 1977: chapters 6 and 7). As it became profitable for these enterprises to transfer production away from the core (see Dixon, Jonas, and McCaughan, 1983), both import substitution industrialization proliferated in the periphery.

Consistent with the argument presented in Chapter 4 on ISI and its effects, Southeast Asia's primate cities served as advantageous locations for such industrialization—and grew more primate as a result (for evidence on the Philippines, see Nemeth and Smith, 1986). This development strategy was also compatible with heightened inequality within the large cities since import substitution is most successful if a society's resources are concentrated in the hands of a group of wealthy consumers (Roberts, 1978a: chapter 3; Catley, 1976: 65–57; Bell, 1978: 65).

The move to ISI, and still later export-oriented manufacturing were partially the result of political processes within Southeast Asian societies. And both these general economic policies, as well as decisionmaking more narrowly designed to influence urban development, were heavily influenced by elite groups concentrated in the primate capital cities.

Politics and the State

In Southeast Asia, just as in the West African cases, politics and the control the elites or powerful classes exercise over government institutions can directly or inadvertently influence urban development. It is necessary to indicate how this occurs in Southeast Asia and discuss the manner in which national class structures and political dynamics are related to the international system.

London's (1979, 1980) analysis of Thai urban development provides a useful starting point. His argument centers on the power of the urban elite and the internal colonialism that has emanated from Bangkok as a result. Explicating the mechanisms by which urban primacy was reinforced, London shows how specific policies designed to further elite interests concentrated resources in the area of the capital. For instance, transportation system development apparently was designed to enhance and consolidate the political and economic dominance of Bangkok and its elite class (London, 1980: 88). A similar strategy of center-oriented transportation development under the direction of Manila elites has been noted for the Philippines (Nemeth and Smith, 1985b). Assuming that similar dynamics affected urban trajectories in other Southeast Asian countries, a discussion of the nature of the state and the interests of the elites who control it is in order.

Paralleling the experiences of other parts of the Third World, the dominant form of government in recent East Asian history is authoritarianism of one type or another (Myrdal, 1971: chapter 10; Sobhan, 1979; Frank, 1981b). Peter Bell

(1978) and Rehman Sobhan (1979) note that the lack of political democracy is compatible with an emphasis on state-directed economic planning. Rehman Sobhan provides evidence of the increasing involvement of the public sector in a number of East Asian economies (presenting statistical data, particularly for Thailand, the Philippines, and South Korea). Justification and legitimation of government intervention and planning is provided by highlighting the goal of national development. But what kind of development? And for whom?

An article on Philippine development by Robyn Lim (1978: 205) provides the most explicit answers to these questions: "It should be noted that what I have been talking about in this paper is 'development' in the sense of capitalist development. It is very clear that the kind of development occuring in the Philippines is to the benefit of the elite. . . . Real wages have fallen substantially under martial law." Lim realizes that this pattern must be located within its international context. As a useful model for the Philippine experience, he points to Cardoso's (1973) notion of "associated-dependent development." London's arguments notwithstanding, the Southeast Asian ruling elites have not consistently struggled for national autonomy; in fact, a number of researchers highlight the *alliances* between indigenous elites and metropolitan capital (Catley, 1976; Bach, 1976; Lim, 1978; Bell, 1978; Sobhan, 1979; Frank, 1981b). Lim's (1978) well-articulated argument emphasizing the ties between the local elite, the state, and the transnational corporation is tantalizingly close to Evans's (1979b) formulation of the triple alliance (see Chapter 5). Similarly, descriptions of an emerging postcolonial bourgeoisie bent on preserving societies that are open to and politically stable enough for core investment (Catley, 1976; Elliot, 1978; Bell, 1978; Sobhan, 1979) are strikingly analogous to the picture of West African urban elites drawn previously.

What does this lead researchers to expect about policies that are planned and implemented by these states and that (implicitly or explicitly) affect urban patterns? Clearly, they are likely to reflect more than a vague type of internal colonialism. They need to be placed in a conceptual framework that highlights the importance of capital accumulation on a world-scale. Southeast Asian elites have acted in ways consistent with their international class alliances. They have provided material incentives and maintained structural conditions conducive to increasing levels of foreign capital investment. Excessive investment in capitals and leading ports or commercial centers is only the most direct way in which political decisionmaking has affected urban patterns. Other policies less obviously related to the creation of urban imbalance but still explicitly tied to the elites' international class interests reinforced these configurations. Policies aiding the highly mechanized agribusinesses that emerged from the "Green Revolution" contributed to the massive cityward migration dispossessed peasants (Catley, 1976: 70; Bell, 1978: 65). Policies designed to create a good business climate (of cheap labor and political stability) led to growing un- and underemployment and declining wage levels (Catley, 1976; Lim, 1978). And policies encouraging import substitution industrialization reinforced the pattern of extreme inequalities in Southeast Asian cities (Bell, 1978: 65; Short, 1979).

In summary, I argue that urbanization patterns in Southeast Asia are the result of a political process. But the politics of urban development are linked to the economic interests of the city-based societal elites. Their interests can only be understood by looking at the position that these elites hold in relation to other powerful actors in the world economy. Uneven urbanization can be explained as the outcome of the political economy of dependent capitalism. Elite class interests, allied with international capital, shape policymaking that both directly and indirectly promotes cityward migration and skewed income distributions. These, in turn, lead to urban primacy and intra-urban inequality.

Intra-Urban Inequality and "The Informal Sector"

Ample discussion has already been devoted to desbribing intra-urban inequality and the swelling ranks of the under- and unemployed in Southeast Asian cities. In addition, McGee's work on the growing urban informal sector was summarized. This uneven pattern is very similar to conditions in West African cities (see Chapter 5). Bell (1978: 65) provides a qualitative description of Bangkok as a city characterized by "an overabundance of posh hotels, a tiny but highly apparent luxury goods market, and a mass of underemployed workers." Sprawling squatter settlements ring most of Southeast Asia's large cities (McGee, 1976) as perhaps the most visible reminder of inequality. Discussing the wretched shantytowns of Manila, Mary Hollensteiner and Miria Lopez (1976: 71) remark: "The most conspicuous indicator of this ironic duality is the proliferation of poverty areas—the slum and squatter enclaves whose residents comprise one-third of the metropolitan population."

Early modernization theory researchers, while downplaying poverty and employment problems as "transitional," tended to see the major cause of such problems in terms of massive demographic influxes from rural areas (Fryer, 1972; Ginsburg, 1972). Using the general logic of functional analysis, these commentators suggested that the disruptive effects of huge population increases could be muted and controlled by planning efforts designed to reequilibrate the urban system. Ultimately, these efforts would lead to modernization and economic development for the whole society, bringing about a widespread distribution of benefits (see, esp. Ginsburg, 1972: 56).

Unfortunately, this process has not occurred. Problems associated with skewed income distribution and poverty did not lessen. They became more pervasive. This is a clear example of the orthodox assumption of the developmentalist perspective failing to square with Third World reality.

McGee's concern with the internal economic structure of Southeast Asian cities and its lack of "fit" with the then-dominant approach prompted him to begin his decade-long search for a more adequate framework. (This has already been discussed in some detail.) His efforts ultimately led him (1979) to conclude that the growth of the informal sector in these cities is an integral part of unequal exchange and capital accumulation on the world scale. This view, also espoused by Portes (1983), holds that rather than being an aberration or a transitional phase, the pattern of structured inequality in Third World cities is an important mechanism of surplus value extraction that helps to maintain the contemporary world economy.

The ubiquity of the informal sector in both West Africa and Southeast Asia lends credence to McGee's (1979) claim that it is a general characteristic of Third World capitalism. This may suggest that those who attempt to ameliorate urban poverty and inequality need to direct their attention toward the context of international economic dependency. Planning efforts designed to alter the relations of dependence and thus begin to change the roles these cities play in the world economy may be the only *practical* policies. Other strategies designed to deal with overpopulation and rapid growth may not be as effective since they would deal with the symptoms rather than the basic cause of the problem.

The Issue of Overurbanization

As in the chapter on West African urban development, this discussion leads us back to the old debate about overurbanization, since the Southeast Asian demographic pattern is very similar. Compared with other world regions, the absolute percentage of Southeast Asians who live in cities is very small. Coupling this with very high urban growth rates and the concentration of city-dwellers in a few very large cities creates a situation strikingly similar to that of West Africa. Are Southeast Asian cities overurbanized in Gugler's (1982) sense? Has the growth of the primate cities created economic inefficiencies in these societies?

To begin to answer that question, I will return to McGee's (1971) contention that the type of urbanization that took place in Southeast Asia failed to produce cities that generated national economic development. This proposition appears to have considerable merit. Yet it goes against the grain of much of the old modernization theory research on development. Adherents of this perspective must have known of urban problems, poverty, and diseconomies. How, then, did they reconcile this knowledge with their theoretical perspective?

Keyfitz (1965) provides a sophisticated analysis of Southeast Asian urbanization from the developmentalist perspective. His article convincingly dismisses simplistic arguments for the overurbanization thesis. But despite its virtues, it also clearly illustrates the fatal weakness of failing to seriously account for the international economy.

Drawing heavily on the historical experiences of the currently advanced countries, Keyfitz argues that the primate cities in Southeast Asia do, in fact, appear to be exerting a parasitic influence on national hinterlands. Why? Because they are fulfilling the necessary function of surplus extraction. This surplus is needed to finance development (Keyfitz, 1965: 279). Capital accumulation, a necessary prerequisite to economic growth, occurs in the cities and can only take place if there is an asymmetrical pattern of exchange concentrating resources in the hands of urban elites. Eventually, as this process proceeds and reinvestment of the surplus leads to economic growth, the positive effects of extractive policies become more obvious. At this point, the long-term generative role of the city is apparent.

Keyfitz makes a number of interesting points in his article. His suggestion that a "strong central administration" may be necessary for development (Keyfitz, 1965: 265–266) presages later work on the importance of "strong states." His argument that peasants in the countryside are the ones who have historically paid for industrialization is a theme that resonates through the work of Moore (1966), Chirot (1977), and Skocpol (1979). Unfortunately, however, his long-run optimism about cities and development in Southeast Asia appears misplaced.

Reviewing Keyfitz's (1965) argument using a dependency/world-system approach reveals a rather simple problem in his analysis. His general thesis that the governments, corporations, and elites of Southeast Asia's primate cities are involved in the business of surplus extraction seems irreproachable. Keyfitz saw this as primarily involving the unequal relationship between the city and the countryside. This type of asymmetrical exchange undoubtedly existed and continues to be important. Contemporary analysts would also point to the articulation between the formal and informal economies within cities as a more subtle form of surplus extraction. That Keyfitz failed to notice this exchange mechanism is hardly surprising: Scholars began to understand these processes only in the late 1970s and early l980s (see the earlier discussion). The real weakness of Keyfitz's argument lies elsewhere. The reason his implicit prediction of ultimately generative cities has not held lies with his unit of analysis. Like other writers of the modernization theory era, Keyfitz focused his attention on the internal dynamics of Asian societies. Assuming that they were relatively well-bounded systems, he neglected to consider the possibility that the surplus extraction that was occurring would lead to capital accumulation and economic development not in the great capital cities of Southeast Asia but primarily in the metropolises of the core countries. The continuing relative economic stagnation of many parts of this and other dependent regions suggests that, at least to some extent, this is the case.

As with West Africa, the label "overurbanized" captures some of the problems that primate cities create for national economies in Southeast Asia. They *do* seem to represent a spatial misallocation of human and material resources, and they *are* places of lavish consumption for elites in countries that are desperately poor. In these senses, the patterns of urbanization in Southeast Asia can be seem as parasitic in regard to some rationally planned, balanced, and equitable types of economic growth.

In another way, however, this uneven pattern of urban development—manifest in both urban primacy and urban poverty and inequality—is anything *but* dysfunctional—quite to the contrary! Viewed from a political economy of the world-system perspective, this social ensemble is an extremely efficient pattern of surplus extraction under dependent capitalism. From this perspective, one can see the high level of "efficiency" in capital-intensive export agriculture and import substitution industrialization. Even the urban informal sector, which, viewed in isolation, appears relatively nonproductive, becomes a highly "efficient" operation when it is conceptualized as a mechanism of surplus extraction linked to the world economy. Conditions that might be seen as problematic effects of overurbanization and impediments to national development may actually play an important role in maintaining profitability in the international economy.

This is not to say that the problems of the primate city in Southeast Asia are not real. Poverty and inequality are an undeniable part of the lives of millions of people who live in these nations. The point, however, is that the problem is not merely one of too much city growth. Demographic solutions designed to direct populations from the primate cities will not bring about real change because they do not address the real problem. Meaningful solutions must address the *causes* of the problems. The most basic of these, I maintain, is the role that the Southeast Asian region plays in the world economy. Real progress will be made only when the pattern of its external dependency relations with the centers of the world economic system is restructured.[6]

Disclaimer

As in Chapter 4, it is necessary to point out to the limits of this chapter. Even more clearly than in the West African case, a tremendous amount of diversity was summarized in a fairly superficial manner here. An attempt was made to place countries into four subregional patterns and give the reader an idea of how the theoretical model of urbanization in the world-system might explain the various trajectories. Though the bulk of the chapter concentrated on Southeast Asia and peripheral urbanization there, even that analysis must be considered preliminary and suggestive rather than conclusive.

In the next chapter, another deviant case is examined in depth. South Korea's pattern of urbanization and development is very different from that in the parts of East Asia most readily associated with the Third World. As a part of the East Asian semiperiphery, South Korea merits a more detailed investigation that will highlight the strengths and weaknesses and the urban impacts of dependent development.

7

South Korean Urbanization and Semiperipheral Development

South Korea epitomizes one of the distinct paths of urbanization sketched in the last chapter. In a sense, it represents a middle way between highly urban Japan and China and Southeast Asia, which are just seeing the beginnings of city growth. It is also intermediary in terms of what I have called uneven urbanization. South Korea's urban primacy is well below that of Thailand and a number of other Southeast Asian countries; even Tokyo is more primate than Seoul. Intra-urban inequality, while probably relatively high compared to that in Western nations or Japan, appears to be much lower in Seoul and other Korean cities than in the primate cities of Southeast Asia (see Chapter 6).

Why are South Korean urban patterns so different? That is the primary question addressed in this chapter. Consistent with the political economy of the world-system approach, it is reasonable to begin the search for an answer by exploring the role that this nation plays in the world economy. Is it different from other Third World East Asian countries? An ancillary issue, which will be taken up near the end of the chapter, is the contemporary pattern of urbanization in South Korea. Preliminary evidence suggests some changes occurred in the 1980s—what implications do these have for the notion of semiperipheral urbanization?

According to nearly every classification schema, South Korea is a semiperipheral country. This is true whether one uses quantitative gauges like the Bollen (1983)/Snyder and Kick (1979) measure (used in Chapter 3), the Nemeth and Smith (1985a) measusre, or the Smith and White (1992) measure. South Korea also makes the list of semiperipheral countries posed by Wallerstein (1976b), Chirot (1977), and Chase-Dunn (1983). The only other East Asian nation that is uniformly accorded semiperipheral status is Taiwan (and perhaps the city-states of Hong Kong and Singapore). Most Southeast Asian countries are generally classified as members of the periphery, although various researchers classify Indonesia (Wallerstein, 1976b, Chirot, 1979), the Philippines (Snyder and Kick, 1979;

Caporaso, 1981; Nemeth and Smith, 1985a), Malaysia (Snyder and Kick, 1979), and even Burma (!) (Snyder and Kick, 1979) as semiperipheral.

The lack of complete consensus on the world-system roles of Southeast Asian societies suggests that caution must be used in tying urban pattern to world-system role. James Caporaso's (1981) in-depth analysis of industrializing semiperipheral countries includes South Korea and the Philippines, and this presents a problem for my analysis. The Filipino urban pattern is a sharp contrast to South Korea's more balanced configuration of urban growth. Manila's high urban primacy and squalid shantytowns seem much more similar to factors of city growth in the periphery rather than in semiperipheral South Korea. The hypothesized relationship between world-system role and urban outcome appears to have broken down in this specific case.

Upon closer examination, however, the Filipino case may not be as anomalous as it seems. Caporaso's (1981) detailed data show that South Korea and the Philippines are about as different as two supposedly semiperipheral countries can be, even by his own criteria. South Korea scores very high on each of three indexes for semiperipheral status (economic growth, manufacturing growth, and manufacturing as a proportion of GNP), while the Philippines barely scored high enough to make the category. Caporaso (1981: 359, 361) notes that South Korea's growth rate for the period was nearly three times that of the Philippines, and that the South Korean economy dominates East Asian export-manufacturing trade. In sum, his work provides evidence that the Philippines is, at best, a marginal member of the semiperiphery. If the global hierarchy is conceptualized as a continuum rather than as categorically bounded, distinct strata (Chase-Dunn, 1989, provides a compelling argument for this view), South Korea clearly ranks considerably higher than the Philippines (or, for that matter, any of the Southeast Asian countries).

Even an insistence that South Korea really does share semiperipheral status with a nation like the Philippines does *not* invalidate the general approach I have developed in this book. One of my basic contentions is that urbanization is a historical process tied to the changing economic functions that cities and regions play in different periods. The Philippines (and two or three other Southeast Asian countries) may be semiperipheral in the late twentieth century, but this does not mean that they did not go through a long period of peripheralization during the colonial period. In fact, as Chapter 6 demonstrates, the entire Southeast Asian area functioned as a periphery in the world economy from at least the mid-nineteenth century until the post-World War II period. Regardless of later changes in that country, the Philippines, because of their relatively primitive indigenous level of development and very early incorporation into the Spanish colonial empire, were thoroughly peripheralized. This may explain why its urban patterns there continue to be very imbalanced (see Nemeth and Smith, 1985b, for a full analysis).

The Korean peninsula's incorporation into the modern world-system was very different. There was no prolonged period of peripheralization. In a very short span of time, Korean society was transformed from an external arena operating beyond the reach of the world economy to a contemporary semiperiphery. This is the key to understanding South Korea's seemingly deviant pattern of urbanization and development. The historical-structural analysis that follows traces the linkages between Korea's distinct pattern of incorporation into the capitalist world economy, its subsequent role in the world-system, and its divergent urban trajectory.

Indigenous Urbanization: Cities and Agrarian Kingdoms

While Spain and other European powers were consolidating their colonial dominion over Southeast Asia, Korea remained relatively remote and isolated. [1] Location played a role in this. The Korean peninsula was located far north of the Asian trade routes that initially allowed Europe to partake of the riches of "the Spice Islands." For many centuries, little was known about Korea in the West; one early historian points out that parts of the rugged Korean coast were so unfamiliar to foreigners that they did not even appear on Japanese or Chinese maps until the early nineteenth century (Hamilton, 1904). On charts prior to this date, "the space now occupied by the Korean Archipelago was covered with the drawing of an elephant—the conventional sign of ignorance for cartographers of that time" (Hamilton, 1904: 1). With publication of one late-nineteenth-century volume on "Corea" in English, the publishers proclaimed: "Corea stands in much the same relation to the traveller that the region of the pole does to the explorer, and menaces with the same penalty the too inquisitive tourist who ventures to penetrate its inhospitable borders" (Griffis, 1971: VII).

But geography alone does not sufficiently explain why Korea remained free of Western domination into the twentieth century. Unlike some other parts of East Asia (particularly the Philippines), Korea had developed an advanced agrarian society long before its incorporation into the modern world economy. Evidence of metallurgy and rice cultivation can be traced back to the first century A.D. (Hatada, 1969: 5–8). At about the same time, the politico-administrative apparatus typical of agrarian societies was beginning to develop. Although some of the early Korean agrarian states were apparently under Chinese influence and control, a series of indigenous kingdoms gradually emerged that unified large areas and were capable of defending their territories against outside aggression (McCune, 1956: chapter 3; Henthorn, 1971: chapter 4; Hatada, 1969: chapter 2).

At first, there were a fairly large number of these "states" scattered over the peninsula (Hatada, 1969: 14–18). Gradually, three particularly powerful kingdoms came to dominate all of Korea. Each of these competing political systems controlled significant land areas, possessed large standing armies, and developed sophisticated administrative and taxation systems (Hatada, 1969: chapter 2). After

250 years of struggle, the Silla Empire succeeded in extending its control over a unified peninsula in the early eighteenth century (Hatada, 1969: 26–30; Henthorn, 1971: 59). State development continued. The Shilla and their dynastic successors constructed strong, efficient administrative units capable of mobilizing and maintaining large armies. The height of politico-military development was realized in the Chosun state under the control of the Yi dynasty. This government maintained control from 1392 until 1910. During this 500-year period the, Chosun state, despite occasional military setbacks, managed to maintain its sovereignty and repulsed a number of attacks by its hostile neighbors (Hatada, 1969: chapter 5; Henthorn, 1971: 136–226). This high level of indigenous political control and military power, coupled with relative geographic isolation from Western Europe, combined to prevent the area's early incorporation into the Western-controlled world economy.

As in other agrarian states, the nerve centers for these Korean kingdoms were preindustrial cities (see Sjoberg, 1965). In the earlier period of multiple states, a number of large capital cities were built. Their growth was tied to military successes and the rise and fall of dynastic lines, so that political capitals were moved frequently (see, for example, Hatada, 1969: 16, 18). Many regional cities emerged as a result. After Silla unification, the first national capital was established at Kyongju (Hatada, 1969: 27). Although reliable estimates of precolonial city size are difficult to obtain, primary sources estimate the population of Kyongju during its "great period" (the mid-thirteenth century) at over 800,000 (see Henthorn, 1971: 66).

Clearly, a figure of this size even in a very advanced agrarian economy must be viewed with some degree of skepticism (see Lenski and Lenski, 1978: 192). Nonetheless, historians claim that the eleventh-century capital of Kaesong was even larger Kyongju at its apex (Henthorn, 1971: 101). Allowing that the numerical estimates of these urban populations may be inflated, it is reasonable to conclude that these cities were probably nearly as large as the largest cities of China or Japan during roughly equivalent periods.

It is important to note that the structure of the indigenous Korean kingdoms also promoted city growth in other old and new centers. Provincial capitals were key components of the central administration from the sixth century onward (Henthorn, 1971: 49). The exact bureaucratic arrangements varied with changing dynasties (see Hatada, 1969, for details), but in general, the country was divided into eight or nine districts, each largely administered from its own capital. Shannon McCune (1956: 31–32) explains for the Yi dynasty: "The provincial system was reorganized giving governors of the provinces considerable authority. . . . Each province was intended to be a major geographic and economic region. Each had major cities, from which the name of the province was derived." Comparison of maps of the various dynastic periods with contemporary maps of Korea clearly shows the gradual emergence of most of the modern cities as provincial or subprovincial capitals (see Henthorn, 1971: 87, 133). Additionally, by the late Yi period, commerce had become very important. A number of state monopolies were established to handle certain types of goods, such as silks, ramie, cotton, paper, and marine products (Henthorn, 1971: 204). By the early nineteenth century, some cities had developed specialized markets and trade fairs (Henthorn, 1971: 205–206).

Precolonial Korea possessed a system of relatively large urban centers that were based on an incipient politically and economically based geographical division of labor and linked together by established trade routes. Although population data are scant, it seems reasonable to assume that this precontact urban system was relatively balanced demographically (with the Yi capital of Seoul at the top).

The earliest reliable figures on urban populations are the Japanese counts taken soon after annexation. In 1920, only 3.2 percent of the nation's people lived in urban areas with populations over 20,000 (Renaud, 1974: 26). There were eight cities of this size. Seoul was the largest, with a population of about 250,000, followed by Pusan (74,000), Pyongyang (72,000), Taegu (45,000), Kaesong (37,000), Incheon (36,000), Wonsan (28,000), and Jinnampo (21,000). All these cities were either ports or colonial administrative centers and had served similar functions in the precolonial period (Renaud, 1974).

Precolonial Korea had reached a very advanced level of indigenous development by the late nineteenth century. Though like all advanced agrarian societies, the peninsula's population was overwhelmingly rural, a sophisticated national city system was well established. This system was composed of urban areas that were older, larger, and more tightly integrated with each other than preindustrial cities in most parts of the world—including much of Southeast Asia and all of West Africa. The interaction effect of this sophisticated level of development and late incorporation into the modern world economy affected the path of subsequent urbanization and development.

Japanese Colonialism: Imperialism and Rational Planning

After the Japanese arrived in Korea at the beginning of this century, Korean cities experienced a period of growth, but all increased at rates commensurate with their earlier positions in the urban hierarchy (see Kwon et al., 1975: appendix, table 1). Seoul did not become increasingly primate, and, in fact, the ratio actually declined slightly. What is perhaps even more remarkable is that after World War II, the liberation from Japan, the division of the country, the Korean War, and the industrial transformation of the economy, the major cities of South Korea retained their 1920 rank order without a single alteration (Mills and Song, 1979: 48).

The persistence of this urban configuration might be explained as an example of the momentum of institutionalized patterns of social organization. Powerful groups in society often act in their own interests to preserve the status quo. But no argument based on social inertia is very compelling in the absence of an explanation of *how* this occurs. This is particularly true in the present case since Korean society was undergoing a series of jarring social changes. The following analysis highlights the mechanisms that operated to maintain a balanced urban hierarchy in Korea. To this end, the manner in which the urban structure was compatible with the changing political and economic needs of Korea's ruling elites is explored. Throughout the analysis, internal policies that affected urban growth are examined in light of the changing role Korea came to play in the modern world-system.

Internationally, the period following 1870 was one of renewed imperialism for most core and some semiperipheral nations. Stimulated by the belief that continual expansion and permanent security of raw material sources and markets were necessary for economic survival, these countries began to prepare for what they perceived to be the inevitable conflict over a declining number of unclaimed peripheral areas (Chirot, 1977: 48–54). As the core countries enlarged their militaries, the weaker semiperipheral nations (most notably, Russia and Japan) struggled to keep pace in order to avoid being reduced to peripheral status (Chirot, 1977: 50). In this international setting, Japan began its imperialistic expansion seeking raw materials and new markets. Taiwan, parts of China, and Korea became Japan's early colonies during this period (Chirot, 1977: 82).

Trade between Korea and Japan officially began in 1876 with the coerced signing of the Kanghwa Treaty. Pusan officially became an open port, although after 1894, Japan was the only country involved in trade with Korea. In 1905 (following Japan's victory in the Russo-Japanese War), the Protectorate Treaty was signed between Korea and Japan, and in 1906, Japan established the inspector general post to oversee all domestic administration and diplomatic activities. From 1910 to the end of World War II, the Korean political and economic systems were completely controlled by the Japanese colonial government. Not surprisingly, Japanese policies in Korea almost entirely reflected the needs of Japan. Therefore, any analysis of policies during this period "must be carried out with reference to the changing conditions of the Japanese economy during the period under review. Only in this way will the major factors that shaped the pattern of the Korean economy be made clear" (Suh, 1978: 6).

During the initial period of colonization (1910–1930), Japan's major policy objectives were directed at developing Korea into a classic colony, with special emphasis placed on the export of agricultural produce. The Decree on Business Entities, which required the licensing of all business firms in Korea, enabled the Japanese to discourage development of modern manufacturing industries and "furthered their policy of making the Korean colony chiefly a supplier of grains and industrial raw materials to Japan and a market for Japanese manufacturers" (Kim and Roemer, 1979: 3).

This imperial "need" to transform the Korean mode of production necessitated a more complete penetration of Korea by Japan. This was facilitated by continued development of the transportation and communication systems.

Although development of a transportation and communication network had begun long before incorporation, the road system connecting the major urban areas (while adequate for maintaining governmental administration between and within provinces) was inadequate for Japan's planned transformations of the Korean economy (Hulbert, 1906; Reeve, 1963; Cumings, 1981). Thus, in the early period, transportation development became a policy priority of the colonial government. Because of the opening of Pusan as free port and the increased trade with Japan, a railway was built to connect Pusan with Seoul in 1896. By 1928, an entire system of railways and bridges linking Manchuria with Korea had been built (Reeve, 1963). The major north-south line connected Pusan with Siniuju on the Manchurian border with a linkage to the Manchurian rail lines. This north-south line included Pusan, Taegu, Seoul, and Pyongyang. Another major rail line connected Seoul and Wonsan, and yet another connected Taejon to the port city of Mokpo. In spite of the rugged terrain, nearly 4,000 miles of rail line were completed by 1944 (Chang, 1971; Wood, 1977). The colonial government was also responsible for beginning construction of a highway and telecommunication network, along with improvements in maritime transportation. New ports (mostly on the eastern coast) were opened as trade with Japan increased during the colonial period (Suh, 1978; Cumings, 1981).

These advances in the transportation and communication systems served to maintain and strengthen the existing urban hierarchy by increasing the flow of interactions between cities. Lacking an adequate port and located on the western side of the peninsula (the region farthest from Japan), Seoul became dependent on intermediate rail and port cities for its trade with Japan. These intermediate cities were nodes in the developing trade system, and as such, they became functionally important as junctions where freight from one transport system was shifted to another system. Thus, while massive investment in transportation and communication by Japan served to transform Korea into an export agricultural economy, it also strengthened an already existing urban hierarchy.

Between 1900 and 1929, Japan enjoyed a period of tremendous economic growth, with increases in GNP that far exceeded those of any contemporary core power (Kuznets, 1971: 38–40). It was primarily during this period that Japan made the transition from semiperipheral to core status. In its effort to become an established power in the world political and economic system, however, Japan became heavily dependent on its export trade to finance the import of vital raw resources. With the Great Depression of the 1930s, internal protectionist pressure led Western industrial nations to create tariffs to protect their domestic economies.

Japan, more than any other core power, was vulnerable to the imposed trade restrictions (Chirot, 1977: 103).

The military and the large corporations, which were in control of the Japanese economy and polity by 1930, directed Japan on a policy of heavy military industrialization. Given the international situation, this was clearly needed for strategic as well as economic reasons. And as early as the period of annexation, some Japanese leaders had viewed the Korean peninsula as an avenue to colonial penetration into continental Asia (Kim and Kim, 1967).

This strategic element meant that Korea was more than merely an economic satellite to exploit and underdevelop. Even prior to the 1930s, a number of the colonial policies had a developmental effect on Korea—particularly those regarding advances in transportation. The development of fairly extensive rail lines reaching up to Manchuria was obviously designed to enhance imperial Japan's potential for expansion. But it also resulted in closer economic integration within Korea. Similarly, the conscious development of an industrial base in Korea was intended to promote Japan's strategic power. But it, too, resulted in the location of modern industrial facilities in a number of Korean cities.

In this manner, policies geared to the needs of Japanese political and economic expansion later redounded to Korea's benefit. For instance, in an attempt to reduce domestic economic competition, Japan enacted the Law for Regulation of Major Industry in 1931, which controlled heavy industrial production within Japan (Kim and Roemer, 1979: 5). The fact that industries in Korea were not subject to this law was very influential in the decisions of many Japanese firms to establish plants in Korea. In addition, Korea possessed a variety of mineral resources, an abundant supply of hydroelectric power, and a cheap supply of labor—all of which helped create a setting that offered cost advantages to heavy industry. Furthermore, as a result of an agricultural depression experienced by Japan in the late 1920s, the initial plan for the development of large-scale agribusiness in Korea came under review (Suh, 1978: 13). In an effort to avoid any further damage to their own economy, Japanese leaders decided to discontinue expansion of Korean agricultural production.

As a result of these policy shifts, manufacturing output in Korea grew rapidly with heavy Japanese investment between 1930 and 1937. For the most part, this growth was entirely unrelated to Korean entrepreneurship, which was limited mainly to small industries.[2] With Japan's invasion of Manchuria, a conscious policy was instituted to expand heavy industries in Korea for military purposes (Suh, 1978).

The capture of Manchuria in 1931 in a sense actualized Korea's potential strategic importance for the Japanese empire. The country became a corridor for trade between Tokyo and the frontier areas, as well as a staging ground for subsequent Japanese pushes into Asia (Suh, 1978). Japan's interests, more clearly than ever before, rested with continued infrastructural and industrial development of its colony.

As the foregoing analysis indicates, Japanese colonialism in Korea did not result in the pattern of underdevelopment experienced by most areas incorporated into the world economy in early periods. In part, this can be attributed to the peninsula's strategic position and proximity to the colonizing power. But the very different form of colonialism undertaken by Japan can also be understood as a "period effect." This early-twentieth-century imperialism, to be sure, displays some important parallels with previous colonization efforts carried out by the Spaniards, the British, the French, and other world powers. But Japanese imperial needs during the "early monopoly capital" phase of the world-economy were very different from previous drives for colonies merely as a source of primary products and "primitive accumulation" (see Frank, 1979). Like other imperialists, the Japanese were not concerned with the needs and desires of Korea or Koreans; they were motivated by self-interest, and at times, they brutalized the Korean population (see Hatada, 1969: chapter 7; McCune, 1956: 37–38). In the 1920s and 1930s, however, Japan's need for increased military preparedness and for outlets for capital investment facilitated the development of Korean industry (see Cumings, 1984).

This, in turn, had its effect on the Korean urban pattern. The diversification of the Korean economy resulted in industries locating near the factors of production. Regional specialization and interregional dependencies increased (Wood, 1977: 32). This conscious policy of diversifying the Korean economy served to further develop urban areas in all regions of the country and to incorporate these cities in a system of interdependencies. Thus, the nature of Japanese imperialism reinforced the balanced urban hierarchy that had its origin in much earlier times.

U.S. Domination and "Dependent Development"

Once incorporated into the modern world-system, it is very difficult for a nation to reisolate itself. This is particularly obvious for Korea, which one writer suggests has functioned as a veritable vortex of international activity in the recent past (Henderson, 1968). With the end of World War II, Korea, while liberated from Japanese rule, once again was dominated by foreign powers. In the South, a U.S. military government was established, while in the North, the Soviet Union gained control.

The partitioning of Korea had a dramatic disorganizing effect on the economy and the functional relationships within the urban hierarchy. The South contained a larger population and the most productive agricultural land, while the North possessed most of the important mineral resources and the country's heavy industry and power plants (Hatada, 1969; Kim and Roemer, 1979). In addition, the cities in the two regions had developed a system of interdependencies that (given the removal of the colonizers and their Japan-oriented growth policies) had the potential of developing much stronger complementary relationships. With the separation of the two regions, South Korea was forced to become heavily dependent on the United States to supply both manufactured goods and a large proportion of its food (Kim and Roemer, 1979). These shortages were further compounded when an estimated 2.3 million Korean emigrants from Japan and North Korea entered South Korea between 1946 and 1948 (Kim and Roemer, 1979: 25).[3]

Although this influx of people created many short-term problems, it also stimulated the growth of urban areas in the southeastern provinces. These areas had been the principal source of prewar migrants to Japan and were the points of entry for most of those who returned (Mills and Song, 1979: 70). Additionally, "the vast majority of the Koreans from Japan had been living in urban areas or industrial areas and upon their return a large proportion—at least 40 percent—settled in urban areas, chiefly in their native provinces" (Mills and Song, 1979: 70). Primarily as a result of this postwar migration, the proportion of the total population living in urban areas grew from 13 to 17 percent between 1944 and 1949. Furthermore, this growth was widely distributed, with ten cities having growth rates of 8 per cent of more (Mills and Song, 1979: 70).

As a result of the almost complete prior domination of the Japanese, there remained little of an elite class in Korea after World War II. The egalitarian effect of the war was further enhanced by a series of successive land reforms initiated in 1947 by the U.S. military government. These reforms, which redistributed the land previously held by Japanese landlords, were apparently quite effective in equalizing income distribution (Kim and Roemer, 1979: 164; Repetto, 1979).

The U.S. interest in Korea was primarily geopolitical. Korea's strategic location vis-à-vis China, Japan, and the Soviet Union makes it an important military position for the United States. Furthermore, Korea became a "quasi-experiment" for the testing of the dominant economic systems: capitalism and communism. For this reason, the economic success of South Korea was of immense importance to the United States.

Despite the severe disruptions of World War II, industrial production began recovering by 1948, the year that the Republic of Korea was formally established. The economy continued to improve until the outbreak of the Korean War in 1950.

After the war, South Korea was more dependent on the United States than ever before. The total amount of economic relief and aid given by the United States increased from $58 million in 1950 to $194 million in 1953 (Kim and Roemer, 1979: 33). It was this massive foreign aid that sustained South Korea during the reconstruction following the war and continued to do so up through the early 1960s. U.S. aid continued for decades—between 1945 and 1980, South Korea received nearly 6 percent of the total nonmilitary grants given by the United States (United States Bureau of the Census, 1980: 868–869). This is more aid than was given to any other nation in Asia, Africa, or Latin America, except for Israel and India. The long-term assistance from the United States reflected ongoing perception of South Korea's geopolitical importance. The extent of its strategic importance becomes clear when one considers that in the 1970s, South Korea also received nearly $3.5 billion in U.S. military assistance—over three times more than was given to any other East Asian country, except for Vietnam (United States Bureau of the Census, 1980: 870).

Strategic considerations have also influenced Korean city location since ancient times. Early towns were located in river valleys some distance inland as a defense against marauding Japanese pirates (McCune, 1960: 30).[4] In recent years, particularly after the partitioning of the country, security is again a major concern. The proximity of Seoul to North Korea is often cited as a particular reason for concern.[5] Although cities were once important as fortresses to protect populations and economic functions, it has been argued that large cities have become vulnerable with the changes in military technology and that population spread to a number of centers is now strategically more desirable (Boulding, 1978). The rapid urban growth of the southeastern coastal region is, in part, the result of a conscious policy to focus industrial growth away from North Korea (Mills and Song, 1979: 53). During the 1970s, the growth rates of the major cities in the southeastern region were substantially higher than those for other cities—including Seoul.

Between 1953 and 1960, the South Korean economy grew slowly. Paralleling developments elsewhere in the Third World, industry was characterized by production for the domestic market, and a policy of import substitution was pursued (Kim and Roemer, 1979: 153; Cumings, 1984). This sluggish growth pattern ended in the 1960s. Early in that decade, South Korea began one of the most rapid and sustained rates of growth ever recorded. For the period between 1963 and 1976, the South Korean GNP grew at an average rate of over 10 percent per year. Unemployment dropped precipitously, and average real wages grew at 7 percent per annum. The key to the Korean "economic miracle" was a basic shift to labor-intensive export manufacturing (Cumings, 1984, 1989; Amsden, 1989).

How can this economic transformation be explained? Development economists focus on the indigenous characteristics of Korean society. Parvez Hasan (1976: 29–30) identifies three key factors: (1) the nature of the labor force, (2) "historical and cultural" predispositions to utilize "entrepreneurial talent," and (3) the alliance between business and government. Other economists discuss these factors but also speculate about the possible effects that large amounts of U.S. foreign aid and investment may have had in promoting this economic transformation (Kim and Roemer, 1979: 155–156).

At least two of these factors—the nature of the labor force and the relationship between the state and capital—seem to be crucially important (Amsden, 1989). But it is obvious that South Korea's economic transformation based on export manufacturing needs to be placed in its international context. From a world-system perspective, this semiperipheral East Asian society is playing a distinct world economic role. Its global niche in the "new international division of labor" (Froebel, Heinrichs, and Kreye, 1981) is one that only emerged quite recently in response to a "crisis" in world-system development.

A number of analysts address this contemporary crisis issue (Frank, 1981a and 1981b; Amin et al., 1982; Bergesen, ed., 1983). The fine points of these theoretical debates need not concern us, but the overall thrust of the argument is that in the 1960s and 1970s, businesses involved in production in core zones of the world economy began to face mounting economic difficulties. Among the reasons for this "crisis of profitability" were rising labor costs, obsolete technology, and the high cost of financing advanced welfare states. The result has been a "restructuring of the international division of labor" (Dixon, Jonas, and McCaughan, 1983: 175; see also Froebel, Heinrichs, and Kreye, 1981). Capital began to leave the core in search of lower wages and a better business climate. One of the earliest and most obvious manifestations of this process was the rise of the multinational corporation (Barnet and Mueller, 1974). Evans (1979b) argues that dependent development in the semiperiphery of the world economy has changed the global division of labor in a more complex and subtle manner (see also Caporaso, 1981).

South Korean development is a direct result of this geographic reorientation of world industrialization. Frank (1981a: 320) explains the process:

> From the point of view of the world capitalist economy this is a transfer of part of the industrial production from high- to low-cost areas. From the point of the Third World, this move represents a policy of export promotion. This movement started in the 1960s with Mexico . . . and in South Korea, Taiwan, Hong Kong and Singapore. . . . These economies offer cheap labor, and they compete among each other with state subsidies to provide plant facilities, electricity, transportation, tax relief, and every other kind of incentive for foreign capital to come to their countries to produce for the world market.

Frank (1981a: 320) goes on to explain the government's active role in this process:

> To provide these low wages and indeed to reduce wages from one country to another competitively, as each tries to offer more favorable conditions to international capital, requires political repression, the destruction of labor unions and/or the prohibition of strikes and other labor union activity, the systematic imprisonment, torture, or, assassination of labor and other political leaders and in general the imposition of emergency rule, martial law, and of military government. In fact, the whole state apparatus has to be adapted to the Third World role in the new division of labor.

This is the backdrop for semiperipheral industrial development in South Korea. Within this context Hasan's (1976: 29) comments on South Korean workers becomes fully intelligible: "[This] labor force is unusually well educated, vigorous and industrious. Labor's acceptance, until recent years, of wages that lagged behind productivity, its adaptability to exacting industrial discipline, and an absence of labor militancy have all been conducive to rapid industrialization." Similarly, the role of the "bureaucratic-authoritarian state" in dependent development (see O'Donnell, 1978; Cumings, 1984) helps to explain "the apparent paradox that the Korean economy depends in large measure on private enterprise operating under highly centralized government guidance" (Hasan, 1976: 29).

Obviously, this pattern of development involves trade-offs. The failure of democracy and the imposition of authoritarian rule in South Korea has been a long-standing concern among both scholars and politicians (see, for example, Han, 1974; Wright, ed., 1975; McCormack and Selden, 1977). Even recent widely heralded moves toward political liberalization are fraught with contradictions and difficulties (Smith and Lee, 1990). One is tempted to suggest that semiperipheral development may mirror social change in Eastern bloc nations: Gains in economic equality may come at the expense of losses in political equality. But speculation of this type is not central to the current argument.

More germane is the effect that the shift to labor-intensive export manufacturing has on urban patterns. This type of industrialization operates most efficiently when plants locate close to the factors of production and are able to utilize regional resource advantages. In contrast, under the policy of import substitution industrialization, it is more advantageous to locate manufacturing close to a concentrated domestic market (this pattern is evidenced by a number of the Southeast Asian primate cities) (see Chapter 6). Export manufacturing industries need not consider this market element when making locational decisions (Roberts, 1978b: 603–604). In Korea, these locational decisions are given further latitude by the continued development of the already relatively sophisticated transportation infrastructure. All major cities are now connected not only by railroads but also by an elaborate highway system similar to interstate routes in the United States (Hasan, 1976: 30–35). This transportation system minimizes the economic advantages of any one node and further encourages the relatively even spread of population and economic activity. Particularly given this level of transportation efficiency, export manufacturing has reinforced deconcentrated patterns of urban growth and mitigated any trend toward urban primacy.

What about the low level of intra-urban inequality and the relatively small size of the South Korean urban informal sector through most of the period of rapid economic growth? Does this make sense given South Korea's new semiperipheral role in the world economy?

One reason intra-urban inequality has stayed relatively low is the connection between export manufacturing and low urban primacy. One key economic function of a city and its population is to provide a market for goods and services. Import substitution policies required a sufficient internal market to generate demand (see the discussion in Chapter 6). Given limited societal resources, the only way to ensure the marketability of indigenously produced consumer goods is to concentrate income in the hands of elites. But when the economy is geared toward producing products for foreign sales, national markets are irrelevant. Discussing the general logic of export industry in the Third World, Marlene Dixon, Susanne Jonas and Edward McCaughan (1983: 177) assert: *"The key is that the producers in a number of these countries are no longer the consumers of what they produce (in contrast to the import-substituting model)"* (italics in original). Under an economic regime that stresses export manufacturing, concentration of wealth is not so important.

Another argument focuses attention directly on the size and importance of the urban informal sector. Portes (1983) has reiterated his claim that urban informal economies often function to provide cheap wage subsidies to formal sector firms. He claims, "Different informal production arrangements have been reconstituted in recent years as so many mechanisms to help retard or bypass wage gains and state-enforced labor legislation" (Portes, 1983: 63). This explains the proliferation of these economic activities in various parts of the Third World (and even in a number of poverty areas in large U.S. cities). But this does not mean that *all* Third World countries dependent on low-wage economic growth will necessarily have large urban informal sectors. Instead, the effect of international dependence on urban informal sector size and vitality will be mediated by the role of the state (Portes, 1983: 164–168). Therefore, the existence of a large informal sector and high urban inequality are the results of political as well as economic needs (Portes, 1983: 168).

Discussing some Latin American examples, Portes points to pronounced differences between countries that play the essentially similar semiperipheral role of exporting industrial products. A number of these states have traditions of political democracy and long histories of factory production and trade unionism. In these nations, development policies imposed by recent military authoritarian governments, designed to attract international capital, have resulted in rapid increases in unemployment and growing informal sector activity. Brazil, by contrast, has "followed a consistently anti-labor course" for many years, and repression has been used to hold down wage demands (Portes, 1983: 167). Many of the features characteristic of a large informal economic sector are absent in Brazil's large cities. Contrasting the pattern in the formerly more "liberal" Southern Cone countries with the situation in Brazil, Portes (1983: 166) explains how the political system leads to different degrees of urban informal sector activity:

The continuation of anti-labor policies by an authoritarian government may lead to a different outcome. If trade union activity and enforcement of labor legislation are sufficiently disorganized, firms will have little incentive to engage in sub-contracting practices, preferring instead to take advantage of rationalized methods of factory production. In addition, if wages are sufficiently low and the labor supply sufficiently elastic, formal enterprises can successfully compete in the low-income market with small, informal ones, whose only advantage consists in a sub-remunerated labor force. The end result of this process is not the swelling of the informal sector, but the elimination of the formal/informal dichotomy and the return to unfettered capitalist practices. Under these conditions, unemployment may actually be reduced, since lower wages and freer use of labor will encourage firms to expand their work force.

From the beginnings of the Park Chung Hee regime in the 1960s until the mid-1980s, this Brazilian model seemed to fit South Korea well. South Korea's late incorporation and relatively long period of Japanese rule precluded the development of either democracy or the premature proletarianization of the workforce. Throughout the period of economic upswing, it was ruled by a rigid authoritarian regime comparable, in some ways, to Brazil's bureaucratic-authoritarian state (Caporaso, 1981; Cumings, 1984). Lower levels of informal sector activity and the general pattern of more equitable growth have been possible despite a semiperipheral role in the international economy because South Korea's leaders have been able to impose a strong state capable of maintaining economic stability and stringent labor discipline.

In sum, South Korea's more balanced urban system together with its relatively low degree of informal sector activity and intra-urban inequality throughout the period of "the economic miracle" must be tied to the nation's changing role as a relative latecomer in the modern world-system. The Korean peninsula's relatively advanced agrarian economy and the fairly balanced system of preindustrial cities before incorporation into the modern world economy have had a historical impact that weighed against a pattern of urban primacy. Subsequent social changes in the twentieth century have reinforced this pattern. Both the logic of Japanese colonialism and the restructuring of the international division of labor in the post–World War II period provided a situation of dependency that mitigated against the uneven urbanization characteristic of many other parts of the Third World. From the mid-1960s to the mid-1980s, the key was a strong state apparatus capable of enforcing policies allowing for the rapid growth of a labor-intensive export manufacturing sector.

Urbanization in the Late 1980s: Some Unexpected Changes?

The 1980s were a tumultuous period in the Republic of Korea (ROK) as the contradictions of the Korean model of dependent development came to the fore.

Economic growth slowed; political upheaval grew (Cumings, 1989; Smith and Lee, 1990). It is not surprising that some aspects of the urban system and city growth showed signs of change as well. New evidence suggests that the more even pattern of urbanization may be changing: Seoul's rate of in-migration recently surged, uncontrolled settlement is becoming an increasing problem in several cities, and the informal sector appears not only viable but perhaps also on the upswing.[6]

Most prior research shows that Seoul, while still experiencing demographic increase, was not becoming dramatically more primate. Data cited by Myong-Chan Hwang and Jin-Ho Choi (1987) and Sunghee Nam (1987) clearly show a reduced rate of growth for the capital city and accelerated growth in small and medium-sized cities in the 1970s. This pattern seemed to hold in the 1980s, with regional cities continuing to grow and migration to the capital gradually on the decline (National Bureau of Statistics, 1989). The number of net immigrants to Seoul dropped steadily for a decade, from a high of over 260,000 in 1976 to a net *out*-migration of nearly 6,000 in 1986. But in 1987, the metropolitan area population increased by 84,399 due to migration. The next year, the net in-migration reached 188,556—the highest total since 1978. These same data show more modest growth via migration for outlying provinces like Taegu, Kwangju, and Kyonggi. In 1988, Pusan, the country's second largest city, lost 23,225 people to out-migration. Obviously, a two-year change in a long-term pattern might be just an aberration. But the magnitude of the reversal suggests that we may be witnessing an important turning point.[7]

A second major theme of research on South Korean cities has been the stress on the relatively low level of intracity inequality. The argument is that South Korea's economic miracle was particularly impressive because it was accompanied by little national income inequality (see Jain, 1975, for data).[8] But In-Joung Whang (1986: 215) notes that "the distribution of income has deteriorated since the late 1970s." Statistical information on the degree of inequality in urban areas in South Korea (or, for that matter, in most countries) is notoriously difficult to find. Housing provision and land ownership provide rough proxies. One surprising indicator of inequality in Seoul was data released in early 1988 that showed that 60 percent of the real estate in the city was owned by 5 percent of the population. This fact and rampant speculation in land and buildings has sent housing costs skyrocketing in the capital.[9] A more standard indicator of housing provision in non-Western countries is the extent of illegal dwelling units. Mills and Song (1979) report a decline in illegal squatter settlement housing during the 1970s. But Whang (1986: 270) reports figures that reveal a substantial increase in both squatter settlements (from 111 to 227) and illegal housing units (from 59,525 to 186,436) between 1966 and 1979. In 1988, one urban expert estimated that up to 1 million people (or about 10 percent of Seoul's total population) resided in illegal settlements (interview with Tae-Joon Kwon, July 15, 1988).

In the absence of hard data, generalization is perilous. It seems reasonable to conclude, however, that illegal housing is not on the decline in Seoul and probably is increasing. Apparently, Pusan is also experiencing housing problems. Urban sociologists at Pusan National University have reported that the number and extent of squatter settlments are definitely increasing in and around that city (interview with Dae-Ki Kang and Dong-A Hong, July 22, 1988).

The urban informal sector is empirically coextensive with squatter settlements. Illegal housing is a subset of informal sector activity, as are petty commodity production, various and sundry casual services, and informal vending. Again, good data are virtually impossible to obtain. Nam (1987: 8) uses information on "self-employed and family workers" to argue that the portion of informal sector workers rose from 25.2 to 29.7 percent of Seoul's total employed population during the 1970s. Similar data for the 1980s are not yet available. But every visitor to Seoul knows that the informal sector is thriving—in the sprawling but congested market areas, vendors sell a wide array of items ranging from baked goods and fresh fruit to shoes, luggage, and electronic equipment. The urban experts I spoke with in 1988 agreed that the informal sector was still large and that it absorbed a large portion of urban employment in both Seoul and Pusan. While detailed statistical data are lacking, again it seems unlikely that the informal sector is declining with modernization.

This section suggests a recent change in South Korean urbanization. Although it is clear that urban problems and inequalities remain less severe in South Korea than in many peripheral Third World societies (see Chapter 6), patterns of urban concentration and inequality have not disappeared. In fact, the (admittedly sketchy) data suggest that new concerns about urban unevenness in the late 1980s may be warranted. How can this be explained? Does it cast doubt on the political economy approach used to account for the earlier South Korean trajectory?

I would argue that the recent changes in urbanization can be directly linked to current political changes in South Korea. For many years, the ROK state played a critical role in the South Korean economic miracle through its control and repression of labor (Deyo, 1987, 1989; Amsden, 1989). But in the mid-1980s, the military dictatorship of Chun Doo-Hwan faced a legitimation crisis and a popular mobilization of disgruntled students, workers, and members of the middle classes (Smith and Lee, 1990). The result has been a period of political liberalization. This political loosening makes it increasingly difficult to depress wages through direct labor repression. In global markets, South Korean industry faces "the sandwich effect," in which the nation's niche in the world economy becomes increasingly squeezed between the hi-tech innovative core and the very low-wage periphery. As democratization and concomitant forces like unionization occur, South Korean wages rise and its industries cannot compete at either end of the global spectrum.

This forces business leaders and the state to face a tough question: How can labor costs be controlled to maintain international competitiveness?

One possible answer is to allow the urban informal sector to swell. I am not suggesting that the government and business elite of the ROK conspiratorially decided to promote imbalanced urban growth in the late 1980s. But a growing informal sector could provide a functional alternative to the labor repression of previous bureaucratic-authoritarian regimes. Consistent with discussions in Chapters 4 and 6, Nam (1987) argues that a large urban informal sector in Korean cities has tended to depress formal wages. This function is probably only necessary when other mechanisms to "discipline" labor are weak or absent. The semiproletarianized labor of the informal sector (see Wallerstein, Martin, and Dickinson, 1982) is not necessary when sufficiently repressive controls are in place to keep workers' pay relatively low (Portes, 1983). But as these controls are eased, informalization is one likely result. Since the informal sector particularly thrives in the largest cities, it would make sense that migrants would flow to these centers to take advantage of the new economic opportunities. Additionally, political liberalization may directly reduce the coercive power of the state to enforce policies designed to decentralize population and resources.

One advantage of this explanation is its consistency: It allows us to account for the long-term trend toward more balanced South Korean urban patterns between the mid-1960s and mid-1980s, as well as the recent reversals. For the previous period of the Korean "economic miracle," lower levels of informal sector activity (as well as the general pattern of more balanced city growth) were possible because the ROK's leaders succeeded in deploying a strong state capable of maintaining economic stability and tight labor control. During the political crisis of the mid-1980s, the state was forced to cede some basic democratic reforms—and the urban patterns soon began to change. Given the country's continuing niche in the international economy as a source of export manufactured goods, whose competitiveness is at least partially dependent on inexpensive labor, the future trajectory of South Korean cities may be closely tied to the type of *political* solutions the state employs to address economic problems.

Present and Future: Semiperipheral Urbanization

South Korea is often held up as a model of development for other Third World countries (see Hasan, 1976; Hasan and Rao, 1979; Kim and Roemer, 1979; Mills and Song, 1979). It is easy to see why. By the 1980s, the Republic of Korea had achieved results that planners and policymakers in most other Third World countries could only dream about. But the lessons of the South Korean model may not be as simple as they seem. Recent political unrest and the challenges it presents highlight this strategy's inherent limits and the contradictions within the country itself. Furthermore, the transferability of this model to other countries may run into a number of obstacles. In his article on the Northeast Asian semiperiphery, Bruce Cumings (1984: 38) points out that "the developmental 'success' of Taiwan and Korea are historically and regionally specific, and therefore provide no readily adaptable models for other developing countries interested in emulation." A major reason for South Korea's success may be related to its rather unique position in the international economic and political system.

The key to South Korea's success (at least in comparison with other less developed countries) has been its ability to take on a semiperiheral role in the world economy. In contrast to Nigeria (see Chapter 5), South Korea plays an unambiguous role. Because of the country's solid membership in the semiperiphery, there is more reason for confidence that the South Korean patterns of relatively balanced urbanization and development will continue. Until very recently there was little doubt that the ROK possessed a very strong "bureaucratic authoritarian industrializing regime (BAIR)" (Cumings, 1984). But one characteristic of the semiperipheral zone is political volatility (Wallerstein, 1976b; Chirot, 1977). As early as 1977, Gavan McCormack and Mark Selden argued that the real threat to the South Korean pattern of dependent development was political not economic. If recent changes are any indication, the decline of the BAIR and the emergence of a genuine popular movement for democratization could present an important challenge to South Korea's erstwhile smooth upward mobility in the global system. The tumultuous years of the late 1980s may have already altered South Korea's urban trajectory.

Setting aside moralistic concerns about the desirability of economic development under political authoritarianism, as well as consideration of the recent economic setbacks and political turmoil, there were always strict *limits* to South Korea's potential. Despite the growth rates and balanced urban patterns during the height of the South Korean economic miracle, this country was still an example of dependent development. Like other members of the modern semiperiphery, South Korea is dependent on the core to provide capital, technology, and markets (Evans, 1979b; Caporaso, 1981; Cumings, 1984, D. Smith, 1993).[10] Though the restructuring of the world economy that created the conditions for semiperipheral industrialization may create serious problems for industrial labor in the advanced countries, few commentators believe that South Korea, Taiwan, or even powerful Brazil will achieve core status anytime soon. The transition from semiperiphery to core is an exceedingly difficult one, with only Japan succeeding in this century. Short of making this leap into the core, South Korean urbanization and development patterns will continue to follow a dynamic distinct from the more autonomous growth in the core areas of the world economy.

Recognizing the likely limits of dependent development should not obscure its successes. But can other nations replicate the South Korean model? Some unique and "accidental" factors recommend pessimism. One of Korea's key advantages was its late incorporation into the world economy and the planned development of infrastructure and industry under Japanese imperial rule. Another advantage accrued to South Korea because of an accident of geography that placed it in a location of great geopolitical importance. These factors allowed for a different urban and economic trajectory than in most other Third World countries, peripheralized during much earlier periods. Planners in other countries cannot go back and change their nations' histories. Yet the success of a strong state committed to economic development and not encumbered by entrenched elites (after the Japanese expulsion) may lead to some policy implications. A fuller development of these implications must be set aside here.

Conclusion

The main theme of this chapter is by now a very familiar one. In analyzing the development of South Korea's urban system and the internal characteristics of its cities, it is of tantamount importance to examine the world-systemic context in which changes take place. This is not to say that the prior level of development of Korean society is not important. The presence of a relatively advanced agrarian nation with a well-developed system of cities is influential—and this influence is heightened given the very late timing of Korean incorporation. Nor should the internal processes of Korean society be trivialized. Indeed, the importance of transportation and communication infrastucture (factors usually understood as "ecological") was already stressed. But rather than see these as isolated variables explaining urban patterns, this analysis places them in their historical and political economic context. It attempts to link external and internal dynamics. This is not always easy, and sometimes it leads to a complicated series of linkages. But this chapter (as well as each of the other case studies) is designed to demonstrate that this historical-structural analysis can point to general patterns and mechanisms of dependent urbanization in the world-system.

What conclusion can be drawn about the utility of the concept of "semiperipheral urbanization"? On the one hand, this chapter clearly demonstrates that South Korea's semiperipheral status is a crucial context for understanding the form and function of cities and city growth. On the other hand, the South Korean case also cautions against overgeneralization. Too rigidly linking semiperipheral status with a definitive urban pattern (e.g., less uneven urbanization than in the periphery) is perilous since a variety of other factors impact urban processes. In particular, politics and the state appear to be very important determinants of the trajectory of economic growth, urbanization, and other macrostructural change in South Korea (and, most likely, in other newly industrializing semiperipheral societies as well).

Obviously, there are many significant difference between the urban dynamics and outcomes of various semiperipheral countries. For instance, it is clearly necessary to distinquish between recently industrialized, upwardly mobile members of this stratum (such as South Korea and Taiwan) and declining, older industrial semiperipheral states (for example, Spain or New Zealand). And even among non-Western semiperipheral countries, there are many salient differences: indigenous development prior to contact, timing and historical context of incorporation, contemporary state strength and institutionalization of democracy, degree of societal proletarianization, power and economic base of the dominant classes, and so forth. Each of these factors can have major implications for urbanization. Aware of these distinctions, I am wary of applying a unitary concept of "semiperipheral urbanization" to all countries occupying this international status. It is better to use ideas like semiperipherality as a starting point for detailed studies that carefully consider world historical, national, and local political economic factors as proximate determinants of urbanization. That is precisely the sort of analysis offered here and in Chapter 5.

8

Urbanization in Global Perspective: Summary, Synthesis, and Policy Recommendations

The rapid growth of cities in the contemporary Third World raises interesting intellectual issues for social scientists and presents vexing problems for planners and policymakers. The overriding theme of this book is that a proper understanding of this pattern of urbanization, as well as any useful diagnosis of its pathologies, must begin by locating cities and the decisionmakers who shape them in their world-systemic context. City growth is part of a set of a truly global processes that reproduce and extend hierarchial social, political, and economic relationships in the capitalist international system. Failure to grasp this fundamental reality leads, at best, to a partial and distorted view of the urban process. Research that fails to adopt the global perspective has limited social science value; policy planning and implementation that ignores it is unlikely to succeed.

To empirically ground my global perspective on cities, I used both quantitative and qualitative techniques. The cross-national statistical analysis presented in Chapter 2 demonstrates that there are general patterns of urbanization that vary by world-system zone. Regression analysis shows that a quantitative measure of the roles nations play in the international system is causally related to temporal changes in overall level of urbanization and lead-city primacy.

Based on this quantitative evidence, the historical case studies begin with the premise that world-system roles are important and that membership in the peripheral stratum may lead to more urban unevenness than is experienced in semiperipheral countries. To be "macroanalytical," these studies focus on world regions that are largely peripheral, but they also contain deviant cases that are distinctly semiperipheral. In one sense, this historical research offers in-depth follow-ups on the quantitative results, providing richer data on the differences and similarities between the periphery and semiperiphery in terms of urbanization and development.

The historical case studies also perform another function: They get at the *mechanisms* of urban processes and expose the subtleties of "conjuctural causation" (Ragin, 1987). In this way, the analysis moves beyond the relatively static generalizations of cross-national quantitative research and on to the complexity of concrete historical chains of causation. This strategy not only illuminates the origins and dynamics of long-term urban growth (and its relationship to development) but also provides some insight into how and why certain nations and regions experienced peripheralization while others followed paths of dependent development. At the general level of methodological axioms, the point is that "history really does matter" (Tilly, 1982) and that our goal should be to arrive at historically grounded "bounded generalizations" (Skocpol and Somers, 1980) about uneven urbanization and socioeconomic development.

For example, one key finding is that the timing and nature of incorporation into the modern world-system has important implications on development trajectories in general and urban origins and growth in particular. Early European penetration into non-Western areas generally led to primate city patterns (either by promoting the growth of an indigenous center or by initiating the establishment of a new settlement). These unbalanced urban systems tended to be further reinforced if the newly penetrated area followed the prototypical pattern of primary product extraction, which was characteristic of the nineteenth-century periphery. Later capitalist penetration often had a very different effect, enhancing the likelihood of dependent development into a semiperipheral zone and promoting more even urban growth. The basic reasons are twofold. First, late incorporation, in a number of instances, was highly correlated with higher levels of indigenous socioeconomic and urban development. Second, later penetration occurred in a different phase of world-system expansion and development, when dependent cities and the surrounding societies came to play different roles in the international system. The need to be sensitive to the world historical timing of incorporation and city origin reminds us of the limited role of sweeping, nomothetic generalizations about "the city" or even "the Third World city" (for similiar arguments, see Armstrong and McGee, 1985; Sachs, 1988).

Building Synthetic Urban Theory

While my research cautions against formulating overly general propositions about urbanization and development, theory building *is* one of its explicit goals. At the broadest level, of course, I am identifying with a political economy of the world-system view of cities and urban processes. But this does not imply a blanket rejection of opposing theoretical traditions. Human ecological approaches to Third World cities and modernization theory research on socioeconomic development generated important empirical results and often highlighted key variables. To avoid "throwing the baby out with the bathwater," researchers should not ignore the insights of these traditions.

The research presented in this book and other recent studies of cities in the Third World (see Meyer, 1986; Bradshaw, 1987; London, 1987; London and Smith, 1988) provides evidence that both world-system analysis and ecological-developmentalist perspectives are analytically useful. As a result, some researchers conclude that we should avoid "current theoretical and ideological particularism" by modeling research to simultaneously assess the competing approaches, without giving logical priority to either paradigm (Bradshaw, 1987). While this may be a reasonable strategy for some types of quantitative analysis, it provides little theoretical guidance for more detailed historical work. More critically, it represents a retreat into eclecticism. It sidesteps the real challenge; which is to construct a synthetic theoretical approach that melds the useful theoretical elements of the competing approaches into coherent guiding principles and explanations. That is the purpose of the following discussion.

A Historical Aside

Perhaps the major failing of developmentalist approaches was the tendency to fixate on Third World cities or national urban systems as relatively closed system, ignoring these societies' dependency relations with the international system. But actually, the notion of the importance of the global economy's effect on urbanization and cities roles within the international system is not a new one. In fact, a global perspective on urban organization did *not* originate in the 1970s with the political economy of the world-system school or with the new urban sociology. Surprisingly, most of the pieces of this theoretical orientation were already present in the writings of the "classical" human ecologist, Roderick McKenzie.[1]

In a series of articles written in the late 1920s and early 1930s, McKenzie claims that an understanding of the expanding world market and world economy critically affected the growth of cities and the organization of industrial society. His 1926 article in the *American Journal of Sociology*, outlining "the scope of human ecology," places the world as a social system at center stage: "Civilisation, with its vast galaxy of communities, each of which is more or less dependent upon some or all of the others, may be thought of as an ecological distribution or organization" (McKenzie, 1926: 21). In a later essay, "Industrial Expansion and the Interrelations of Peoples" (1933), McKenzie argues that "the history of modern civilisation is the history of European expansion" in which "different European peoples have taken the lead at different times" (McKenzie, 1933: 123). Noting the "center"/"frontier" structure and "cyclic pattern" of the process, he claims that this process has "furnished the most effective territorial division of labor the world has ever known" (McKenzie, 1933: 126). But he also asserts that the "backward countries . . . have come to depend on the United States as a source of capital and as a market for their export products, they have come under the economic dominance and, in some cases, the political hegemony of this country" (McKenzie, 1933: 129).

To contemporary readers, this sounds eerily familar. Even some of the language foreshadows Wallerstein's descriptions of the modern world-system. Although he was certainly no Marxist, McKenzie emphasizes the role that 400 years of capitalist expansion has had on social change, the ubiquity of core-periphery structures, patterns of cyclic uneven development, and the exploitative nature of dependency relations.

With this brief digression into the history of sociological thought, my intent is not to claim that McKenzie was, in fact, the first world-system theorist. He apparently never fully developed the implications of his seminal ideas about the world economy. And other parts of his work clearly fit with the developmentalist assumptions of later modernization theorists. But McKenzie's legacy offers some threads to which the themes of this book can be knitted in the human ecology tradition. Of course, my research also draws theoretical inspiration from neo-Marxist political economy. Thus, I would argue that a global perspective on urbanization provides an intellectual juncture where the theoretical perspectives meet and offers an opportunity for synthesis.

The World-System and Human Ecology

Human ecology and various forms of urban political economy are almost invariably seen as theoretical (and even ideological) foes (Walton, 1979b, 1981; Feagin, 1988: chapter 2). The differences between the basic ecological and world-system perspectives on Third World cities are fundamental and should not be minimized. Human ecological studies tend to ignore "the built environment," make technological determinist assumptions, downplay political forces that shape cities, and assume that urban systems functionally adapt in ways that maximize benefits for the aggregate (Feagin, 1988: chapter 2).

Nevertheless, there are some points of convergence and potential synthesis (Hawley, 1984). For example, the political economy of the world-system's emphasis on international stratification and class structures is consistent with ecological notions of the ubiquity of hierarchy and dominance. Human ecology provides a very general image of the emergence of hierarchies based on "key functions" in particular communities, regions, or larger systems (Hawley, 1950). The dependency/world-system analysis of the type presented in this book focuses on historically and empirically specific systems, and it explicitly links dominance and subordination to the capitalist organization of the world-economy. But both approaches stress the material basis of social organization (whether as "sustenance organization" or "mode of production") and asymmetrical relations of power and exchange. The international political economy approach pours particular content into the extremely abstract form of human ecological models. While this abandons strict "all times/all places" nomotheticism in favor of a more nuanced historical understanding, it is consistent with the scientific goal of building bounded generalizations, discussed earlier.

The emphasis on materialist factors affecting urbanization and other macrostructural change prompts ecologists to take a special interest in the impact of technology. Technology helps communities to adapt to the natural and social environment. In turn, it impacts the spatial distribution of population and the social organization of activities. Unfortunately, this is a variable that political economy approaches, including world-system analysis, tend to downplay or ignore. Yet the importance of technology and technological change in setting broad parameters for urbanization and/or economic development are obvious. Particularly in reference to spatial dimensions of an urban system or the extent of urban primacy, transportation and communication network are crucial. Consistent with standard human ecological arguments, infrastructure shapes and reinforces patterns of city and urban system growth. Cities that grew in the era of the automobile *are* very different from those that developed when railroads predominated or during the days of the horse and buggy.

But while technology is critical, my research shows that it must be seen as more than a collective adaptation the environment. The way technology is used (and even how it is developed) is the product of struggles between societal groups with conflicting political and economic interests. Roads, railroads, shipping facilities, airports, telegraph or telephone lines, and telecommunications networks are all outcomes not of smooth, natural processes of innovation and diffusion but of political economic battles. In most cases, these contests are rather one-sided, and the resultant transportation and communications systems are much more likely to facilitate the interests and needs of wealthy and powerful people.

The provision of specific types of infrastructure (where and when to build highways, ports, rapid transit, "smart-wired" buildings, and so on) becomes implicit urban policy. The construction or selective upgrading of particular roads, railroads, and ports to accommodate the evacuation of particular export products and the disproportionate expenditure of scarce national resources on telecommunication and highway grids in capital cities are bound to skew city growth and settlement patterns. It is a mistake to see these changes as driven by blind technological change: They are the result of policymaking decisions that usually reflect dominant class interests. Elite power and class structures influence urban outcomes in this way, as well as through more explicit policymaking at the level of national and local government action. Traditional human ecological studies often do not fully develop the political economic nature of this process. They miss the extent to which urban patterns are channeled by the interests of elites or the prerogatives of capital accumulation.

A global perspective helps unravel the *specificity* of these class and power dynamics. Especially in peripheral and semiperipheral zones of the international system, the interests and policies of urban elites must be placed in the context of their international class alliances. As we have seen, when power is concentrated in a single city in a peripheral society, elite decisions seem to reflect an urban bias. But probing deeper, what appears to be a city-versus-countryside resource issue actually reduces to the interests of Third World elites and their transnational allies versus the interests of the masses and genuine socioeconomic development. The crucial lesson is that urbanization is a political economic process hinging on explicit or implicit policymaking by societal elites who are tied to the international system in particular ways. This suggests that city growth under traditional dependency in a monoexporting peripheral area should be quite different from urbanization in the new international division of labor in a semiperipheral nation dependent on export-oriented industry. In this way, placing cities and urban dynamics in both world historical time and world-system zone helps us to make sense of the key functions that human ecologists conceptualize as central to determining social and spatial organization.

Unlike more flaccid variants of modernization theory, human ecological models of city growth suggest some concrete starting points for investigations of cities and urbanization. The idea of asymmetrical hierarchies, the key role of transportation and communication systems, and the focus on sustenance organization are useful and mesh with the perspective developed in this book. But ecological research results need to be interpreted using a theoretical filter, *beginning with* the orienting assumptions of international political economy. The initial unit of analysis can only remain the "community" in so far as that is "the global village." The driving force behind urbanization and development must be located in the political and economic interests of key actors and the imperatives of capital accumulation on a world scale.

Overurbanization, Proletarianization, and the State

Modernization theory argued that urbanization, industrialization, and human progress reinforced one another and grew together. But as early as the 1950s and 1960s, scholars became aware of the possible negative developmental effects of overurbanization (see, for example, Davis and Golden, 1954; Gibbs and Martin, 1962). They argued that population concentration in large Third World cities was increasing so quickly that demographic growth was outstripping the newly urbanized societies' ability to adjust, absorb, and cope with the human influx. The result was the generation and intensification of serious problems: grinding poverty, massive unemployment, inadequate services, social unrest, increasing crime, political instability, and so forth.

While the conditions described were real, the concept of overurbanization was subject to a great deal of criticism. N.V. Sovani (1964: 21) provides a comprehensive critique, concluding "that the definition of over-urbanization is unsatisfactory and vague; that the analysis of the causes and consequences of over-urbanization developed so far is tenuous and oversimplified." Major monographs on comparative urbanization in subsequent decades emphasizes the ambiguity of the idea of overurbanization (Breese, 1966; Hawley, 1971; Castells, 1977). But recently, "the overurbanization thesis" has made a comeback. A number of authors claim that rapid population increases in large cities in the the underdeveloped world constitute a major obstacle to economic, social, and political development (Riddell, 1978, 1980; Todaro, 1981; Gugler, 1982; Bienen, 1984; Rondonelli, 1985).

Previously, I have addressed the multifarious aspects of the renewed debate about overurbanization (D. Smith, 1987a). To reiterate, my argument is that framing the issue simply in terms of urban-rural disparities or "spatio-demographic imbalance" is misleading. Conceptualizing overurbanization as the basic problem focuses attention on urban bias and spatial antagonism. But this may actually obfuscate the true nature of domination and class conflict in these societies. It is true that Third World cities are centers of power and privilege. But there is also a great deal of inequality *within* these urban areas. The basic conflict really is not between rural and urban classes; rather, it pits the urban-based elite (in alliance with international capital) against both urban and rural masses. While the conditions associated with overurbanization may mean misery and hardship for most city residents and may be quite a burden on efforts to generate genuine socioeconomic development in a poor nation, they may actually benefit some people. They also may actually be *functional* for surplus extraction under the conditions of dependent capitalism.

The existence of large urban informal sectors illustrates this argument. Modernization theory anticipated that the traditional bazaar economy would gradually be replaced by modern capitalist firms. But as we have seen, even in a relatively advanced semiperipheral nation like South Korea, informal sector activity appears to be increasing rather than declining.

A global perspective explains this apparent paradox. The conditions that force people into informal labor—high rates of inequality and poverty in rapidly growing cities—are very undesirable for the masses of people. But they also provide business opportunities for formal sector companies and entrepreneurs. Informal sector workers perform many types of socially useful and necessary but extremely inexpensive work.

Once again, my working hypothesis is that this phenomenon would vary between periphery and semiperiphery. The case studies show that this relationship does not always hold. Noncore societies do *not* always evolve toward this form of labor control. Intra-urban economic structure, like systems of cities, emerge over long periods of history. Portes (1983) argues that historical factors explaining the political relationship between the state, labor, and capital are critical. Since the defining characteristic of informal economic activities is their "common functional relationship to the modern capitalist economy" (Portes, 1983: 163), the extent to which the state has consistently repressed labor to control wage demands affects the size and importance of this sector. Where government repression has always been high and formal sector wages depressed, the cost advantages of informal enterprises are drastically reduced. In areas where the the historical pattern of incorporation and subsequent economic change laid the groundwork for a strong bureaucratic-authoritarian state, capable of promoting dependent development while repressing labor, the informal sector will be smaller and less important and extreme levels of urban poverty and inequality will be less pronounced. But in nations following a more "liberal" tradition (early industrialization and worker organization, establishment of postcolonial democratic governments), high levels of informal sector activity are likely. The comparative case studies support these arguments. The South Korean case is particularly interesting since recent political loosening and liberalization seems to have stimulated urban informal sector growth. Ironically, Third World variants of democracy and unionization, by making regulated labor more costly, increase the need for a large informal sector to buoy global competitiveness.

A focus on the issues of the "informalization" of work, and the role of the informal sector in the global economy provides a link to a general issue in macrosociological theory while countering a standard critique of depdendency/world-system analysis. This perspective is frequently charged with overemphazing international processes and placing too much stress on external determination of change in Third World societies. There is a need to link broad world-system dynamics to internal national and local changes. My analysis suggests that one of the ways this can be done is by studying the international division of labor's effect on the master process of proletarianization in different societies. Tilly (1981: 174) provides a concise definition:

> Proletarianization is a set of processes that increases the number of people who lack control of the means of production and who survive by selling their labor power. From the perspective of ordinary peoples' lives, proletarianization is the single most far-reaching social change that has occurred in the Western world over the past few hundred years and that is going on in the world as a whole today.

But this is not a gradual, uniform process that leads inexorably to free wage labor everywhere. Instead, areas and nations that play different roles in the world-economy and/or follow different historical trajectories will vary in their form of "labor control" and the extent to which their workforces are composed of wage laborers. My case studies show that in noncore African and Asian countries, there are large semiproletarianized labor forces involved in informal sector activity (on the similar pattern in Latin America, see Portes, 1985b; Safa, 1987). Both urban primacy and high levels of intra-urban inequality appear to be linked to economies at intermediary levels of proletarianization. Urbanization patterns may be only one of a number of important social changes associated with proletarianization levels. Tilly (1981) suggests that a better understanding of this process could be the key to explaining a whole range of social and demographic changes that are usually vaguely linked to modernization and development. Recent research shows that informalization is becoming increasingly integral to advanced core economies as they adapt to changes in the new international division of labor (Mingione, 1987; Portes and Sassen-Koob, 1987; Lozano, 1989; Ross and Trachte, 1990). This suggests that the process is not only uneven but may also be reversible. Some writers believe this may herald the beginning of an era where "the Third World comes home" to advanced industrial cities (and brings its attendant problems) (Ross and Trachte, 1983). At any rate, further empirical research on full and partial proletarianization and theoretical refinement in this area provides a conceptual bridge between international and local dynamics. It promises real progress in the construction of better theories of macrostructural change.

The discussion of the informal sector and proletarianization reminds us of the key role *politics* plays in the process of urbanization. This is something that both human ecologists and world-system analysts have tended to slight. But it is crucial to "bring the state back in" (see Evans, Rueschmeyer, and Skocpol, 1985). Local and national governments are the loci of explicit (and probably more importantly) implicit urban policymaking. The state becomes the fulcrum that elites and dominant classes, in tandem with transnational allies, use to propel macrostructural change in directions favorable to their interests.

The role of states in the process of informalization has been discussed. The state also directly and indirectly influences urban concentration and unevenness in systems of cities. In the West African or Southeast Asian peripheral countries, government policies reinforce and exacerbate urban bias. The role of the state is particularly crucial in semiperipheral nations undergoing dependent development. This process requires "negotiated dependency" through strategies such as primary product cartels, restrictions on foreign capital, state partnerships with multinational corporations, and geopolitical maneuvering between core superpowers (see Chirot, 1977; Evans, 1979b, Evans, 1985). The South Korean case illustrates this particularly well. The "bureaucratic-authoritarian industrializing regime" (Cumings, 1984) successfully planned and coordinated "the economic miracle" from the mid-1960s to the mid-1980s. Many of the development strategies had spatio-demographic consequences, either concentrating population in Seoul (the growth of the government technocracy) or dispersing growth to the provinces (the development of regional industrial complexes). This prompts Nam (1987) to conceptualize "the state as an 'urban manager'" directing spatial planning processes in the interests of capital. While this may accord even the South Korean bureaucracy a planning efficacy greater than it truly possesses, it underlines the myopia of models of urbanization that leave the state out. Urbanization is a political process. Both ecological theories that ignore politics in favor of technodemographic determinism and world-system approaches that ignore the state because they insist on economic reductionism fail to grasp an essential aspect of city growth.

Vertically Integrated Theory

To digest and organize this book's theoretical lessons, the reader is referred back to Figure 1.1. This schematic shows a sequence of macrostructures, beginning with the global system itself, that set progressively narrower parameters for urban outcomes. I have chosen the image of smaller "windows" of possible variability, instead of deterministic causal arrows, because this figure is intended to provide a general theoretical orientation for research (i.e., to point to the key elements) rather than pretending to provide a verifiable model for testing. In directly linking infrastructure to urbanization, I am acknowledging the proximate causal effect of transportation and communication networks and technology on the evolution of cities and urban systems. For this causal link, the human ecology perspective deserves acknowledgment. But infrastructure provision itself is a product of political economic processes emanating from the state and class structure. At this point, political struggle comes in. In turn, basic political economic conditions within a society are constrained by the nation's role in the international system. And this role is limited by the phase of world-system development: Certain international niches are more likely to be available during periods of expansion or contraction; particular economic specialization arises in response to historical economic imperatives of the system as a whole. By depicting an image of *"vertically integrated processes* passing through a network from the international level to the urban hinterland" (Walton, 1979a: 164), Figure 1.1 begins to capture the complexity of the global perspective on urbanization developed in this book.

Practical Implications

Urban planners and policymakers rarely dialogue with world-system researchers. World-system analysts are good at critiquing development policy, but they rarely recommend concrete policy alternatives.[2] Much of the planning literature eschews "radical" analysis altogether. This concluding section is designed to stimulate a little dialogue.

A major problem with the planning literature lies in its uncritical implicit reliance on the developmentalist perspective for theoretical guidance. One example is a World Bank publication (Renaud, 1981) that provides an overview of national urbanization policies in developing countries and is explicitly designed to give strategic advice to practitioners. It cites a wealth of quantitative data and lists a series of valid empirical generalizations about urban patterns and trends. While the explicit goal of the volume is to redress problems of urban imbalances and inequalities, the analysis focuses exclusively on particular nations' political and economic policy failures and repeatedly suggests that urbanization in developing countries is in the "expanding" phase of a transition to the "mature" city-systems of the "advanced economies" (Renaud, 1981: esp. pp. 57–59). By uncritically accepting this implicit modernization theory stance, the author discounts the possibility of external constraints due to international dependency. This leads to an incomplete and slanted assessment of specific national situations, and it vitiates the efforts to provide useful policy recommendations. The analysis in my book suggests that the global perspective on urbanization may have some practical implications that could lead to more pragmatic policy formulation.

The Constraints of International Dependence

The two most basic findings relevant to policy in this book are (1) that all nations have not, cannot, and will not follow "the Western path" of urbanization and development, and (2) that the external effects of various types of international dependence do impose major constraints on urban development in noncore Third World societies. To be effective, policies intended to control rapid cityward migration, excessive urban migration, uncontrolled growth, squatter settlements, and a multitude of other urban problems *must* consider the economic and political effects of factors such as international trade and export concentration, foreign investment, and global political alliances.

For example, I have shown that certain types of investment policies promote different types of urban growth. Policies to promote import substitution industrialization often lead to both a concentration of people and resources in very large cities and higher levels of intraurban inequality. But development strategies based on export manufacturing may lead to a more balanced intra-urban and city system patterns since proximity to large income-skewed urban markets is irrelevant for this type of industry. Of course, successful implementation of a self-sustained, export-led strategy is not a viable option for many countries that have undergone peripheralization. Both class structure and infrastructure mitigate against this type of activity in some of these societies. Entrenched classes with long-standing material interests in a agrarian monoexport status quo, for instance, are likely to resist policies that would lead to autonomous industrial growth (for a particularly interesting historical example of this in colonial Charleston, South Carolina, see

D. Smith, 1987b).   Similarly, "dendritic" patterns of transportation and communication designed for evacuating primary products are poorly suited to the type of integrated economic space conducive to export-led industry.

One of the lessons of this book is that historical patterns *do* matter. This makes it impossible to provide generic responses to dependent urbanization across various countries. To provide a useful diagnosis of specific Third World urban problems, it is necessary to perform concrete analysis of the ways in which class relations, infrastructural development, production facilities, and spatial distribution of people and resources are articulated with the global system. Close attention to what Raymond Duvall (1978) calls "the general referential contexts" of dependency requires specialized knowledge of particular countries, which is readily available to indigenous scholars and planners but only accessible to outside researchers through intensive case studies. For both, sensitivity to the conceptual apparatus of the global perspective on urbanization is necessary in order to filter out the specific manifestations of dependent urbanism in particular cases. While this call for more research may seem odious to practical-minded planners, it is clearly superior to the alternative: continued reliance on cross-national generalizations and recipes that ultimately are based on unwarranted (and inaccurate) assumptions about the universality of urbanization and development trajectories.

Lessons of Semiperipheral Urbanization?

In this book and elsewhere (Smith and Nemeth, 1990) I have argued that urbanization in the semiperiphery should be considered distinct from city growth in the periphery. While the evidence was a bit spotty, it appears that semiperipheral urbanization is less uneven (in terms of both city systems and intracity inequality), more generative of economic growth, guided by stronger states more dedicated to genuinely development-oriented planning, and so on.

If this is the case, what can planners and policymakers in peripheral countries learn from the experiences of the relative success stories of the semiperiphery? Taiwan and South Korea, for instance, are often held up as shining examples for others to follow. Two distinct types of caveats are in order. First, the historical conditions that gave dependent development its initial impetus are usually missing from more underdeveloped peripheral regions. This means that there is reason to doubt that the semiperipheral models will be readily transferable. For example, the Northeast Asian model cannot be abstracted from a concatenation of historical events and geographic accidents in South Korea and Taiwan. The context is not very similar to those of, say, contemporary peripheral Southeast Asia. Mechanical imitation of South Korean or Taiwanese development strategies is not a panacea for peripheral societies, for the same reason that policies imported directly from the industrial core often fail. Different urbanization and development trajectories necessitate the formulation of distinct planning strategies.

Second, it is important to qualify the semiperipheral success stories. In Chapter 5, the mixed results of dependent development in Nigeria are reviewed (and the results on urbanization were inconsistent, too). One could argue that Nigeria is a very marginal case, and perhaps this country has not really moved into the semiperiphery after all. But even the less ambiguous cases of Taiwan and South Korea have a downside. These nations remain in subordinate, constrained positions in the international system. Like other semiperipheral societies, they still rely on core nations to supply capital, technology, and markets (Evans, 1979b; Caporaso, 1981; Cumings, 1984; Deyo, 1987). Few commentators predict that South Korea, Taiwan, or even powerful, resource-abundant Brazil will join the elite circle of core nations anytime soon. And the economic advances of these nations have not come without costs. The price of semiperipheral dependent development has been the rise of bureaucratic-authoritarian states (Frank, 1981b; Cumings, 1984).

The lack of political democracy in countries like South Korea is a long-standing concern of scholars and politicians (Han, 1974; Wright, ed., 1975; McCormack and Selden, 1977; Koo, 1987; Smith and Lee, 1990). Furthermore, repression is a costly way to govern. South Korea's and Taiwan's economic vulnerability to global recessions (or increasing core protectionism), combined with these nations' ostensible commitment to the ideology of Western democracy, make them particularly susceptible to large-scale unrest and political vulnerability (events in South Korea in the late 1980s bear this out). So even if it were possible to replicate this path, peripheral planners should recognize that the model has pitfalls, too.

Nevertheless, recognizing the limits of dependent development should not obscure its real accomplishments. While planners in peripheral countries cannot orchestrate the historical conjuctures of the Korean or Taiwanese experiences, there are some general lessons. First, cases like South Korea and Taiwan, whatever their weaknesses and however specific their historical context, do demonstrate that it is possible to achieve economic growth without increasing inequality. Although these countries provide no simple prescription for this desirable pattern, they do suggest that planning for individual and interregional equity can promote economic growth and vice versa. Second, the East Asian newly industrializing countries (NICs) and other semiperipheral nations make the case for active, effective, enforceable, state-directed planning. Strong, even repressive, governments among "late developers" appear to be the norm for even moderately successful cases (Chirot, 1977). Throughout the twentieth century, South Korea, for instance, was ruled by colonial and later national bureaucrats and military men. Neither a traditional elite nor free enterprise played a leading role. In spite of the danger of repression and the loss of political freedoms that state planning implies (and the wariness that Western-trained intellectuals harbor for it), this form of state control may be necessary to solve the pressing economic and demographic problems facing underdeveloped societies (see Heilbroner, 1980).

Cities and Politics

The political nature of cities is quite obvious to planners. As practitioners trying to formulate and implement various types of policies on a day-to-day basis, they need no theoretical argument to convince them of the reality of political conflicts, struggles, and compromises. Texts and articles on planning allude to its political nature as an important issue (see, for example, Lo and Salih, 1978; Mehmet, 1978; Renaud, 1981; Rodwin, 1981). But there are crucial differences in the way politics are conceptualized.

One common approach focuses on "political constraints" to the formulation and implementation of well-designed policies (Renaud, 1981). Planning itself is a purely technical matter of solving problems to maximize social welfare. Politics, like a storm or an earthquake, can upset the planning process. It has stochastic effects, except that political stability is better for policy implementation than instability. This is a technocratic and functional model that ignores the real substance of political power and conflict. Social classes or even competing "interests groups" are rarely mentioned. This has practical implications. Bertrand Renaud (1981), for instance, makes a number of recommendations to promote more balanced urban and development patterns that would require the redistribution of resources, power, and privilege. These policies probably would be social desirable, but they run directly into conflict with the interests of urban businesses, elites, and dominant classes. Ignoring (or failing to comprehend) those interests hardly improves the prospects that these suggestions will be implemented.

A second planning approach to politics is more cognizant of the powerful in society and the effect they have on policymaking (Mehmet, 1978; Rodwin, 1981). This view acknowledges that elites, usually based in large cities, are an obstacle to equitable planning. The political process is likely to result in urban policies biased toward creating cities and urban systems fitting the needs of the powerful. These policies take many forms: explicit or implicit, national or local, active or passive. The resultant pattern of city growth embodies urban bias, disproportionately benefits urban elites, and exerts a parasitic effect on national development. While this approach begins to identify obstacles to equitable planning, it shares the problem of all urban bias views: It overemphasizes spatial conflict (city versus countryside), and it remains very vague about the precise material interests of the urban elites.

A global perspective suggests that urban "imbalances" and inequality are better understood by focusing on the economic function of the "overurbanized" city in peripheral capitalism. These inequalities and the elites who often oppose policies to remedy them are linked to the role dependent societies play in the world-economy. To redress the problems of uneven urbanization, planners must consider external dependency relationships, indigenous power structures, and the links between the two. The nature of the alliances with multinational capital, the types of products manufactured and exported, and the strength and composition of the state and/or the national bourgeoisie are some of the factors establishing political economic constraints for policymaking in the Third World. If planners are to arrive at truly practical policies for addressing the urban problems of these societies, they will have to take the impact of international dependence into account.

Global Urbanization: A Research Agenda

Calling for further research is a rather hackneyed device for drawing a book or article to a close. But in this case, it seems particularly appropriate. By its very nature, the terrain this book covers is limited. While the cross-national analysis of Chapter 2 attempts to provide a genuinely global view of urbanization in the world-system, the case studies that make up the bulk of the volume cover just two world regions. They fill holes in prior research by applying dependency/world-system concepts to areas where this perspective had been less extensively used. These case studies, in conjunction with the existing body of literature on dependent urbanization in Latin America, provide a relatively sound empirical foundation for tentative generalizations about dependent cities in the Third World. But they only raise tantalizing questions about how a global perspective on urbanization might address cities in the rest of the world.

One theoretical task that comparative case studies facilitate is demarcating the limits of conceptual analogies (see Stinchcombe, 1979, discussed in Chapter 3). Further historical-structural analysis of urbanization patterns in different contexts could help deepen or limit the analogy of dependent urbanization. More case studies are also needed to assess the usefulness of discussing semiperipheral urbanization. Further research on urban growth in the contemporary Third World might contribute to both of these projects. But historical research on colonial cities in early stages of world-economy expansion, regardless of their contemporary world-system status, also provides fertile ground for theoretically productive studies. My research on colonial Charleston, South Carolina, is explicitly designed to deepen the analogy of dependent urbanization (D. Smith, 1987b). Anthony King's (1976, 1990a) comparative research on colonial cities also provides a wealth of theoretically rich empirical material.

Another potentially fruitful focus is on the Second World. One of the major critiques of the world-system perspective in general involves its putative inability to deal with noncapitalist societies (see Chirot, 1986). Recent events in Eastern Europe forcefully remind scholars that even those self-proclaimed "socialist" societies were always part of the modern world-system. This suggests the need for a serious investigation of the degree to which macrostructural patterns and changes in places like Eastern Europe, China, or Cuba can be related to the role these nations play in the overarching world-system. Has Eastern Europe undergone dependent development and become part of the semiperiphery? Can we meaningfully talk about peripheral or semiperipheral urbanization in so-called "socialist" societies? A timely article (Kennedy and Smith, 1989) explored these issues for a small portion of Eastern Europe; obviously, much more research is needed.

Touching on a current "hot topic": How does global economic restructuring impact urban patterns? Is there a fundamental change in a global system based on "flexible production," "global post-Fordism," and so on. We must poise these questions and move on.

Finally, if a comprehensive understanding of urbanization in the world-system is the goal, the implications of this perspective for core cities and the urban systems of advanced nations must be developed and studied. This book focuses on the way in which world-system development channeled and constrained city growth in the periphery and semiperiphery. What of the cities and urban societies at the other end of the dependency relationships? Obviously, *these* urban patterns and processes are intermeshed in global dynamics, too. The process of capital accumulation on a world scale deeply affects their structures, as well. What effects, for instance, does the restructuring of the international division of labor have on U.S. urban areas and on cities in other core nations? Fortunately, preliminary work is also being done on this topic. Joe Feagin's (1988) study of Houston and King's (1990b) of London, as well as several chapters in a book edited by Smith and Feagin (1987), stand out as pioneering exemplars of research linking the growth of particular core cities to global restructuring. Studies are also needed that focus on city systems of core nations and the changes in urban hierarchies, tying these to world-system dynamics.

This book does not suggest simple formulaic answers to questions about the impact of global changes on core cities. My attention has been focused on dependent urbanization: city growth in the core should follow a very different trajectory. But if the basic argument of the global perspective on urbanization is correct, it suggests a reorientation in the way we look at cities in our own and other core societies. The pattern of uneven development that is so pronounced in the Third World may be present in core economies as well. Urban policymakers who consider the changing role of the United States in the contemporary world economy may arrive at quite different national urban strategies from those suggested by traditional social science. At the very least, a conceptual shift of this type would force urban sociologists and planners to face an undeniable reality: that our cities, like those of the Third World, are enmeshed in the diverse global processes that constitute the modern world-system.

Notes

Introduction

1. The cited article appeared in a special section of the *Los Angeles Times,* entitled "Seeking a New World," on December 18, 1990.

2. The following observations on Jakarta are based on my impressions when I visited the city during September 1994 as part of a research trip, sponsored by a University of California-funded project on "Commodity Chains and Industrial Districts in the Pacific Rim." During the visit, my major focus was on visiting factories and interviewing businesspeople and experts associated with the garment industry.

3. For two excellent summaries of the general debate about the demise of modernization theory and the rise of the dependency/world-system approach, see Portes, 1976, and Valenzuela and Valenzuela, 1978.

4. This discussion of basic assumptions draws on a similar treatment by Feagin, 1988: chapter 2 (esp. pp. 23 and 24). But while Feagin is defining the features of a critical urban paradigm in referenct to contemporary Western core societies, my focus is on noncore cities over a longer historical period.

Chapter 1

1. See Note 3 in the Introduction.

2. David Harvey (1973: 232, quoted in Walton, 1979b: 14) conceptualizes cities' role in advanced capitalist countries in a similar way in *Social Justice and the City* (but note his sensitivity tothe larger international system, as well): "Within countries functioning hierarchies of city types provide channels for the circulation and concentration of surplus value while at the same time providign for the spatial integration of the economy. Swirls in circulation occur too within the large metropoli (between, for example, city and suburb in the contemporary United States); these, however, are minor compared to the massive global circulation of surplus value in which contemporary metropolitanism is embedded."

3. Parenthetically, it is possible that the periodizations that world-system analyst use may be based, at least in part, on changing forms of technology that are available in the world-system at various points in time (Chase-Dunn, 1979). Perhaps this is another place where the world-system and ecological-evolutionary perspectives may be complementary.

4.   See Bornschier, Chase-Dunn, and Rubinson, 1978; Gereffi, 1979; Chase-Dunn, 1981a; and Rubinson and Holtzman, 1981, for reviews and critiques of this literature.

5.   For these authors, this is a variable measuring the ratio of population in large cities (20,000 and over) to the number of workers in industrial occupations.

6.   A general approach to the issue of proletarianization, its link to a nation's role in the world economy, and its effect on a variety of demographic phenomena will be explored in the concluding chapter of the book.

7.   The desirability of combining the quantitative and qualitative methodologies is highlighted by Chase-Dunn (1982: 4).

Chapter 2

1.   This chapter draws on and updates the analysis of world urban patterns that appeared inan article in *Urban Affairs Quarterly* (1990), which I co-authored with Bruce London.

2.   Obviously, there is the omnipresent problem with any comparative research using cross-national demographic data of reliability and validity. The fact that this information is generated by Third World governments with a wide range of statistical competence is a problem. Nevertheless, the data used in this chapter are considered the best available.

3.   The earlier analysis reported in Smith and London (1990) included a measure of overurbanization, as well. Although there are various ways of indexing this variable (Kentor, 1981; Timberlake and Kentor, 1983; Bradshaw, 1985; London, 1987), all involve some indicator of "fit" between a country's level of urbanization and its degree of industrialization. The measure used in Smith and London, 1990 compared the population in cities to the percentage of the labor force in the manufacturing sector.   When we examined the trends on this operationalization of overurbanization, we found that there *was* some convergence between core and periphery on this indicator between 1960 and 1970. Interpreting this was substantively difficult since, in a sense, we faced the old problem of comparing apples to oranges—relatively low employment in the manufacturing sector has vastly different implications in societies in different world-system zones. For example, the data showed that core North American nations scored very high in terms of overurbanization. But these nations are not overurbanized in the sense that the concept normally implies. Instead the score reflected structural changes in the United States and Canada, where a very large proportion of the population lives in urban areas but a declining percentage of the labor force remains in manufacturing. North America underwent a process of "deindustrialization" over the last quarter-century in which automation and capital flight reduced manufacturing employment (see Bluestone and Harrison, 1982; Ross and Trachte, 1990), at the same time that more and more people moved into highly paid

professional and service sector jobs (Reich, 1991). Rapidly urbanizing peripheral Third World societies teeming with informal sector workers but few industries would also score high on this measure—closer to the meaning of overurbanization in the literature. But a variable that confounds these situations is of dubious value, at best. As the process of global restructuring progressed in the 1980s and 1990s (see Smith and Böröcz, 1995, for various perspectives), a variable that gauged development as linked to the labor force in manufacturing became even more questionable. Because of this weakness, it is omitted from the analysis in this chapter.

4. A superior indicator for standardizing "urban" uses the percentage of thepopulation living in cities of 100,000 or more. This measure is compiled in the *World Handbook of Political and Social Indicators* (most recently edited by Taylor and Jodice, 1983), but unfortunately, this volume has not been updated past 1980.

5. This indicator of urban primacy measures the dominance of the largest city relative to the second largest, but it (1) fails to specify situations of two-city primacy, and (2) does not capture "the shape of the total city-size distribution" beyond these two places (Walters, 1985: 75). Future research might attempt to operationalize the "standard primacy ratio," a measure developed by Christopher Chase-Dunn and his associates. They painstakingly collected information on the ten largest cities in over 120 countries using archival information from the U.S. Library of Congress. Their summary measure (explained by Walters, 1985) estimates the deviation from lognormality for each of the top ten cities in each nation. Unfortunately, their data were collected in the mid-1980s and have not been updated since then.

6. The particularly small N for the most recent paper (Smith and White, 1992) is the result of stringent selection procedures that only include countries for which complete data are available for 1965, 1970, and 1980. We will be redoing this analysis with all nations for which there are a single year's data—which will push the sample size up to nearly 100 cases. One possible way to improve on the Snyder and Kick work and incorporate the advantages of our recent efforts would be to combine the two by correcting differences where appropriate (using the newer results) but retaining data on all 120 nations.

7. But it should be noted that this may be an artifact of the Snyder and Kick classificatory scheme that places countries like Brazil and Nigeria in the periphery and Peru, Malaysia, and the Philippines in the semiperiphery. The combined coding scheme mentioned in Note 4 might yield quite different results.

Chapter 3

1. For a pioneering attempt to build the time dimension into cross-national quantitative studies of dependence, see Bornschier, Chase-Dunn, and Rubinson, 1978. Some researchers argue that, despite being less than entirely satisfactory,

twenty-year time lags are long enough to detect certain types of macrostructural changes (Kentor, 1981; Chase-Dunn, 1982).

2.   These two regions, West Africa and East Asia, were also chosen because these areas traditionally received relatively little attention from researchers working out of the dependency perspective. By studying a variety of geographical regions, the dependency/world-system approach should transcend its early preoccupation with development and underdevelopment in Latin America.

Chapter 4

1.   In this chapter, the term *West Africa* refers to all the countries in sub-Saharan Africa west of Nigeria and east of Senegal (including those two nations). This follows the standard United Nations definition of world regions.

2.   The deviant case is Cotonou in Benin, which is larger than the capital of Porto Novo.

3.   Gugler and Flanagan (1977: 286) discuss the paucity of data on urban living conditions in some detail, concluding that the lack of information on urban inequality and poverty for West African cities is "remarkable."

4.   Cohen reports these rents in francs CFA, which are converted to 1969 U.S. dollars, with 260 francs CFA equal to US$1. The currency conversion is based on data from the World Bank (1980: 112).

5.   For examples of the articles in this planning tradition, see recent issues of *African Urban Studies* or the book edited by El-Shakhs and Obudho (1974).

6.   For a definition of urban policy and a discussion of it as incorporating both "decisions" and "nondecisions," see Cohen, 1974: 4–5.

7.   Wallerstein (1989: 130) distinquishes between "incorporation" and "peripheralization": incorporation involves 'hooking' the zone into the orbit of the world-economy in such a way that it virtually can no longer escape, while peripheralization involves a continuing transformation of ministructures of the area in ways that are sometimes referred to as the deepening of capitalist development. He proceeds to describe the rise of plantation economies and new political institutions in peripheralized areas. The key point is that the more thoroughgoing transformation that occurs as a result of peripheralization is more that just the type of structural exploitation that occurs when surplus is drained away. It involves basic changes in the "ministructures" that define everyday life: families, settlement patterns, subsistence organization, etc.

8.   One possible exception is Nigeria. Evans (1979b: 308–314) claims that this nation has recently become semiperipheral. At any rate, this type of "moving up" in the world-system would result in the transformation of the bonds of dependency, not a break in them. See a fuller discussion of this in the next chapter.

9.   In the following discussion, the debate about the desirability of one term or the other is not addressed (see Moser, 1978). Generally, the notion of "the

informal sector" is more inclusive (it can include service work, illegal housing, etc.) and less judgmental (it leaves the relationship of labor to the mode of production as an empirical issue) (see Portes and Walton, 1981: chapter 3). But the terms are used interchangeably here.

10.   Elsewhere, I provide a general critique and theoretical reconceptualization of the overurbanization thesis (D. Smith, 1987a). The following discussion addresses some of the major points and specifically relates them to the West African cases.

Chapter 5

1.   See Wallerstein, 1989: 130, as mentioned in Note 7, Chapter 4.

2.   Lord Frederick Lugard, in a 1922 volume entitled *The Dual Mandate in Tropical Africa*, cited by Hopkins, 1973: 192.

3.   In a "dendritic" system, a strict hierarchy of urban places develops where smaller towns at each level are engaged in close trade relationships with a single larger place but do not trade with each other. Depicted graphically, such systems resemble a dendrite nerve ending or the tributary system of a river. For details, see C. Smith, ed., 1976.

4.   Using data from Chase-Dunn and his associates, we calculated the 1970 Nigerian primacy score was .984 (compared to a similar calculation of .848 for U.S. metropolitan regions that same year). A more recent estimate of the population of the four largest cities in 1975 yields an even lower Davis Index of .75 (Kirk-Greene and Rimmer, 1981: 63). Of course, all recent data are strictly estimates because of the paucity of census information (see Note 5). All discussions of city sizes in the following section are based on the Chase-Dunn estimates.

5.   A major difficulty in any discussion of current trends in Nigerian urbanization is the lack of hard data. All these numbers are estimates; there simply are no reputable census figures on Nigerian population in recent years. The problem is more than just a technical one of a poor country lacking the resources and expertise to make the count. Censuses in 1963 and 1973 were heavily politicized since they were supposed to determine regional representation in parliment, and they were subject to manipulation. The 1963 results are considered very suspect; the 1973 data were voided and never released (see Gugler and Flanagan, 1978: 189, n. 13; Kirk-Greeene and Rimmer, 1981: 62-63). Therefore, discussions of patterns must rely on fairly gross estimates and qualitative descriptions. Nevertheless, I am confident that the Chase-Dunn estimates are the very best data available and that they provide a reasonalby accurate picture of the overall urban pattern.

Chapter 6

1. In this chapter, the term *East Asia* refers to all countries east of and including Burma and China. This combines the United Nation's "East Asia" region with "Eastern South Asia."

2. Martin Whyte and William Parish (1984) also claim that Chinese urbanization followed a distinctive path between the Revolution of 1949 and the mid-1970s (when they collected their data). Their analysis shows the successes and failures of Maoist attempts to create more productive and egalitarian cities, and the costs an dbenefits of these policies. While this book was arguably the best sociological analysis of Chinese urbanization during the 1980s, it adopts the implicitly developmentlaist assumption that there is a typical "modern city" form that was deviated from in this case. My claim here is more specific—that the Chinese urban experience during this period stands in sharp contrast with city growth in other non-core societies.

3. One might, of course, argue that political development here has not been nearly so successful. See Smith and Lee (1989) for a full discussion of the South Korean case.

4. Evans (1979b: 11) writes: "If classical dependence was associated with weak states, dependent development is associated with the strengthening of strong states in the 'semiperiphery.' The consolidation of state power may even be considered a prerequisite for dependent development."

5. I will return to this issue in Chapter 7, when discussing the South Korean case.

6. At this point, I should clarify my position on directions for change. As argued in Chapter 2, the world-system perspective emphasizes the possibility of mobility in the global hierarchy. Dependent development is one route. Some Marxist analysis on Southeast Asia calls for social revolution as a means of destroying peripheral capitalism and its associated ills. For instance, Catley (1976: 63) holds up Vietnam and Cambodia as examples of successful transformations; of these postwar societies he says, "The development of underdevelopment has ended; development has started." It is easy to be skeptical, given these examples with twenty years of hindsight. But my perspective, which stresses the importance of the subordinate roles these countries play in the world-economy, suggests that internal political change may not be enough. New revolutionary regimes face many of the same external constraints that the old ruling elites did. Those hoping to bring about genuinely transformative change, whether directed by revolutionary or nonrevolutionary developmentalist states (Evans, 1990), need to tailor policy changes that maximize the possibility of balanced generative development *despite* continuing situations of trade, aid, and investment dependency.

Chapter 7

1. Unless otherwise indicated, the term *Korea* refers to what is now North and South Korea.

2. It should be noted that a relatively small Korean bourgeoisie had developed by 1930. This group, for the most part, was so closely aligned with the Japanese occupiers that, for purposes of discussion, we can assume the interests of these two groups were nearly identical (see Cumings, 1981: chapter 1, for a fuller treatment of the origins and early development of capitalism in Korea).

3. Related to the wartime mobilization was the dramatic increase in migration of Koreans to Japan. The Personnel Draft Law of 1939 made Korean men eligible for military conscription. As a result, between 1939 and 1941, nearly 700,000 men were sent to Japan for military duty (Mills and Song, 1979: 66). An additional 250,000 men were forced to migrate to Japan or northern Korea to work in labor-scarce industries (especially in the mines). After the war, many of these migrants returned to South Korea.

4. This explains Seoul's seemingly curious location. In the modern era, the capital's inland location has undoubtedly contributed to the rapid growth of Inchon, its port city.

5. During the Korean War, Seoul suffered tremendous damage. So complete was the devastation that civilian movement to the city was severely restricted in the immediate postwar years, and it was not until the late 1950s that Seoul recovered its full complement of political and economic functions. In recent years, it is safe to say, the balance of power on the peninsula has shifted decisively to South Korea. It seems likely that regular air-raid drills and restrictions on photography in parts of Seoul as late as the mid-1980s, putatively based on security considerations, were motivated as much by a desire on the part of successive military regimes for ideological legitimation as by genuine fear of North Korean attack.

6. Cited interviews and most of the data for this section of the chapter were collected while I was a 1988 Summer Research Fellow at Kyungnam University's Institute for Far Eastern Studies in Seoul. I thank the faculty and staff there, who graciously provided facilities and support.

7. The rise and decline of Pusan and that city's link to *specific* patterns of export-led industrialization are particularly instructive. They illustrates both the fragile nature of semiperipheral development and the importance of understanding the details of particular types of industrial growth. In the late 1970s and early 1980s, the Pusan area boomed, driven to a large extent by the rapid growth of athletic shoe manufacturing for export (Korzeniewicz 1994). With Korea's dominant port and a large supply of workers eager for factory work, this southeastern city was well positioned for rapid demographic and economic growth. Area sports footwear factories were established based on large mass production lines, designed to produce enormous quantities of particular shoe designs to meet

the global demand for the products of core-based companies like Nike and Reebok (Chon, 1994). But as often happens in a capitalist economy (and especially in a contemporary world with extremely fluid corporate "sourcing" strategies), the boom turned to bust. As Korean wages rose, local producers were priced out of the world market. The giant core-based firms that market athletic shoes turned their sights on Southeast Asia, where wages were considerably lower than in South Korea. The sourcing shift by these industry leaders "literally annihilated the footwear industry in Pusan, Korea" (Chon, 1994: 21). This type of industrial catastrophe may help to explain some recent changes in Pusan's urban trajectory (i.e., slowed population growth and increased informalization).

8.   Some of these claims may be overblown. In her recent book, Alice Amsden (1989: 39) argues that the nation's "reputation among developing countries as one with a relatively equitable income distribution . . . has become increasingly undeserved as industrialization has advanced." She provides several technical objections to the way South Korean income data are compiled, particularly for wealthier families and individuals, which would systematically underestimate inequality.

9.   News articles in South Korea suggest that in 1989, income from urban land speculation reached twice the gross national product for that year, with *chaebols* (giant Korean business conglomerates) as major players in this lucrative financial game (personal communication, Su-Hoon Lee, April 1990).

10. Cumings's (1984) prescient discussion of the limits of South Korea's international mobility, in a section entitled "Many Are Called but Few Are Chosen: Korea's Export-Led Trap," is particularly relevant.

Chapter 8

1.   This section draws on a longer, more specific discussion in D. Smith 1995.

2.   D. Smith (1985) provides a much more detailed exploration of the policy and planning implications of the dependency/world-system perspective on East Asian urbanization.

References

Abu-Lughod, Janet, and Rucgard Hay, eds. 1978. *Third World Urbanization*. New York: Methuen.

Ake, Claude. 1976. "The Congruence of Political Economies and Ideologies in Africa." Pp. 198–211 in P. Gutkind and I. Wallerstein, eds., *The Political Economy of Contemporary Africa*. Beverly Hills, Calif.: Sage.

Allen, R.G.D., and J. Edward Ely. 1953. *International Trade Statistics*. New York: Wiley.

Amarshi, Good, and Mortimer. 1979. "Political Economy of Contemporary New Guinea." *Journal of Contemporary Asia*.

Amin, Samir. 1973. "Underdevelopment and Dependence in Black Africa—Their Historical Origins and Contemporary Forms." *Social and Economic Studies* 22: 177–196.

———. 1974. *Accumulation on a World Scale*. New York: Monthly Review.

Amin, Samir, Giovanni Arrighi, Andre Gunder Frank and Immanuel Wallerstein. 1982. *Dynamics of Global Crisis*. New York: Monthly Review.

Amsden, Alice. 1989. Asia's Next Giant: *South Korea and Late Industrialization*. New York: Oxford University Press.

Armstrong, Warwick, and T. G. McGee. 1985. *Theatres of Accumulation: Studies in Asian and Latin American Urbanization*. London: Methuen.

Association of Japanese Geographers. 1970. *Japanese Cities*. Tokyo: Kokusai Printing.

Ayeni, Bola. 1978. "Urban Planning and Urban Problems in Nigeria." *Nigerian Behavioral Sciences Journal* 1(2): 61–73.

Bach, Robert. 1976. "Historical Patterns of Capitalist Penetration in Malaysia." *Journal of Contemporary Asia* 6: 458–475.

Bairoch, Paul. 1975. *The Economic Development of the Third World Since 1900*. Berkeley: University of California Press.

———. 1988. *Cities and Economic Development: From the Dawn of History to the Present*. Chicago: University of Chicago Press.

Baldwin, D. 1980. "Interdependence and Power: A Conceptual Analysis." *International Organization* 34(4): 471–506.

Barnet R., and P. Mueller. 1974. *Global Reach*. New York: Simon and Schuster.

Barrett, Richard, and Soomi Chin. 1987. "Export-Oriented Industrializing States in the Capitalist World System: Similarities and Differences." Pp. 23–43 in Fred Deyo, ed., *The Political Economy of the New Asian Industrialism*. Ithaca: Cornell University Press.

Barrett, Richard, and Martin Whyte. 1982. "Dependency Theory and Taiwan: Analysis of a Deviant Case." *American Journal of Sociology* 87(5): 1064–1089.

Bell, Peter. 1978. "'Cycles' of Class Struggle in Thailand" *Journal of Contemporary Asia* 8(1): 51–79.

Bergesen, Albert, ed. 1983. *Crises in the World-System.* Beverly Hills, Calif.: Sage.

Berry, Brian. 1971. "City Size and National Development." Pp. 111–152 in P. Jakobson and V. Prakash, eds., *Urbanization and National Development.* Beverly Hills, Calif.: Sage.

———. 1973. *The Human Consequences of Urbanization.* London: Macmillan.

Berry, Brian, and John Kasarda. 1977. *Contemporary Urban Ecology.* New York: Macmillan.

Bienen, Henry. 1984. "Urbanization and Third World Stability." *World Development* 12(7): 661–691.

Birkbeck, Chris. 1978. "Garbage, Industry and the 'Vultures' of Cali, Columbia." Pp. 163–183 in R. Bromley and C. Gerry, eds., *Casual Work and Poverty in Third World Cities.* New York: John Wiley & Sons.

Bluestone, Barry and Bennett Harrison. 1982. *The Deindustrialization of America.* New York: Basic Books.

Bollen, Kenneth. 1983. "World System Position, Dependency, and Democracy." *American Sociological Review* 48: 468–497.

Bornschier, Volker, and Thanh-Huyen Ballmer-Cao. 1979. "Income Inequality: A Cross-National Study of the Relationship between MNC–Penetration, Dimensions of the Power Structure and Income Distribution." *American Sociological Review* 44: 487–506.

Bornschier, Volker, and Christopher Chase-Dunn. 1985. *Transnational Corporations and Underdevelopment.* New York: Praeger.

Bornschier, Volker, Christopher Chase-Dunn, and Richard Rubinson. 1978. "Cross-National Evidence of the Effects of Foreign Investment and Aid on Economic Growth and Inequality: A Survey of Findings and a Reanalysis." *American Journal of Sociology* 84: 651–683.

Bornschier, Volker, and Peter Heintz, eds. 1979. *Compendium of Data for World-System Analysis.* Zurich: Bulletin Soziologisches Institut des Universitat Zurich.

Bose, Ashish. 1971. "The Urbanization Process in Southeast Asia." Pp. 81–109 in Leo Jakobson and Ved Prakash, eds., *Urbanization and National Development.* Beverly Hills, Calif.: Sage.

Boulding, Kenneth. 1978. "The City as an Element in the International System." Pp. 150–157 in L. S. Bourne and J. W. Simmons, eds., *Systems of Cities.* New York: Oxford University Press.

Bousquet, N. 1980. "From Hegemony to Competition: Cycles of the Core." Pp. 46–83 in T. K. Hopkins and I. Wallerstein, eds. *Processes of the World System.* Beverly Hills, Calif.: Sage.

Bradshaw, York. 1985. "Overurbanization and Underdevelopment in Sub-Saharan Africa: A Cross-National Study." *Studies in Comparative International Development* 20: 74–101.

————. 1987. "Urbanization and Underdevelopment: A Global Study of Modernization, Urban Bias and Economic Dependency." *American Sociological Review* 52: 224–239.

Braudel, Fernand. 1977. *Afterthoughts on Material Civilization and Capitalism.* Baltimore: Johns Hopkins University Press.

Breese, Gerald. 1966. *Urbanization in Newly Developing Countries.* Englewood Cliffs, N.J.: Prentice-Hall.

Breiger, Ronald. 1981. "Structures of Economic Interdependence Among Nations." Pp. 353–380 in Peter Blau and Robert Merton, eds., *Continuities in Structural Inquiry.* New York: Free Press.

Breiger, Ronald, Scott Boorman, and Phillip Arabie. 1975. "An Algorithm for Clustering Relational Data with Applications to Social Network Analysis and Comparison with Multidimensional Scaling." *Journal of Mathematical Psychology* 12: 328–383.

Brenner, Robert. 1977. "The Origins of Capitalist Development: A Critique of Neo-Smithian Marxism." *New Left Review* 104: 25–92.

Bromley, Ray. 1978. "The Urban Informal Sector—Why Is it Worth Discussing?" *World Development* 6(9/10): 1033–1039.

Bromley, Ray, and Chris Gerry. 1979. *Casual Work and Poverty in Third World Cities.* New York: John Wiley & Sons.

Burt, Ronald. 1978. "Cohesion Versus Structural Equivalence as a Basis for Network Subgroups." *Sociological Methods and Research* 7(2): 189–212.

Caldwell, John. 1968. *Population Growth and Family Change in Africa: The New Urban Elite in Ghana.* Canberra: Australian National University Press.

Caporaso, James A. 1981. "Industrialization at the Periphery: The Evolving Global Division of Labor." *International Studies Quarterly* 25(3): 347–384.

Cardoso, Fernando H. 1973. Associated-Dependent Development." Pp. 142–176 in A. Stepan, ed., *Authoritarian Brazil.* New Haven, Conn.: Yale University Press.

Cardoso, Fernando H. and Enzo Faletto. 1979. *Dependency and Development in Latin America.* Berkeley: University of California Press.

Castells, Manuel. 1977. *The Urban Question: A Marxist Approach.* Cambridge, Mass.: MIT Press.

Catley, Bob. 1976. "The Development of Underdevelopment in Southeast Asia." *Journal of Contemporary Asia* 6(1): 54–74.

Chang, Yunshik. 1971. "Colonization as Planned Change: The Korean Case." *Modern Asian Studies* 5(2): 161–186.

Chase-Dunn, Christopher. 1975. "The Effects of International Economic Dependency on Development and Inequality." *American Sociological Review* 40(6): 720–738.

———. 1978. "Core-Periphery Relations: The Effects of Core Competition." Pp. 159–176 in B. Kaplan, ed., *Social Change in the Capitalist World Economy*. Beverly Hills, Calif.: Sage.

———. 1979. "World Division of Labor and the Development of City Systems." Grant proposal to the National Science Foundation.

———. 1980. "The Development of Core Capitalism in the United States: Tariff Politics and Class Struggle in an Upwardly Mobile Semiperiphery." Pp. 189–230 in Albert Bergesen, ed., *Studies of the Modern World-System*. New York: Academic Press.

———. 1981a. "The Uses of Formal Comparative Research on Dependency Theory and the World System Perspective." Pp. 117-137 in Harry Makler, Alberto Martinelli, and Neil Smelser, eds., *The New International Economy*. London: Sage Publications.

———. 1981b. "Interstate System and Capitalist World Economy: One Logic or Two?" *International Studies Quarterly* 25(1): 19–42.

———. 1982. "World Division of Labor and the Development of City Systems: A Longitudinal Cross National Study." Grant renewal proposal to the National Science Foundation.

———. 1983. "Inequality, Structural Mobility, and Dependency Reversal in the Capitalist World-Economy." Pp. 73–95 in Charles Doran, George Modelski, and Cal Clark, eds., *North/South Relations: Studies of Dependency Reversal*. New York: Praeger.

———. 1984. "Urbanization in the World-System: New Directions for Research." Pp. 111–120 in Michael P. Smith, ed., *Cities in Transformation*. Beverly Hills, Calif.: Sage.

———. 1985a. "The Coming of Urban Primacy in Latin America." *Comparative Urban Research* 11: 14–31.

———. 1985b. The System of World Cities, A.D. 800-1975." Pp. 269–292 in Michael Timberlake, ed., *Urbanization in the World-Economy*. New York: Academic Press.

———. 1989. *Global Formation: Structures of the World-Economy*. New York: Basil Blackwell.

Chase-Dunn, Christopher, and Richard Rubinson. 1977. "Toward a Structural Perspective on the World System." *Politics and Society* 7(4): 453–476.

Chirot, Daniel. 1977. *Social Change in the Twentieth Century*. New York: Harcourt Brace Jovanovich.

————. 1986. *Social Change in the Modern Era*. New York: Harcourt Brace Jovanovich.

Chon, Soohyun. 1994. ". . .."

Clarke, John. 1972. "Urban Primacy in Tropical Africa." Pp. 447–453 in *La croissance urbaine en Afrique Noire et a Madagascar* Vol. 1. Paris: Centre National de la Recherche Scientifique.

Cohen, Michael. 1974. *Urban Policy and Political Conflict in Africa: A Study of the Ivory Coast*. Chicago: University of Chicago Press.

Coll, Steve and Cindy Shiner. 1994. "Military Rulers Drained Nigeria, Enriched Selves." *The Washington Post*, July 23, pp. 1 and 16.

Coquery-Vidrovitch, Catherine. 1977. "La Mise en Dependence de l'Afrique Noire: Essai de Periodisation, 1800–1970." *Cahiers d'Etudes Africaines* (16)1–2.

Cumings, Bruce. 1981. *The Origins of the Korean War*. Princeton: Princeton University Press.

————. 1984. "The Origins and Development of the Northeast Asian Political Economy: Industrial Sectors, Product Cycles, and Political Consequences." *International Organization* 38: 1–40.

————. 1989. "The Abortive Apertura: South Korea in the Light of the Latin American Experience." *New Left Review* (173)5–32.

Davidson, Basil. 1966. "The Outlook for Africa." *The Socialist Register*. London: Merlin Press.

Davis, Kingsley. 1972. *World Urbanization: 1950–1970*. Berkeley: University of California Press.

Davis, Kingsley, and Hilda Golden. 1954. "Urbanization and the Development of Pre-Industrial Areas." *Economic Development and Cultural Change* 3(1): 6–24.

Delacroix, Jacques. 1977. "The Export of Raw Materials and Economic Growth: A Cross-National Study." *American Sociological Review* 42: 795–808.

Deyo, Frederic. 1987. "State and Labor: Modes of Political Exclusion in East Asian Development." Pp. 182–202 in Frederic Deyo, ed., *The Political Economy of the New Asian Industrialism*. Ithaca: Cornell University Press.

————. 1989. *Beneath the Miracle: Labor Subordination in the New Asian Industrialism*. Berkeley: University of California Press.

Dixon, Marlene, Susanne Jonas, and Edmund McCaughan. 1983. "Changes in the International Division of Labor and Low-Wage Labor in the United States." Pp. 173–191 in A. Bergesen, ed., *Crises in the World-System*. Beverly Hills, Calif.: Sage.

Drakakis-Smith, David. 1980. *Urbanisation, Housing and the Development Process*. New York: St. Martin's Press.

Dudley, Billy. 1982. *An Introduction to Nigerian Government and Politics.* Bloomington: Indiana University Press.

Duncan, Beverly, and Stanley Lieberson. 1970. *Metropolis and Region in Transition.* Beverly Hills, Calif.: Sage.

Duncan, Otis D., William R. Scott, Stanley Lieberson, Beverly Duncan, and Hal Winsborough. 1960. *Metropolis and Region.* Baltimore: Johns Hopkins.

Durand, E. D. 1953. "Country Classification." Pp. 117–129 in R.G.D. Allen and J. E. Ely, eds., *International Trade Statistics.* New York: Wiley.

Durand, John and César Palaez. 1969. "Patterns of Urbanization in Latin America." Pp. 166–188 in Gerald Breese, ed., *The City in Newly Developing Areas.* Englewood Cliffs, N.J.: Prentice-Hall.

Duvall, Raymond. 1978. "Dependence and Dependencia Theory: Notes Toward Precision of Concept and Argument." *International Organization* 32(1): 51–78.

Elliot, David. 1978. "The Socio-Economic Foundation of Modern Thailand." *Journal of Contemporary Asia* 8: 21–50.

El-Shakhs, Salah. 1974. "Development Planning in Africa: An Introduction." Pp. 3–12 in Salah El-Shakhs and Robert Obudho, eds., Urbanization, National Development, and Regional Planning in Africa. New York: Praeger.

El-Shakhs, Salah and Robert Obudho, eds. 1974. *Urbanization, National Development, and Regional Planning in Africa.* New York: Praeger.

Emmanuel, Arghiri. 1972. *Unequal Exchange: A Study of the Imperialism of Trade.* New York: Monthly Review.

Evans, Peter. 1979a. "Beyond Center and Periphery: A Comment on the World System Approach to the Study of Development." *Sociological Inquiry* 49(4): 15–20.

———. 1979b. *Dependent Development.* Princeton: Princeton University Press.

———. 1985. "Transnational Linkages and the Economic Role of the State: An Analysis of Developing and Industrializing Nations in the Post-World War II Period." Pp. 192–226 in Peter Evans, Dietrich Rueschemeyer, and Theda Skocpol, eds., *Bringing the State Back In.* Cambridge: Cambridge University Press.

———. 1990. "Predatory, Developmental and Other Apparatuses: A Comparative Analysis of the Third World State." *Sociological Forum* 4:561–587.

———. 1995. *Embedded Autonomy: States and Industrial Transformtion.* Princeton, N.J.: Princeton University Press.

Evans, Peter, and John Stephens. 1988. "Development and the World Economy." Pp. 739–773 in Neil Smelser, ed., *Handbook of Sociology.* Beverly Hills, Calif.: Sage.

Evans, Peter, and Michael Timberlake. 1980. "Dependence, Inequality, and the Growth of the Tertiary: A Comparative Analysis of Less Developed Countries." American Sociological Review 45(4): 531–555.

Evans, Peter, Dietrich Rueschemeyer, and Theda Skocpol, eds. 1985. *Bringing the State Back In*. Cambridge: Cambridge University Press.

Fanon, Frantz. 1965. The *Wretched of the Earth*. C. Farrington, trans. New York: Grove Press.

Fava, Sylvia. 1968. Urbanism *in World Perspective*. New York: Crowell.

Feagin, Joe. 1988. Free *Enterprise City: Houston in Political-Economic Perspective*. New Brunswick, N.J.: Rutgers University Press.

Frank, Andre Gunder. 1969. Latin *America: Underdevelopment or Revolution?* New York: Monthly Review.

———. 1977. "'Long Live Transideological Enterprise' The Socialist Economies in the Capitalist Division of Labor." *Review* (Fernand Braudel Center) 1: 91–140.

———. 1978. World *Accumulation 1492–1789*. New York: Monthly Review.

———. 1979. Dependent *Accumulation and Underdevelopment*. London: Macmillan.

———. 1981a. *Crisis in the World Economy*. New York: Holmes & Meier.

———. 1981b. *Crisis: In the Third World*. New York: Holmes & Meier Publications.

Friedmann, Harriet. 1981. "The Political Economy of Food: The Rise and Fall of the Postwar International Order." Working Paper Series no. 5A. Department of Sociology, University of Toronto.

Friedmann, John. 1978. "The Role of Cities in National Development." Pp. 70-81 in L. S. Bourne and J. W. Simmon, eds., *Systems of Cities*. New York. Oxford University Press.

Friedmann, John, and Tomas Lackington. 1967. "Hyperurbanization and National Development in Chile: Some Hypotheses." Urban *Affairs Quarterly* 2: 3–29.

Froebel, Folker, Jurgen Heinrichs, and Otto Kreye. 1981. The *New International Division of Labor*. Cambridge: Cambridge University Press.

Fryer, Donald W. 1972. "The Primate Cities of Southeast Asia." Pp. 31–42 in Alice Taylor, ed., *Focus on Southeast Asia*. New York: Praeger.

Fuchs, Roland, Gavin Jones, and Ernesto Pernia, eds. 1987. Urbanization *and Urban Policies in Pacific Asia*. Boulder: Westeview Press.

Galtung, John. 1971. "A Structural Theory of Imperialism." Journal *of Peace Research* 2: 81–117.

Geertz, Clifford. 1963. Peddlers *and Princes: Social Development and Economic Change in Two Indonesian Towns*. Chicago: University of Chicago Press.

Gereffi, Gary. 1979. "A Critical Evaluation of Quantitative Cross-National Studies of Dependency." Paper presented at the annual meeting of the International Studies Association, Toronto, Ontario.

Gereffi, Gary, and Peter Evans. 1981. "Transnational Corporations, Dependent Development, and State Policy in the Semiperiphery: A Comparison of Brazil and Mexico." Latin *American Research Review* 16(3): 31–64.

Gerry, Chris. 1978. "Petty Production and Capitalist Production in Dakar: The Crisis of the Self-Employed." World Development (6)9/10: 1147–1160.

Gibbs, Jack, and Walter Martin. 1962. "Urbanization, Technology, and the Division of Labor: International Patterns." Pp. 309–321 in G. Breese, ed., The *City in Newly Developing Areas*, Englewood Cliffs, N.J.: Prentice-Hall.

Giddens, Anthony. 1982. Sociology: *A Brief but Critical Introduction*. New York: Harcourt Brace Jovanovich.

Gilbert, Alan, and Josef Gugler. 1982. Cities, *Poverty, and Development*. Oxford: Oxford University Press.

Ginsburg, Norton. 1972. "Planning the Future of the Southeast Asian City." Pp. 43–59 in Alice Taylor, ed., Focus *on Southeast Asia*. New York: Praeger.

Gras, N.S.B. 1922. An *Introduction to Economic History*. New York: Harper and Row.

Griffis, William E. 1971. *Corea: The Hermit Nation*. New York: AMS Press.

Grindal, Bruce. 1973. "Islamic Affiliations and Urban Adaptations: The Sisala Movement in Accra, Ghana." *Africa* 43: 333–346.

Gugler, Josef. 1982. "Overurbanization Reconsidered." Economic *Development and Cultural Change* 31(1): 173–189.

———. 1988. "Overurbanization Reconsidered." (Revised version.) Pp. 75–92 in Josef Gugler, ed., *The Urbanization of the Third World*. New York: Oxford University Press.

Gugler, Josef, and William Flanagan. 1977. "On the Political Economy of Urbanization in the Third World: The Case of West Africa." International Journal of Urban and Regional Research 1(2): 272–292.

———. 1978. Urbanization and Social Change in West Africa. New York: Cambridge University Press.

Gutkind, Peter, and Immanuel Wallerstein. 1976. "Editors' Introduction." Pp. 7–29 in P. Gutkind and I. Wallerstein, eds. *The Political-Economy of Contemporary Africa*. Beverly Hills, Calif.: Sage.

Hackenberg, Robert. 1980. "New Patterns of Urbanization in Southeast Asia: An Assessment." *Population and Development Review* 6(3): 391-419.

Hamilton, Agnus. 1904. *Korea*. New York: Charles Scribner's Sons.

Han, Sung-ju. 1974. The Failure of Democracy in South Korea. Berkeley: University of California Press.

Hance, William. 1970. *Population, Migration, and Urbanization in Africa.* New York: Columbia University Press.

Hannan, Michael. 1979. "Issues in Panel Analysis of National Development: A Methodological Overview." Pp. 17–33 in John Meyers and Michael Hannan, eds., National *Development in the World System.* Chicago: University of Chicago Press.

Hardoy, Jorge, ed. 1975. Urbanization *in Latin America: Approaches and Issues.* Garden City, N.Y.: Anchor.

Hart, Keith. 1973. "Informal Income Opportunities and Urban Unemployment in Ghana." Journal *of Modern African Studies* 11: 61–89.

Harvey, David. 1973. Social *Justice and the City.* London: Edward Arnold.

Hasan, Parvez. 1976. Korea*: Problems and Issues in a Rapidly Growing Economy.* Baltimore: Johns Hopkins University Press.

Hasan, Parvez, and D. C. Rao. 1979. Korea*: Policy Issues for Long Term Development*, World Bank report. Baltimore: The John Hopkins University Press.

Hasselman, Karl-Heinz. 1981. "Liberia." In Harm de Blij and Esmond Martin, eds., African *Perspectives.* New York: Methuen.

Hatada, Takashi. 1969. A *History of Korea.* Santa Barbara, Calif.: Clio Press.

Hawley, Amos. 1950. *Human Ecology: A Theory of Community Structure.* New York: Ronald Press.

———. 1968a. "Human Ecology." Pp. 328–337 in D. Sills, ed., International *Encyclopedia of the Social Sciences.* New York: Crowell, Collier, and Macmillan.

———, ed. 1968b. *Roderick D. McKenzie on Human Ecology.* Chicago: University of Chicago Press.

———. 1971. Urban *Society: An Ecological Approach.* New York: The Ronald Press.

———. 1984. "Human Ecological and Marxian Theories." *American Journal of Sociology* 89(4): 904–917.

Heilbroner, Robert. 1980. *An Inquiry into the Human Prospect: Updated and Reconsidered for the 1980's.* New York: W. W. Norton.

Heise, David. 1970. "Causal Inference from Panel Data." Chapter 1 in E. Borgatta and G. Bornstedt, eds., *Sociological Methodology* San Francisco: Jossey-Bass.

Henderson, Gregory. 1968. Korea: *The Politics of the Vortex.* Cambridge, Mass.: Harvard University Press.

Henthorn, William. 1971. A *History of Korea.* New York: Free Press.

Hollensteiner, Mary and Miria E. Lopez. 1976. "Manila: The Face of Poverty." Pp. 69-86 in Social Science Research Institute, International Christian

University, ed., *Asia Urbanizing: Population Growth and Concentration—& the Problems Thereof.* Tokyo: Simul Press.

Holt, Robert, and John Turner. 1966. *The Political Basis of Economic Development.* Princeton: Van Nostrand.

Home, Robert K. 1976. "Urban Growth and Urban Government: Contradictions in the Colonial Political Economy." Pp. 55–75 in Gavin Williams, ed., *Nigeria: Economy and Society.* London: Rex Collings.

Hopkins, Anthony. 1973. *An Economic History of West Africa.* New York: Columbia University Press.

Hoselitz, Bert. 1954. "Generative and Parasitic Cities." *Economic Development and Cultural Change* 3: 278–294.

Hulbert, Homer. 1906. *The Passing of Korea.* New York: Doubleday, Page.

Hwang, Myong-Chan, and Jin-Ho Choi. 1987. "Evolution of the Settlement System in Korea: Historical Perspective." Pp. 35–58 in Harry Richardson and Myong-Chan Hwang, eds., *Urban and Regional Policy in Korea and International Experiences.* Seoul: Kon-Kuk University.

Imoagene, Oshomha. 1974. "Some Sociological Aspects of Modern Migration in West Africa." In S. Amin, ed., *Modern Migrations In West Africa.* New York: Praeger.

Inikori, Joseph E. 1982. *Forced Migration.* New York: Academic Press.

International Labor Organization. 1971. *Labor Force Projections.* Parts 1–5. Geneva: ILO.

International Labor Office. 1972. *Employment, Incomes and Equality: A Strategy for Increasing Productive Employment in Kenya.* Geneva: ILO.

Jackman, Robert. 1980. "A Note on Measurement of Growth Rates in Cross-National Analysis." *American Journal of Sociology* 86: 604–617.

Jain, Shail. 1975. *Size Distribution of Income: A Compilation of Data.* Washington, D.C.: World Bank.

Jefferson, Mark. 1938. "The Law of the Primate City." *Geographical Review* 29: 226–282.

Kay, Geoffrey. 1975. *Development and Underdevelopment: A Marxist Analysis.* London: Macmillan.

Kennedy, Michael, and David Smith. 1989. "East Central European Urbanization: A Political Economy of the World System Perspective." *International Journal of Urban and Regional Research* 13(4): 597–624.

Kentor, Jeffrey. 1981. "Structural Determinants of Peripheral Urbanization: The Effects of International Dependence." *American Sociological Review* 46: 201–211.

———. 1985. "Economic Development and World Division of Labor." Pp. 25–39 in M. Timberlake, ed., *Urbanization in the World Economy.* New York: Academic Press.

Keyfitz, Nathan. 1965. "Political-Economic Aspects of Urbanization in South and Southeast Asia." Pp. 265–310 in P. Hauser and L. Schnore, eds., *The Study of Urbanization*. New York: Wiley.

Kim, Chong Ik, and Han-Kyo Kim. 1967. *Korea and the Politics of Imperialism*. Berkeley: University of California Press.

Kim, Kuang suk, and Michael Roemer. 1979. *Growth and Structural Transformation*. Cambridge, Mass.: Harvard University Press.

King, Anthony D. 1976. *Colonial Urban Development: Culture, Power, and Environment*. Boston, Mass.: Routledge & Paul.

———. 1990a. *Urbanism, Colonialism and the World-Economy: Cultural and Spatial Foundations of the World Urban System*. London: Routledge.

———. 1990b. *Global Cities: Post-Imperialism and the Internationalization of London*. London: Routledge.

Kirk-Greene, Anthony, and Douglas Rimmer. 1981. *Nigeria Since 1970: A Political and Economic Outline*. New York: Africana Publishing.

Koo, Hagen. 1987. "The Interplay of State, Social Class, and World System in East Asian Development: The Cases of South Korea and Taiwan." Pp. 165–181 in Frederic Deyo, ed., *The Political Economy of the New Asian Industrialism*. Ithaca: Cornell University Press.

Kornhauser, David. 1982. *Japan: Geographical Background to Urban-Industrial Development*. New York: Longman.

Korzeniewicz, Miguel. 1994. "Commodity Chains and Marketing Strategies: Nike and the Global Athletic Footwear Industry." Pp. 247–265 in Gary Gereffi and Miguel Korzeniewicz, eds., *Commodity Chains and Global Capitalism*. Westport, Conn.: Greenwood Press.

Kronholz, J. 1983. "City Limits: In China, Rigid, Pervasive Controls Developing Nations Face." *Wall Street Journal*, June 6, 1983.

Kuznets, Simon. 1971. *Economic Growth of Nations: Total Output and Production Structure*. Cambridge, Mass.: Belknap Press of Harvard University.

Kwon, Ta H., HwanY. Lee, Y. Chang, and E. Y. Yu. 1975. *The Population of Korea*. Seoul: Seoul National University.

Lenski, Gerhard. 1976. "History and Social Change." *American Journal of Sociology* 82: 548–564.

Lenski, Gerhard and Jean Lenski. 1978. *Human Societies: An Introduction to Macrosociology*. (Third edition.) New York: McGraw-Hill.

Levy, Marion. 1955. "Contrasting Factors in the Modernization of China and Japan." Pp. 496–536 in Simon Kuznets, Wilbert Moore, and Joseph Spengler, eds., *Economic Growth: Brazil, India, Japan*. Durham, N.C.: Duke University Press.

————. 1962. "Some Aspects of 'Individualism' and the Problem of Modernization of China and Japan." *Economic Development and Cultural Change* 10: 225–240.

Light, Ivan. 1983. *Cities in World Perspective.* New York: Macmillan.

Lim, Robyn. 1978. "The Philippines and the 'Dependency Debate': A Preliminary Case Study." *Journal of Contemporary Asia* 8(3): 196–209.

Lincoln, James. 1977. "Organizational Dominance and Community Structure." In R. Liebert and A. Imerschein, eds. Power *Paradigms in Community Research.* Beverly Hills: Sage.

Linnemann, Hans. 1966. *An Econometric Study of World Trade Flows.* Amsterdam: North-Holland.

Linsky, Arnold. 1969. "Some Generalizations Concerning Primate Cities." Pp. 285–294 in G. Breese, ed., *The City in Newly Developing Countries.* Englewood Cliffs, N.J.: Prentice-Hall.

Lipton, Michael. 1977. *Why Poor People Stay Poor: Urban Bias in World Development.* Cambridge, Mass.: Harvard University Press.

————. 1984. "Urban Bias Revisited." Journal of Development Studies 20: 139–166.

Lo, Fu-Chen, and Kamal Salih. 1978. *Growth Pole Strategy and Regional Development.* New York: Pergamon Press.

Lofchie, Michael F. 1976. "Political and Economic Origins of African Hunger." *Journal of Modern African Studies* 13: 551–567.

London, Bruce. 1979. "Internal Colonialism In Thailand: Primate City Parasitism Reconsidered." *Urban Affairs Quarterly* 14(4): 485–514.

————. 1980. *Metropolis and Nation in Thailand: The Political Economy of Uneven Development.* Boulder: Westview Press.

————. 1987. "The Structural Determinants of Third World Urban Change: An Ecological and Political Economic Analysis." *American Sociological Review* 52: 28–43.

London, Bruce, and David Smith. "Urban Bias, Dependence, and Economic Stagnation in Non-Core Nations." *American Sociological Review* 53: 454–463.

Lozano, Beverly. 1989. *The Invisible Workforce: Transforming American Business with Outside Home-Based Workers.* New York: The Free Press.

Lubeck, Paul. 1977. "Contrasts and Continuity in a Dependent City: Kano, Nigeria." Pp. 281–289 in J. Abu-Lughod and R. Hay, eds., *Third World Urbanization.* Chicago: Maaroufa Press.

Mabogunje, Akin. 1968. *Urbanization in Nigeria.* London: University of London Press.

————. 1974. "Urbanization Problems in Africa." Pp. 13–26 in Salah El-Shakhs, and Robert Obudho, eds., *Urbanization, National Development, and Regional Planning in Africa*. New York: Praeger.

————. 1975. "Migration and Urbanization." Pp. 153–168 in John Caldwell, ed., *Population Growth and Socio-Economic Change in West Africa*. New York: Columbia University Press.

Magubane, Bernard. 1976. "The Evolution of Class Structure in Africa." Pp. 169–197 in P. Gutkind and I. Wallerstein, eds., *The Political Economy of Contemporary Africa*. Beverly Hills: Sage.

Marx, Karl. 1959 (1887). *Capital, Vol. 1*. London: Lawrence and Wishart.

McCall, Daniel. 1955. "Dynamics of Urbanization in Africa." *Annals of the American Academy of Political and Social Science* 298: 151–160.

McCormack, Gavan, and Mark Selden. 1977. *Korea, North and South: The Deepening Crisis*. New York: The Monthly Review Press.

McCune, Shannon. 1960. *Korea's Heritage: A Regional & Social Geography*. Tokyo: Charles E. Tuttle.

McGee, T. G. 1969. *The Southeast Asian City*. New York: Praeger.

————. 1971. "Catalysts or Cancers? The Role of Cities in Asian Society." Pp. 157–181 in L. Jakobson and V. Prakash, eds., *Urbanization and National Development*. Beverly Hills: Sage.

————. 1973. "Peasants in the Cities: A Paradox, A Paradox, A Most Ingenious Paradox." *Human Organization* 32(2): 135–142.

————. 1976. "The Persistence of the Proto-proletariat: Occupational Structures and Planning of the Future of Third World Cities." *Progress in Geography* 9: 3–38.

————. 1979. "The Poverty Syndrome: Making Out in the Southeast Asian City." In B. Bromley and C. Gerry, eds., *Casual Work and Poverty in Third World Cities*. New York: John Wiley & Sons.

McGreevey, W. P. 1971. "A Statistical Analysis of Primary and Lognormality in the Size Distribution of Latin American Cities, 1750-1960." Pp. 116–129 in R. Morse, ed., *The Urban Development of Latin America, 1750–1920*. Palo Alto, Calif.: Stanford University Center for Latin American Studies.

McKenzie, Roderick D. 1968 (1926). "The Scope of Human Ecology." Pp. 19–32 in Amos Hawley, ed., *Roderick D. McKenzie on Human Ecology*. Chicago, Ill.: University of Chicago Press. (Reprinted from *Publications of the American Sociological Society*, xx: 141–154.)

————. 1968 (1927). "The Concept of Dominance and World Organization." Pp. 205–219 in Amos Hawley, ed., *Roderick D. McKenzie on Human Ecology*. Chicago, Ill.: University of Chicago Press. (Reprinted from *American Journal of Sociology* 33: 28–42.)

————. 1968 (1933). "Industrial Expansion and the Interrelations of Peoples." Pp. 121-133 in Amos Hawley, ed., *Roderick D. McKenzie on Human Ecology*. Chicago, Ill.: University of Chicago Press. (Reprinted from *Race and Culture Contacts*, ed., E. B. Reuter, pp. 19–33. New York: McGraw-Hill.

McNulty, Michael, and Isaac Adalemo. 1988. "Lagos." Pp. 212–234 in Mattei Dogan and John Kasarda, eds., *The Metropolis Era: vol. 2, Mega-Cities*. Beverly Hills, CA: Sage.

Mehmet, Ozay. 1978. *Economic Planning and Social Justice in Developing Countries*. New York: St. Martin's Press.

Mehta, Surinder. 1969. "Some Demographic and Economic Correlates of Primate Cities: A Case for Revaluation (sic)." Pp. 295–308 in Gerald Breese, ed., *The City in Newly Developing Countries*. Englewood Cliffs, N.J.: Prentice-Hall.

Mera, Koichi. 1978. "On Urban Agglomeration and Economic Efficiency." Pp. 445–456 in L. S. Bourne and J. W. Simmons, eds., *Systems of Cities*. New York: Oxford University Press.

Meyer, David. 1986. "The World System of Cities: Relations Between International Financial Metropolises and South American Cities." *Social Forces* 64: 553–581.

Migdal, Joel. *Strong States and Weak States: State-Society Relations and State Capabilities in the Third World*. Princeton, J.J.: Princeton University Press.

Miller, Jerry L., and Maynard I. Erickson. 1981. "On Dummy Variable Regression Analysis: A Description and Illustration of the Method." Pp. 44–62 in Peter V. Marsden, ed., *Linear Models in Social Research*. Beverly Hills, Calif.: Sage.

Mills, Edwin, and Byung-Nak Song. 1979. *Studies in the Modernization of the Republic of Korea: 1945–1975: Urbanization and Urban Problems*. Cambridge, Mass.: Harvard University Press.

Mingione, Enzo. 1981. *Social Conflict and the City*. New York: St. Martin's Press.

————. 1987. "Urban Survival Strategies, Family Structure, and Informal Practices." Pp. 297–322 in Michael Smith and Joe Feagin, eds., *The Capitalist City: Global Restructuring and Community Politics*. New York: Basil Blackwell.

Mlia, Justice. 1974. "National Urban Development Policy: The Issues and the Options." Pp. 75–89 in S. El-Shakhs and R. Obudho, eds., *Urbanization, National Development, and Regional Planning in Africa*. New York: Praeger.

Moore, Barrington. 1958. "Strategy in Social Science." Pp. 111–159 in B. Moore, ed., *Political Power and Social Theory: Six Studies*. Cambridge, Mass.: Harvard University Press.

————. 1966. *Social Origins of Dictatorship and Democracy*. Boston: Beacon Press.

Moser, Caroline. 1978. "Informal Sector or Petty Commodity Production: Dualism or Dependence in Urban Development?" *World Development* 6(9/10): 1041–1064.

Moulder, Frances. 1977. *Japan, China, and the Modern World Economy.* Cambridge: Cambridge University Press.

Mountjoy, Alan. 1978. "Urbanization, a Squatter and Development in the Third World." Pp. 480–488 in L. S. Bourne and J. W. Simmons, eds., *Systems of Cities.* New York: Oxford University Press.

Munro, J. Forbes. 1976. *Africa and the International Economy, 1800–1960.* Totowa, N.J.: Rozman and Littlefield.

Murdoch, William. 1980. *The Poverty of Nations: The Political Economy of Hunger and Population.* Baltimore, MD.: Johns Hopkins University Press.

Murphey, Rhoades. 1980. *The Fading of the Maoist Vision: City and Country in China's Development.* New York: Methuen.

———. 1988. "Modernization and Urbanization in Asia: Plague or Promise?" Presidential address, Association for Asian Studies. Reprinted in *Asian Studies Newsletter*, Spring: pages A–D.

Murray, Roger. 1963. "Agronomy and Society." *New Left Review* 19: 85–90.

Myrdal, Gunnar. 1971. *Asian Drama: An Inquiry into the Poverty of Nations.* New York: Pantheon Books.

Nam, Sunghee. 1987. "Beyond Overurbanization: The Pattern and Nature of Recent Urban Decentralization in South Korea." Paper presented at the annual meeting of the American Sociological Association, August, Chicago.

National Bureau of Statistics. 1989. *Annual Report on the Internal Migration Statistics, 1988.* Seoul: Economic Planning Board.

Nemeth, Roger, and David Smith. 1985a. "International Trade and World-System Structure: A Multiple Network Analysis." Review 8(4): 517–560.

———. 1985b. "The Political Economy of Contrasting Urban Hierarchies in South Korea and the Philippines." Pp. 183–206 in Michael Timberlake, ed., *Urbanization in the World-Economy.* New York: Academic Press.

Nisbet, Robert. 1976. *Sociology as an Art Form.* New York: Oxford University Press.

O'Brien, Rita Cruise. 1979. "Introduction." Pp. 13–37 in Rita Cruise O'Brien, ed., *The Political Economy of Underdevelopment: Dependence in Senegal.* Beverly Hills, Calif.: Sage.

O'Donnell, Guillermo. 1978. "Reflections on the Bureaucratic-Authoritarian State." *Latin American Research Review* 13(1): 3–38.

Owen Carol, and Ronald Witton. 1973. "National Division and Mobilization: A Reinterpretation of Primacy." *Economic Development and Cultural Change* 21: 325–337.

Park, Robert E. 1916. "The City: Suggestions for the Investigation of Human Behavior in an Urban Environment." *American Journal of Sociology* 20: 577–612.

Park, Robert E., and Ernest W. Burgess. 1925. *The City*. Chicago: University of Chicago Press.

Parsons, Talcott. 1971. *The Evolution of Societies*. Englewood Cliffs, N.J.: Prentice-Hall.

Portes, Alejandro. 1976. "On the Sociology of National Development." *American Journal of Sociology* 82: 3–38.

———. 1979a. "Convergences between Conflicting Paradigms in National Development." Paper presented at the thematic session of "Development" at the meetings of the American Sociological Association, Boston.

———. 1983. "The Urban Informal Sector: Definition, Controversy, and Relation to Development." *Review* (Fernand Braudel Center) 7(1): 151–174.

———. 1985a. "The Informal Sector and the World Economy: Notes on the Structure of Subsidized Labour." Pp. 53–62 in Michael Timberlake, ed., *Urbanization in the World-Economy*. New York: Academic Press.

———. 1985b. "Latin American Class Structures: Their Composition and Change During the Last Decade." *Latin American Research Review* 20(3): 7–40.

Portes, Alejandro, and Saskia Sassen-Koob. 1987. "Making It Underground: Comparative Material on the Informal Sector in Western Market Economies." *American Journal of Sociology* 93(1): 30–61.

Portes, Alejandro, and John Walton. 1976. *Urban Latin America: The Political Condition from Above and Below*. Austin: University of Texas Press.

———. 1981. *Labor, Class, and the International System*. New York: Academic Press.

Ragin, Charles. 1987. *The Comparative Method: Moving Beyond Quantitative and Qualitative Strategies*. Berkeley: University of California Press.

Rayfield, J. R. 1974. "Urbanization and the Colonial City in West Africa." *Africa* 44: 163–185.

Reed, Robert. 1972. *Hispanic Urbanism in the Philippines*. Manila: University of Manila.

———. 1977. *Colonial Manila*. Berkeley: University of California Press.

Reeve, W. D. 1963. *The Republic of Korea: A Political and Economic Study*. New York: Oxford University Press.

Reich, Robert. 1991. *The Work of Nations*. New York: Alfred A. Knopf.

Reissman, Leonard. 1964. *Urban Process: Cities in Industrial Societies*. Glencoe, Ill.: Free Press.

Renaud, Bertrand. 1974. "Evolution of the Urban System in Korea 1910–1940: An Economic Interpretation." *Bulletin of the Population and Development Studies Center* 3(26): appendix table.

————. 1981. National Urbanization Policies in Developing Countries. New York: Oxford University Press.

Repetto, Robert. 1979. *Economic Equality and Fertility in Developing Countries.* Baltimore, Md.: Johns Hopkins University Press.

Republic of China. 1982. *Statistical Yearbook of the Republic of China, 1980.* Taipei: Executive Yuan.

Richardson, Harry, and Myong-Chan Hwang, eds. 1987. *Urban and Regional Policy in Korea and International Experiences.* Seoul: Kon-kuk University Press.

Riddell, J. Barry. 1978. "The Migration to the Cities of West Africa: Some Policy Considerations. The Journal of Modern African Studies 16(2): 241–260.

————. 1980. "Is Continuing Urbanization Possible in West Africa?" *African Studies Review* 23(1): 69–79.

Roberts, Bryan. 1978a. *Cities of Peasants: The Political Economy of Urbanization in the Third World.* Beverly Hills: Sage.

————. 1978b. "Comparative Perspectives on Urbanization." Pp. 592–627 in David Street and Associates, eds., Handbook of Contemporary Urban Life. San Francisco, Calif.: Jossey-Bass.

Rodwin, Lloyd. 1981. *Cities and City Planning.* New York: Plenum Press.

Rondinelli, Dennis. 1985. "Population Distribution and Economic Development in Africa: The Need for Urbanization Policies." *Population Research and Policy Review* 4: 173–196.

————. 1988. "Giant and Secondary Cities in Africa." Pp. 291–321 in Mattei Dogan and John Kasarda, eds., *The Metropolis Era: Vol. 1 A World of Giant Cities.* Beverly Hills, Calif.: Sage.

Ross, Robert, and Kent Trachte. 1983. "Global Cities and Global Classes: The Peripheralization of Labor in New York City." *Review* (Fernand Braudel Center) 6(3): 393–431.

————. 1990. *Global Capitalism: The New Leviathan.* Albany: State University of New York Press.

Rosser, Colin. 1973. *Urbanization in Tropical Africa.* New York: International Urbanization Survey, Ford Foundation.

Rozman, Gilbert. 1973. *Urban Networks in Ch'ing China and Tokugawa Japan.* Princeton: Princeton University Press.

Rubinson, Richard. 1976. "The World Economy and the Distribution of Income Within States: A Cross-National Study." *American Sociological Review* 41: 638–659.

Rubinson, Richard, and Deborah Holtzman. 1981. "Comparative Dependence and Economic Development." *International Journal of Comparative Sociology* 22(1–2): 86–101.

Sachs, Ignacy. 1988. "Vulnerability of Giant Cities and the Life Lottery."
    Pp. 337–350 in Mattei Dogan and John Kasarda, eds., *The Metropolis Era.*
    Vol. 1, A World of Giant Cities. Beverly Hills, Calif.: Sage.

Safa, Helen. 1987. "Urbanization, the Informal Economy and State Policy in Latin
    America." Pp. 252–272 in Michael Smith and Joe Feagin, eds., *The Capitalist*
    City: Global Restructuring and Community Politics. New York: Basil
    Blackwell.

Salau, Ademola. 1978. "The Political Economy of Cities in Tropical Africa."
    Civilisations 28: 281–290.

———. 1979a. "The Urban Process in Africa: Observations on the Points of
    Divergence from the Western Experience." *African Urban Studies* 4: 27–34.

———. 1979b. "Housing in Africa: Toward a Reassessment of Problems,
    Policies, and Planning Strategies." *Civilisations* 29: 322–339.

Santos, Milton. 1979. *Shared Space: The Two Circuits of the Urban Economy in*
    Underdeveloped Countries. London: Methuen.

Schurz, William. 1939. *The Manila Galleon.* New York: E. P. Dutton.

Sethuraman, S. V. 1977. "The Urban Informal Sector in Africa." *International*
    Labor Review 116(3): 343–352.

Short, Kate. 1979. "Foreign Capital and the State in Indonesia: Some Aspects of
    Contemporary Capitalism." *Journal of Contemporary Asia* 9(2): 152–174.

Sjoberg, Gideon. 1965. *The Preindustrial City: Past and Present.* Glencoe, Ill.:
    Free Press.

Skinner, G. William. 1977. "Regional Urbanization in Nineteenth-Century China."
    Pp. 211–249 in G. W. Skinner, ed., *The City in Late Imperial China.* Stanford:
    Stanford University Press.

Sklar, Richard. 1979. "The Nature of Class Domination in Africa." *The Journal*
    of Modern African Studies 17(4): 531–552.

Skocpol, T. 1977. "Wallerstein's World Capitalist System: A Theoretical and
    Historical Critique." *American Journal of Sociology* 82(4): 1075–1090.

———. 1979. *States and Social Revolutions.* Cambridge: Cambridge University
    Press.

Skocpol, Theda, and Margaret Somers. 1980. "The Uses of Comparative History
    in Macrosociological Inquiry." *Comparative Studies in Society and History*
    22: 174–197.

Slater, David. 1978. "Towards a Political Economy of Urbanization in Peripheral
    Capitalist Societies." *International Journal of Urban and Regional Research*
    2(1): 26–52.

Smelser, Neil. 1976. *Comparative Methods in the Social Sciences.* Englewood
    Cliffs, N.J.: Prentice-Hall.

Smith, Carole. 1978. "Beyond Dependency Theory: National and Regional Patterns of Underdevelopment in Guatemala." American Ethologist 5: 574–617.

———. 1982a. "Placing Formal Geographical Models Into Cultural Contexts: The Anthropological Study of Urban Systems." *Comparative Urban Research* 9(1): 50–59.

———. 1982b. "Modern and Premodern Primacy." *Comparative Urban Research* 9(1): 79–96.

———. 1985. "Class Relations and Urbanization in Guatemala: Toward an Alternative Theory of Urban Primacy." Pp. 121–167 in Michael Timberlake, ed., *Urbanization in the World-Economy*. New York: Academic Press.

Smith, Carole, ed. 1976. *Regional Analysis. Vol. 1. Economic Systems.* New York: Academic Press.

Smith, David A. 1984. *Urbanization in the World-Economy: A Cross-National and Historical-Structural Analysis.* Unpublished Ph.D. dissertation, University of North Carolina, Chapel Hill.

———. 1985. International Dependence and Urbanization in East Asia: Implications for Planning." Population Research and Policy Review 4: 203–233.

———. 1987a. "Overurbanization Reconceptualized: A Political Economy of the World-System Approach." *Urban Affairs Quarterly* 23(2): 270–294.

———. 1987b. "Dependent Urbanization in Colonial America: The Case of Charleston, South Carolina." *Social Forces* 66(1): 1–28.

———. 1991. "Semiperipheral Urbanization? South Korea in the 1980s." Pp. 157–173 in Resat Kasaba, ed., *Cities in the World-System*. Westport, Conn.: Greenwood.

———. 1992. "Technology and the Modern World-System: Some Reflections." *Science, Technology, and Human Values* 18(2): 186–195.

———. 1995. "The New Urban Sociology Meets the Old: Rereading Some Classical Human Ecology." *Urban Affairs Review* 30(3): 432–457.

Smith, David A. And Jószef Böröcz. 1995. *A New world Order? Global Transformations in the Late Twentiety Century.* Westport, Conn.: Greenwood Press.

Smith, David and Su-Hoon Lee. 1990. "Limits on a Semiperipheral Success Story? South Korea at the Political and Economic Crossroads." Pp. 79–95 in William Martin, ed., Semiperipheral States in the World-Economy. Westport, Conn.: Greenwood.

Smith, David A., and Su-Hoon Lee. 1991. "Moving Toward Democracy? South Korean Political Change in the 1980s." *Comparative Urban and Community Research* 3: 164–187.

Smith, David, and Bruce London. 1990. "Convergence in World Urbanization? A Quantitative Assessment." *Urban Affairs Quarterly* 25(4): 574–590.

Smith, David, and Roger Nemeth. 1990. "Dependent Urbanization in the Contemporary Semi-Periphery: Deepening the Analogy." Pp. 8–36 in David Drakakis-Smith, ed., *Economic Growth and Urbanization in Developing Areas*. London: Routledge.

Smith, David, and Douglas White. 1992. "Structure and Dynamics of the Global Economy: Network Analysis of International Trade, 1965–1980." *Social Forces* 70(4): 857–893.

Smith, Michael P., and Joe Feagin, eds. 1987. *The Capitalist City: Global Restructuring and Community Politics*. New York: Basil Blackwell.

Snyder, David, and Edward Kick. 1979. "Structural Position in the World System and Economic Growth: A Multiple Network Analysis of Transnational Interactions." *American Journal of Sociology* 84: 1096–1126.

Sobhan, Rehman. 1979. "The Nature of the State and its Implications for the Development of Public Enterprises in Asia." *Journal of Contemporary Asia* 9(4): 410–433.

Solinger, Dorothy. 1995. "China's Urban Transients in the Transition from Socialism and the Collapse of the Communist 'Urban Public Goods Regime.'" *Comparative Politics* 2(27): 127–146.

Sovani, N. 1964. "The Analysis of Over-Urbanization." *Economic Development and Cultural Change* 12: 113–122.

Spates, James, and John Macionis. 1983. *The Sociology of Cities*. New York: St. Martin's Press.

Steiber, Steven. 1979. "The World System and World Trade: An Empirical Explanation of Conceptual Conflicts." *Sociological Quarterly* 20: 23–36.

Stinchcombe, Arthur. 1978. *Theoretical Methods in Social History*. New York: Free Press.

Stokes, Randall, and David Jaffee. 1982. "The export of Raw Materials and Export Growth." *American Sociological Review* 47(3): 402–407.

Suh, Song Chul. 1978. *Growth and Structural Changes in the Korean Economy, 1910–1940*. Cambridge: Harvard University Press.

Sunkel, Osvaldo. 1973. "Transnational Capitalism and National Disintegration in Latin America." *Social and Economic Studies* 22: 132–176.

Taylor, Charles, and David Jodice. 1983. World Handbook of Political and Social Indicators. 2d ed. New Haven: Yale University Press.

Teune, Henry. 1988. Growth and Pathologies of Giant Cities." Pp. 351–376 in Mattei Dogan and John Kasarda, eds., *The Metropolis Era. Vol. 1. A World of Giant Cities*. Beverly Hills, Calif.: Sage.

Tilly C. 1981. *As Sociology Meets History*. New York: Academic Press.

Timberlake, Michael. 1979. "Economic Dependence, Internal Urban and Labor Force Structure, and the Problems of Development: A Quantitative Cross-National Study." Ph.D. diss., Brown University, Providence, R.I.

————. 1985. "The World-System Perspective and Urbanization." Pp. 3–22 in Michael Timberlake, ed., *Urbanization in the World-Economy*. New York: Academic Press.

————. 1987. World-System Theory and the Study of Comparative Urbanization." Pp. 37–65 in Michael P. Smith and Joe Feagin, eds., *The Capitalist City: Global Restructuring and Community Politics*. New York: Basil Blackwell.

Timberlake, Michael, and Jeffrey Kentor. 1983. "Economic Dependence, Overurbanization, and Economic Growth: A Study of Less Developed Countries." *Sociological Quarterly* 24: 489–507.

Todaro, Michael. 1981. "City Bias and Rural Neglect: The Dilemna of Urban Development." Public issue paper. New York: Population Council.

United Nations. 1976. Habitat: Global Review of Human Settlements. A/CONF.70/A/1. New York: United Nations.

————. 1980. Patterns of Urban and Rural Population Growth. ST/ESA/SER.A/68. New York: United Nations.

————. 1988. Prospects of World Urbanization, 1988. ST/ESA/SER.A/112. New York: United Nations.

————. 1992. *United Nations Demographic Yearbook*. ST/ESA/STAT/SER.R/23. New York: United Nations.

————. 1993. *World Urbanization Prospects: The 1992 Revision*. ST/ESA/SER.A/136. New York: United Nations.

United States Bureau of the Census. 1980. Statistical Abstract of the United States. Washington, D.C.: U.S. Government Printing Office.

Uyanga, Joseph. 1979. "Urban Primacy Strategy in Nigeria: The Institutional Policy Perspective." African Urban Studies 8: 49–58.

Vaitsos, Constantine. 1974. Intercountry Income Distribution and Transactional Enterprise. London: Oxford University Press.

Valenzuela, J. Samuel, and Arturo Valenzuela. 1978. "Modernization and Dependency," *Comparative Politics* 10: 535–557.

Vallier, Ivan. 1971. *Comparative Methods in Sociology: Essays in Trends and Applications*. New York: Harcourt, Brace and World.

Vapnarsky, Cesar. 1966. *Rank Size Distribution of Cities in Argentina*. Unpublished Master's Thesis, Cornell University.

Wallerstein, Immanuel. 1974a. *The Modern World-System. Vol. 1*. New York: Academic Press.

————. 1974b. "The Rise and Future Demise of the World Capitalist System: Concepts for Comparative Analysis." *Comparative Studies in Society and History* 16: 387–415.

————. 1976a. "The Three Stages of African Involvement in the World Economy." Pp. 30–57 in P. Gutkind and I. Wallerstein, eds., *The Political Economy of Contemporary Africa.* Beverly Hills, Calif.: Sage.

————. 1976b. "Semi-peripheral Countries and the Contemporary World Crisis." *Theory and Society* 3(4): 461–484.

————. 1979. *The Capitalist World-Economy.* New York: Cambridge University Press.

————. 1980. *The Modern World-System. Vol. 2.* New York: Academic Press.

————. 1989. *The Modern World-System. Vol. 3.* New York: Academic Press.

Wallerstein, Immanuel, and Terrance Hopkins. 1977. "Patterns of Development of the Modern World-System." *Review* 1(2): 11–45.

Wallerstein, Immanuel, W. Martin, and T. Dickinson. 1982. "Household Structures and Production Processes: Preliminary Theses and Findings." *Review* (Fernand Braudel Center) 5(3): 437–459.

Walter, Bob J. 1974. "Planning for Whom?" Pp. 93–109 in S. El-shakhs and R. Obudho, eds., *Urbanization, National Development, and Regional Planning in Africa.* New York: Praeger.

Walters, Pamela. 1985. "Systems of Cities and Urban Primacy: Problems of Definition and Measurement." Pp. 63–85 in Michael Timberlake, ed., *Urbanization in the World Economy.* New York: Academic Press.

Walton, John. 1975. "Internal Colonialism: Problems of Definition and Measurement." Pp. 29–50 in Wayne Cornelius and Felicity Trueblood, eds., *Urbanization and Inequality: The Political Economy of Urban and Rural Development in Latin America.* Beverly Hills: Sage.

————. 1977. "Accumulation and Comparative Urban Systems: Theory and Some Tentative Contrasts of Latin America and Africa." *Comparative Urban Research* 5(1): 5–18.

————. 1979a. "From Cities to Systems: Recent Research in Latin American Urbanization." *Latin American Research Review* 14(1): 159–169.

————. 1979b. "Urban Political Economy: A New Paradigm." *Comparative Urban Research* 7(1): 5–17.

————. 1981. "The New Urban Sociology." *International Social Science Journal* 33(2): 374–390.

————. 1982. "The International Economy and Peripheral Urbanization." Pp. 119–135 in Normal Fainsten and Susan Fainstein, eds., *Urban Policy Under Capitalism.* Newbury Park, Calif.: Sage.

Weber, Adna. 1899 (1963). The Growth of Cities in the Nineteenth Century. Ithaca: Cornell University Press.

Wernstedt, Frederick, and Joseph Spencer. 1967. *The Philippines Island World: A Physical, Cultural, and Regional Geography.* Berkeley: University of California Press.

Whang, In-Joung. 1986. Social Development in Action: The Korean Experience. Seoul: Korea Development Institute.

White, Harrison, Scott Boorman, and Ronald Breiger. 1976. "Social Structure from Multiple Networks, 1. Block Models of Roles and Positions." *American Journal of Sociology* 81: 730–780.

Williams, Gavin. 1970. "The Social Stratification of a Neo-Colonial Economy." Pp. 225-250 in C. Allen and R. Johnson, eds., *African Perspectives: Papers in the History, Politics, and Economics of Africa*. Cambridge: Cambridge University Press.

———. 1976. "Nigeria: A Political Economy." Pp. 11–54 in G. Williams, ed., Nigeria: Economy and Society. London: Rex Collins.

Williams, Gavin, and E. Tumusiime-Mutebile. 1978. "Capitalist and Petty Commodity Production in Nigeria: A Note." *World Development* 6(9/10): 1103–1104.

Wood, L. E. 1977. "South Korea: Geographic Change Through Planning." Master's thesis. University of North Carolina, Chapel Hill.

World Bank. 1980. *World Tables: The Second Edition (1980)*. Baltimore: Johns Hopkins University Press.

Wright, Edward, ed. 1975. *Korean Policies in Transition*. Seattle: University of Washington Press.

Yazaki, Takeo. 1968. *Social Change and the City in Japan*. San Francisco: Japan Publications.

Yeung, Yue-man. 1975. "Hawkers and Vendors: Dualism in Southeast Asia." *Journal of Tropical Geography* 41: 81–86.

About the Book and Author

In this innovative book, David Smith ultimately links what happens "on the ground" in the neighborhoods where people live to the larger political and economic forces at work, putting these connections in an historical framework and using a case study approach.

The societies of the world's underdeveloped countries are now undergoing an "urban revolution" that is drastically altering the fabric of their predominantly rural agrarian societies. Smith takes the emerging political economy perspective on urbanization, with its focus on global inequality and dependency, as the context for city growth in the Third World.

This perspective allows Smith to critique the conventional ecological view of the city, not by rejecting traditional analyses out of hand, but by reformulating the crucial questions. The conventional ecological perspective assumes an equilibrium model, where very rapid city growth and the various types of urban imbalances are transitional phases on the path to modernity; in contrast, the comparative political economy approach conceptualizes uneven development and inequality as an inevitable result of the expansion of the capitalist world-system.

David A. Smith is a professor of sociology at the University of California at Irvine.

Index